The Great Peace of Montreal of 1701
French-Native Diplomacy in the Seventeenth Century

The last decades of the seventeenth century were marked by persistent, bloody conflicts between the French and their Native allies on the one side and the Iroquois Confederacy on the other. In the summer of 1701, 1,300 representatives of forty Native nations from the Maritimes to the Great Lakes and from James Bay to southern Illinois met with the French at Montreal. Elaborate, month-long ceremonies culminated in the signing of the Great Peace of Montreal, which effectively put an end to the Iroquois Wars.

In *The Great Peace of Montreal of 1701* Gilles Havard brings to life the European and Native players who brought about this major feat of international diplomacy. He highlights the differing interests and strategies of the numerous nations involved while giving a dramatic account of the colourful conference. The treaty, Havard argues, was the culmination of the French colonial strategy of Native alliances and adaptation to Native political customs. It illustrates the extent of cultural interchange between the French and their Native allies and the crucial role the latter played in French conflicts with the Iroquois and the British.

As we approach the three hundredth anniversary of the treaty's signing in August 1701, Gilles Havard emphasizes its contemporary significance: in signing a treaty with forty separate parties the French recognized the independent sovereignty of every Native nation. This translation is significantly revised and updated from the original French publication of 1992.

GILLES HAVARD is a historian living in Paris. He is currently writing a book on French-Native relations in the Great Lakes region.

The Great Peace of Montreal of 1701

French-Native Diplomacy in the Seventeenth Century

GILLES HAVARD

Translated by Phyllis Aronoff
and Howard Scott

McGill-Queen's University Press
Montreal & Kingston · London · Ithaca

© McGill-Queen's University Press 2001
ISBN 0-7735-2209-3 (cloth)
ISBN 0-7735-2219-0 (paper)

Legal deposit second quarter 2001
Bibliothèque nationale du Québec

Printed in Canada on acid-free paper

Publication of this book has been made possible
through the assistance of La Corporation des fêtes de
la Grande Paix de Montréal.

McGill-Queen's University Press acknowledges the
financial support of the Government of Canada
through the Book Publishing Industry Development
Program (BPIDP) for its activities. It also
acknowledges the support of the Canada Council for
the Arts for its publishing program.

A version of this work was published in 1992 as *La
Grande Paix de Montréal de 1701: les voies de la
diplomatie franco-amérindienne* by Recherches
amérindiennes au Québec.

Canadian Cataloguing in Publication Data

Havard, Gilles, 1967–
    The Great Peace of Montreal of 1701: French-Native
    diplomacy in the seveententh century
    Translation of: La Grande paix de Montréal de 1701.
    Includes bibliographical references and index.
    ISBN 0-7735-2209-3 (bound) –
    ISBN 0-7735-2219-0 (pbk.)
    1. Treaty of Montréal – (1701) 2. Indians of North
    America – Canada – Government relations – to 1830.
    3. Indians of North America – Treaties, 1701.
    4. Iroquois Indians – Treaties, 1701. 5. Speeches,
    addresses, etc., Indian. 6. Canada – History –
    1663–1713 (New France) I. Aronoff, Phyllis, 1945–
    II. Scott, Howard, 1952– III. Title.
    FC370.H3813 2001   971.01′8   C2001-900150-9
    F1030.H3813 2001

This book was typeset by Dynagram Inc. in 10.5/13 Sabon.

Contents

Preface

This book is much more than a translation of my earlier *La Grande Paix de Montréal: Les voies de la diplomatie franco-amérindienne*, written in 1989 and published by *Recherches amérindiennes au Québec* in 1992. While preserving the earlier work's overall organization, the content has been significantly revised and updated. As well as taking into account new studies and data which have appeared since the original publication, I wanted to improve a work that had, after all, originated as a master's thesis. Error and change are part and parcel of the historian's craft and so the current work also reflects how my views of these events have evolved over the last ten years. Although this book is undoubtedly not perfect, it is certainly improved.

Many people have helped me in the writing of this work. I must especially thank Denys Delâge, who has unfailing advised and encouraged me over the past ten years. For their numerous contributions to this project I am also indebted to Claire Henderson, Lina Gouger, Laurence Johnson, Marine Le Puloch, Moira McCaffrey, Elise Marienstras, Marcelle Roy, Alain Beaulieu, Peter Cook, Emmanuel Désveaux, Dominique Legros, André Lespagnol, Jacques Mathieu, Jean-Pierre Sawaya, George E. Sioui, and Don Smith. I am also grateful to Aurèle Parisien, Joan McGilvray, and Susanne McAdam at McGill-Queen's as well as to my translators, Phyllis Aronoff and Howard Scott. Finally, I am thankful for the support of my family, especially my sister Calissia for her help in proofing the book.

Chronology

1603	First alliance formed at Tadoussac between the French, the Montagnais, the Algonquins, and the Maliseets.
1608	Founding of the town of Quebec by Samuel de Champlain.
1609	Beginning of the French-Huron alliance.
1609, 1610, 1615	French-Huron expeditions against the Iroquois.
1624	French-Iroquois peace agreement at Trois-Rivières.
1642	Founding of Montreal.
1643	Alliance between the Mohawks and the Dutch of Fort Orange.
1645	Signing of a peace treaty at Trois-Rivières between the Mohawks, the French, and the Amerindian allies of the French (Hurons, Algonquins, Montagnais, Attikameks).
1648–50	Destruction of Huronia by the Iroquois.
1653	Separate peace between the French and the Five Nations.

1663	New France declared a royal province.
1664	New Netherland captured by the English and re-named New York.
1666	Expeditions by the Carignan-Salières Regiment against the Mohawks.
1667	General peace agreement signed at Quebec between the French, their allies, and the Iroquois; Jesuits settle in Iroquoia.
	Beginning of Iroquois migration into the French colony.
1673	Voyage by Frontenac to Lake Ontario; founding of Fort Frontenac.
1677	Signing of Albany treaties that founded the Covenant Chain.
1678	Resumption of the Iroquois Wars against the western nations (Illinois, Miamis).
1684	La Barre's failed expedition against the Senecas; signing of a peace treaty at La Famine.
1687	Denonville's expedition against the Senecas.
1688	French-Iroquois negotiations scuttled by Kondiaronk.
1689	Beginning of the War of the League of Augsburg. Iroquois raid on Lachine.
	Return of Frontenac to Canada.
1693	French-Amerindian expedition against the Mohawks. June: Oneida delegation to Montreal.
1694	May: Conference at Quebec between the French, their allies, and the Iroquois.
1696	Louis XIV's edict ordering the closing of posts in the west.
	Expedition by the French and their allies against the Onondagas and Oneidas.

1697   Le Baron secedes from the Huron nation and joins the
            Covenant Chain.
            February: Oneida delegation to Montreal; Mohawk
            delegation to the town of Quebec.
            August: Oneida delegation to Montreal.
            September: Treaty of Ryswick between France and
            England.
            November: Oneida-Onondaga delegation to Quebec.

1698   November: Death of Frontenac; Callière becomes
            governor general of New France.

1698–1700   Victories by the western nations over the Iroquois.

1699   January: Oneida-Onondaga delegation to Montreal.
            March: Onondaga-Oneida delegation to
            Montreal.
            September: Onondaya delegation to Montreal.

1700   March: Onondaga-Seneca delegation to Montreal.
            June: Peace treaty between the western nations and
            the Iroquois.
            July: Onondaga-Seneca delegation to Montreal.
            August: French-Iroquois conference at Onondaga.
            September: Peace treaty between the French, the
            Huron-Petuns, the Odawas, the Abenakis, the Amer-
            indians settled in the colony, and the Five Nations.

1701   Winter: Diplomatic mission by Courtemanche and
            Father Enjalran to the western nations.
            March: Onondaga delegation to Quebec.
            May: Conference at Michilimackinac; Iroquois dele-
            gation to Montreal.
            June: French delegation to Onondaga.
            June–July: Founding of Detroit by Lamothe Cadillac.
            12–21 July: English-Iroquois conference in Albany.
            21–22 July: Amerindian delegations to Kahnawake.
            23 July–7 August: General peace conference in
            Montreal.

1702–13   War of the Spanish Succession (Queen Anne's War).

1713	Treaty of Utrecht: France loses Acadia, Newfoundland, and Hudson Bay.
1744–48	War of the Austrian Succession (King George's War).
1754	Beginning of the Seven Years' War (French and Indian War).
1759	Surrender of Quebec.
1760	Surrender of Montreal.

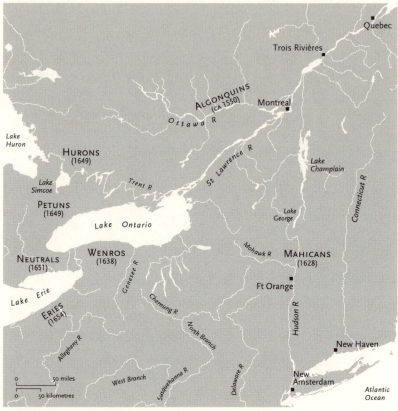

Mid seventeenth-century wars, showing peoples defeated, dispersed, or absorbed by Iroquois

Based on Richter, *The Ordeal of the Longhouse*, 63

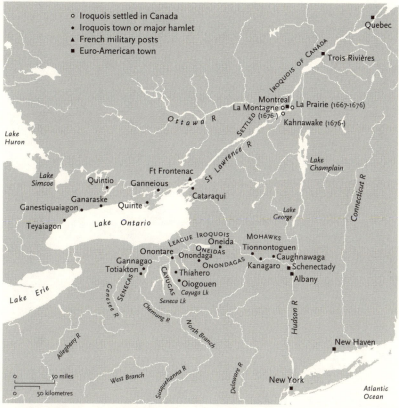

Iroquois villages in the mid 1670s
Based on Richter, *The Ordeal of the Longhouse*, 122

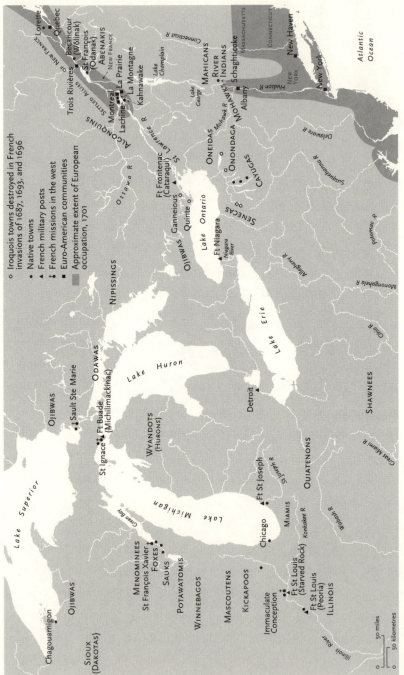

Native and Euro-American settlements, circa 1701

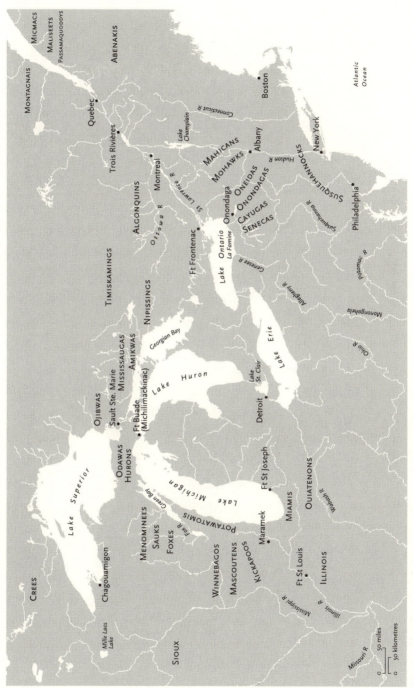

Native signatories of the Great Peace of Montreal, circa 1701

The Great Peace of Montreal of 1701

Introduction

The sun today dissipated the clouds to reveal this beautiful Tree of Peace, which was already planted on the highest mountain of the Earth.

Kondiaronk, Huron chief[1]

On 3 August 1701 in Montreal, French colonial authorities held a grand funeral for the Huron leader Kondiaronk (also known as "Le Rat," or "The Muskrat"). The chief had died the day before, a victim of an epidemic that had struck in the middle of a peace conference. After a solemn procession through the streets of the city, Kondiaronk was buried in Notre Dame Church with the epitaph "Cy git Le Rat, chef des Hurons" ("Here lies The Muskrat, chief of the Hurons"). "Today no trace of Kondiaronk's grave remains," writes W.N. Fenton.[2] Three centuries later, while Kondiaronk and the other significant actors in French-Native relations have not been forgotten, our picture of the Huron leader has become distorted. This process began very soon after the chief's death owing to the works of French chronicler Baron de Lahontan, whose popular *New Voyages to North America* (1703) culminates in "A Dialogue between the Author and Adario, a Noted Man among the Savages." Lahontan's noble savage – a Native philosopher who critiques European society – had a significant influence on notions of primitivism in the eighteenth-century Enlightenment. Adario was taken then and later as a portrait of Kondiaronk, but he is largely Lahontan's literary creation.[3] Although Kondiaronk was an exceptional orator much admired by the French and might sometimes have cast a critical eye on French society, he was no imaginary Indian with an *au courant* flair for social criticism; rather he was a flesh-and-blood person who lived on the shores of Lake Huron. In 1701 he came to a peace conference held in Montreal – like some thirteen hundred other Native ambassadors – to defend the interests of his people. A warrior who yearned "to bury the hatchet deep in the earth,"[4] he was one of the main architects of the peace treaty that the Montreal conference produced. Known as "the Great Peace of Montreal,"[5] this treaty was negotiated between the members of the French-Native alliance and the Iroquois, traditional enemies throughout most of the seventeenth century. While Kondiaronk's tragic death may be seen as illustrating the catastrophic collapse of the Native populations as a result of exposure to diseases carried by the newcomers, this chief was above all the symbol of the French-Amerindian alliance, which was the basis of New France's existence. The goal of this book is to recapture as much as possible the actual motivations, strategies, and outlooks of both the Amerindian and French protagonists of these events.

Shortly after Kondiaronk's burial, the treaty was ratified by the main delegates present. This Great Peace was a key event on the diplomatic and military scene of "colonial" North America. Uniting representatives of New France, the Five Iroquois Nations,[6] and the more than thirty Native nations[7] allied with the French (Amerindians from the Great Lakes, the Atlantic region, and Amerindian mission villages on the St Lawrence), it brought to an end the so-called Iroquois Wars that had occurred sporadically over several decades between the French and their allies on one side and the Iroquois on the other.[8] The Treaty of Montreal thus involved almost forty Amerindian groups and in theory brought peace to an immense geographic area covering, from east to west, from Acadia (Abenakis) to the western and northern shores of Lake Superior (Crees) and, from north to south, from the source of the Ottawa River (Timiskamings) to the confluence of the Missouri and Mississippi rivers (Kaskakias).[9]

Montreal in the summer of 1701 was the political centre of northeastern North America. In fact, for some forty years the town had been at the heart of the great trade networks in this part of America. Founded in 1642, Montreal developed substantially as a result of French expansion into the "Pays d'en Haut" (the Great Lakes region), which started in the 1660s, and the simultaneous extension of the French-Amerindian alliance, although its growth was certainly hampered by the Iroquois Wars. The gateway to a vast hinterland abounding with the furs sought by French merchants, Montreal was for the Amerindians of the Great Lakes an important centre of diplomacy and trade. For a century, from the 1660s until the fall of New France, it was the meeting place par excellence of the French-Amerindian alliance. Each year, from June to September, Montreal received Native ambassadors from the west and sometimes from Iroquoia. It was in a sense the summer capital of Canada; During that season, the governor and the intendant, like a travelling court, would leave the town of Quebec to set up in Montreal, essentially, as an administrator noted, to deal with matters "in relation to the affairs of the savages."[10] In 1701 this change of capital, which shows the importance of the Pays d'en Haut in the political, economic, and military life of the colony, was more than ever on the agenda.

The study of the Great Peace of Montreal, in the context of research on European-Amerindian relations in North America, belongs to the current of ethnohistory, which originated in the early 1950s with work by North American anthropologists and underwent spectacular development in the 1970s and 1980s. Ethnohistory may be defined as a multidisciplinary method combining history and anthropology to reach a better understanding of indigenous peoples.[11] It in turn gave birth to the "new Indian history," which, as R. White writes, "places Indian peoples at the centre of the scene and seeks to understand the reasons for their actions."[12] The Amerindian is thus presented as an agent, on an equal footing with the colonizers. This approach has made it possible to revise the history of the frontier and to demolish the usual prejudices regarding Amerindian inferiority and irrationality.

The history of the New World has traditionally been seen as the gradual victory of "civilization" over "barbarism." From this perspective, historians and anthropologists long agreed that the Native peoples at best played only a passive, marginal role in North American history. Anthropology initially presented itself as the study of peoples who, it was commonly thought, had no history and were fated for extinction because of their "primitive" nature. This view was discredited in the 1960s and 1970s, but the attempt to revise our perceptions, as healthy as that may be, entails risks. "Political correctness" seems to be a dangerous development, since it can lead historians to exaggerate the importance or independence of the Native peoples in the colonial period, to idealize First Nation societies, and to create new stereotypes that, while "positive," are just as false (the ecological Indian, the democratic Indian, the pacifist Indian, etc.) as the old ones.[13]

The peace of 1701 has long been discussed in general histories of New France[14] or in studies of imperial rivalry.[15] It has also often been approached through the Iroquois, who have always held a certain fascination for researchers and who very early, beginning in the eighteenth and nineteenth centuries, became a favoured subject of historical and anthropological study. Three works published in the middle of the twentieth century are well worthy of mention. G.T. Hunt, first of all, left a lasting mark on historiography with his work *The Wars of the Iroquois* (1940), which provides an economist's look at Amerindian behaviour in the fur trade. The Quebec novelist L.P. Desrosiers in 1947 published the first volume of an impressive work entitled *Iroquoisie* (Iroquoia), which was not really a history of the Five Nations but an account of diplomatic and military relations between the French and their allies (Hurons, Algonquins, etc.), on one hand, and the Iroquois, on the other. The title of the book is thus misleading, but it does show the author's interest in the Amerindians.[16] A.F.C. Wallace, finally, in his article "The Origins of Iroquois Neutrality: The Grand Settlement of 1701," was the first historian to relate the Treaty of Montreal to the Albany Agreements concluded by the Iroquois the same year.[17]

Following Hunt, Desrosiers, and Wallace, several researchers in the 1970s took an interest in the history of English-Iroquois relations (F. Jennings, R. Haan, R. Aquila, D.K. Richter, etc.)[18] and, secondarily, in French-Iroquois relations (W.J. Eccles, R.A. Goldstein, Y.F. Zoltvany)[19] in the seventeenth and eighteenth centuries. They all acknowledge the importance of the peace of 1701 but provide a rather sketchy assessment. Since the late 1980s, with the new focus on Native history, there has been much more historiography in the area of intercultural relations. There has been particular progress in the history of the French-Amerindian alliance, initially in Quebec under the impetus of D. Delâge, the author of the important article "L'alliance franco-amérindienne, 1660–1701" (1989), which went unnoticed by American historians. Since then, given the tense relationship between Quebeckers and Native people (the Oka Crisis of 1990), Delâge's research, but also that of A. Beaulieu, J. Grabowski, M. Jetten, and J.P. Sawaya, has mainly focused on the Amerindians living in mission villages within the colony on the St Lawrence – near Montreal, Quebec, and Trois-Rivières – particularly on their relations with the French.[20] As for the written history of the Native peoples of the Great Lakes region, for a long time it consisted of fragmentary monographs,[21] until the publication in 1991 of R. White's innovative *The Middle Ground*, which looks at the process of European-Native accommodation in the Pays d'en Haut over more than one and a half centuries (1650–1815). White defines the "middle ground" as an area of interaction and adaptation for individuals of different cultures who strive to establish a system of mutual understanding and accommodation. Europeans and Native peoples "had to arrive at some common conception of suitable ways of acting"; "people try to persuade others who are different from themselves by appealing to what they perceive to be the values and the practices of those others." This important book, which rejects the traditional history of the North American frontier and distances itself from Hunt's economistic view of the fur trade, provides a stimulating new interpretation of European-Amerindian relations. White discusses the Great Peace of Montreal, but only briefly.[22] The most recent contributions to the understanding of the events of 1701 are works by W.A. Starna and J.A. Brandão, who examine Iroquois strategies in the seventeenth century and conclude that the Five Nations' diplomacy at the turn of the eighteenth century was a success,[23] and a paper by A. Beaulieu and M. Lavoie, who try to explain the policies of the Five Nations in light of the League's message of peace.[24]

The purpose of my work has been threefold. First of all, the Great Peace of Montreal has never been studied specifically. The original (French) version of this book, while drawing very much on the work of F. Jennings,[25] was therefore intended to fill a gap in the historiography.[26] For example, nobody had attempted to identify precisely and exhaustively the Native nations that were signatories of the treaty; this shows a certain lack of interest in First Nations history.

Secondly, this book presents the Great Peace of Montreal in the overall context of European-Amerindian relations in the seventeenth century. Written from a broad perspective, it pays attention to the strategies of all the actors, but also analyses their rivalries on various socio-political levels. I therefore attempt to assess not only French-Iroquois relations, but also the role of the various groups allied with the French, in particular the Great Lakes nations, whose importance in Canadian history has often been neglected.

Thirdly, I review the various interpretations of the Great Peace of Montreal and offer my own. There are many questions that lack obvious answers and that can divide researchers:

1. What are the origins of the Great Peace of Montreal? What explains the resolve of the various groups to sign the treaty? How did they go from war to peace? Was this a capitulation for the Five Nations?
2. What were the main provisions of the treaty: peace? exchange of prisoners? sharing of hunting territories? Iroquois neutrality? the French role as mediator? etc.
3. Who was placed in a position of strength: the French? their allies in the mission villages? the nations of the west? the Iroquois?
4. How did the peace of 1701 differ from treaties concluded previously between the French, their allies, and the Five Nations? Was it a mere truce, or did the peace treaty put an end to the Indian wars in Canada?
5. Finally, what does the Great Peace of Montreal teach us about European-Native relations in New France in the seventeenth century? Does the treaty reveal a particular form of colonization?

To answer these questions, I draw on a relatively homogeneous corpus of sources.[27] The manuscripts of colonial correspondence, histories, reports, accounts of voyages, and documents of missionaries are European writings about Amerindians societies, relations between Natives and non-Natives, and colonial policies. I do not make extensive use of British sources, relying mostly on French documents, in particular the correspondence of the governor, the intendant, and other administrators of New France with France's Minister of marine. English-speaking historians have most often used the English correspondence – in particular with New York – to study European-Iroquois relations and have almost always neglected the French archives. The exclusive use of British documents, which contain copies of French letters (in translation), has led to a certain amount of confusion. It is difficult to understand either French policy or the nature of French-Iroquois relations solely on the basis of these documents. The Canadian historian W.J. Eccles condemns the "American refusal to consult the French sources" and makes this harsh judgment: "American colonial historians are dismayingly unilingual and Americocentric."[28]

Whatever the written sources, they need to be approached carefully. The authors are marked by their time, their social station, their gender, and their personal interests, and it is important to pay particular attention to the distortions and contradictions in their discourse. The *mémoires* and reports sent to Versailles, in addition to their informational purpose, were also intended to justify their authors' activities. The governor, for example, was seeking above all to justify his local policy and reassure his sovereign regarding his management of diplomatic and military interests. Rigorous attention needs to be paid to the contradictions in the colonial discourse. The many authors (officers, merchants, missionaries) were motivated by a range of interests (political, economic, or religious) that were often in opposition, their views of colonization, the fur trade, the Amerindians, and so on, differed profoundly. In this regard, the ethnohistorian B.G. Trigger has defined specific interest groups that form in a society under given historical conditions. These interest groups do not always correspond to the hierarchy of social classes or the logic of organized groups. There were, for example, conflicts among rival groups within the privileged class: between the governor and the intendant, between merchant companies, or between religious orders. It is through the comparative analysis of points of view that we can sometimes deduce the motivations of the Amerindians.[29]

While the motivations of the colonizers are relatively easy to identify, those of the Natives (peoples with an oral tradition) pose a problem for the historian. They were reported by non-Native narrators whose discourse is naturally marked by ethnocentrism.[30] However, although the documents are biased, they are still revealing. Native interests and strategies are not stated explicitly, but it is often possible to infer them. Anthropology is needed here, because only an ethnological understanding of Native life can provide the cultural background that is indispensable for assessing the behaviour of Amerindians as it has been recorded in historical documents. This involves, among other things, studying the speeches of the Native people that have been recorded in the diplomatic minutes. The sources are relatively reliable in this area, because the speeches during negotiations were transcribed almost systematically, either in the colonial correspondence or in the *Histoire de l'Amérique septentrionale* by Bacqueville de La Potherie.[31]

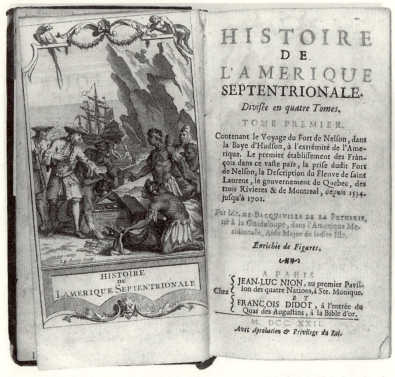

Frontispiece from *Histoire de l'Amérique septentrionale* by Claude-Charles Bacqueville de La Potherie, Paris: Jean-Luc Nion et François Didot, 1722, Vol. 1. McGill University, Rare Books, Lande Collection, #21. Photograph: McCord Museum.

Born in Paris, La Potherie was appointed controller of the Marine and of the fortifications in New France in 1698. He was present at the ceremonies of the Great Peace of Montreal and meticulously recorded aboriginal protocol.

Robert Le Blant has made the following criticism of La Potherie: "Unfortunately La Potherie has taken attention to detail so far as to reproduce in their entirety the contents of the 'collars' or speeches of the Natives, which finally become boring to read. I think, moreover, that these speeches were usually distorted and, especially, toned down out of regard for high-ranking officials."[32] It would be wrong, of course, to claim that these are verbatim transcriptions and that there has been no loss from the speech to its written version, but the loss was more in style than in meaning. The orations in the French diplomatic sources have hardly been altered, as is shown, first of all, by the fact that the orators do not hesitate to take a critical tone towards the French. A scribe was sometimes asked to take down a speech for transmission to the governor, and it was in the interest of the colonial administrators that the orations be recorded in full detail; in order to decide upon the best policy to follow, they had to understand what the Amerindians were asking for.

To refine my analysis, I attempt to weigh the words of the Amerindian speakers where possible by evaluating the symbolic value of the gifts associated with them. This contextualization of the discourse makes it possible to identify what was essential and what was less so for the Amerindians in a given set of negotiations. Generally, it is necessary to systematically decode the language of "forest diplomacy" in order to understand the underlying logic of the Amerindians' actions.[33] Furthermore, where necessary I occasionally use accounts from the oral tradition to analyse the historical context that led to the Great Peace of Montreal. These accounts are at least as biased as the written sources, but they can be relevant when compared against the archival material.[34] In short, my methodological approach ideally allows us to get as close as possible to the Native point of view and thus to avoid a stereotypical, monolithic view of Amerindians as secondary players.

The Treaty of Montreal and the negotiations that preceded it cannot be understood without first placing them in their historical context. In the first part of the book, therefore, I present the geopolitical background, describing the specific forms of European-Amerindian diplomacy and the various actors and their strategies, and placing the peace treaty of 1701 in the diplomatic and military context of the seventeenth century. I then examine the negotiations that took place both among Native peoples and between Europeans and Amerindians during the period 1697–1701.

Finally, I look at the event itself, those days in July and August 1701 in Montreal, describing the lavish and cosmopolitan nature of the conference – including the funeral of Kondiaronk – detailing the agreements that were concluded there, and examining the new political situation that came about as a result.

PART ONE

The Political and Diplomatic Arena

Let us begin by setting the stage and presenting the cast of characters. To put the negotiations for the Great Peace of Montreal in context, three questions may be asked. How did the diplomacy that structured the relationship between Amerindians and Europeans in the seventeenth century function? What actors and networks of alliances defined the international political scene? And in this geostrategic drama, what was the course of war and of peace before the start of the diplomatic process of 1697–1701?

1 Key Elements of Amerindian Diplomacy

The process of European invasion that led to turmoil in America from 1492 on involved more than the conquest of Native societies, the breakdown of their structure, and their exploitation. Any encounter, however violent, between previously distinct civilizations, gives rise to cultural transfers in both directions. This was true in northeastern North America, where at the limit of acculturation, there was a necessary adaptation to Native realities on the part of the first Euro-Americans. Native diplomacy was a key aspect of this cultural adjustment by the colonizers of North America. This does not mean that the Euro-Americans did not contribute new elements and thus modify some aspects of Native diplomacy, nor that Amerindians and Europeans always shared the same conception and the same interpretation of the diplomatic rituals that formalized their political and economic relations; but it is clear that the Europeans, in terms of both the concept of alliances and the mechanisms of protocol, had to conform to rituals that were often completely foreign to their customs.[1]

THE FOUNDATIONS OF ALLIANCE

The distinctiveness of European-Native contact in northeastern North America in the seventeenth and eighteenth centuries lies in the establishment of long-standing alliances – in contrast to the short-lived alliances of the Spanish *conquista*[2] – between the Native nations and the colonies, alliances that cut across the boundaries of ethnicity and culture.[3] These European-Amerindian alliances were influenced both by intercolonial rivalries[4] and by the existence of antagonisms among Native nations. Each party used these divisions to enhance its economic and political interests, or at the very least, for the Native peoples, to manage them as well as possible.

At the end of the seventeenth century, the geopolitical situation in northeastern North America was structured in two great systems of alliances. The first system, to which New France was added, centred around the Huron-Petuns, Odawas, Potawatomis, and Ojibwas, and included most of the Great Lakes nations; the other system, the Covenant Chain, was organized around the Iroquois Confederacy and the New York colony.[5]

Underlying these networks was the Native understanding of trade. As an eighteenth-century Iroquois orator explained, "Trade and Peace we take to be one thing."[6] Beginning in the early seventeenth century, the fur trade was the basis for friendship treaties and political and military pacts, because if there was no peace without trade,[7] there could be no alliance without economic relations.[8] The Europeans had gradually to conform to these traditions of the Native world in order to remain credible as diplomatic partners, and thus adaptation by the Whites was inevitable. Around 1700, the authorities of New France lived in constant fear that their allies in the Pays d'en Haut would trade with the English in Albany, who had the advantage of a more attractive market; that would have meant not only the loss of their economic associates, but also the disintegration of their political and military alliance,[9] "since trade is the strongest bond of alliances and friendship."[10]

The Native peoples were to some extent able to adjust to the competitive spirit of the Europeans by exploiting intercolonial competition in trade and using the weapon of blackmail to obtain the most merchandise for the least furs. But beyond prices and bargaining, they also got the Europeans to accept their practice of gift giving as the basis of social relations; in a context of rivalry and suspicion, it was through the exchange of goods and persons in a spirit of mutual generosity, that trust was established between partners. This Native philosophy was expressed, in political and economic relations within alliances, in terms of the importance of the gifts that were exchanged. The colonizers had to respect this obligation in order to demonstrate their gratitude to their Native hosts; at the same time, it was an essential means of inducing their Native allies to act in favour of their interests. By giving presents to the Amerindians, the colonial power was attempting to place them in the position of debtors and make it a matter of honour for them to repay their debts. In 1692 Governor Frontenac, speaking of the war of the Great Lakes nations against the Iroquois, told the minister of marine, "All these movements are only the effect of the gifts we gave them, for you would not believe, Monseigneur, what an impression they make on their minds."[11]

Gifts also cemented alliances; they fuelled the ritual of trading and that of the diplomatic conference[12] and helped to maintain pacts of friendship.[13] Governor Louis-Hector de Callière and Intendant Jean Bochart de Champigny were very clear on this point. They told the French court in 1699: "It would be unfortunate ... not to give any more gifts to the savages that are allied mainly with the chiefs when they come to deal with affairs of consequence, because these marks of generosity, though extremely limited, are the most tangible signs that one can give them of the protection of the King and our alliance with them. They would view their suspension as formal contempt against their persons."[14]

Gift giving was a fundamental part of Native culture, but when the Euro-Americans gave gifts to the Amerindians, they considered them a diplomatic instrument of payment for military services. In 1701 Louis XIV stated to the authorities in the town of Quebec:

His Majesty is pleased to point out to them regarding these gifts that He has been informed that the savages who received them give others to the officers who present them on behalf of His Majesty, ... he finds it good that they see to it that these savages realize that they are effects of His generosity ... for which He asks them only to continue in the fidelity that they owe to Him by still being attached to the French, but if their customs are such that it would be an insult to them to refuse their friendship in this case His intention is that these gifts be carried to His stores.[15]

The gifts reflected a European model – that of the patron and his dependants, the lord and his vassals, the father and his children[16] – but they were also a means for the colonial authorities to maintain their military alliances regardless of any difficulties concerning trade. The French, whose market was sometimes saturated, were not always able to sell all the furs the Amerindians brought them.

To preserve their friendship, they gave them gifts, which compensated for the lack of trade. The French state, whose desire for imperial expansion extended to all of North America, in this way gave politics precedence over economics.[17]

Thus, the Amerindian practice of gift giving became part of the structure of European diplomacy in North America, serving as a means of preserving essential alliances. The budgets of the colonies felt the effects of these obligations. Each year the colonial powers had to plan the nature and extent of the gifts for the nations (and especially the chiefs) that were allied with them, and each year they were reminded of the necessity of these gifts.[18] Finally, according to Native custom, to remain viable, alliances had to be reaffirmed through frequent conferences.[19] The Europeans thus had to rely on the indigenous culture of negotiation and treaty in order to conclude and maintain pacts of friendship.

THE MECHANISMS OF NEGOTIATION AND TREATY

Like the fundamental principles of alliance, the diplomatic protocol that governed European-Amerindian relations remained primarily Native in nature, although it underwent some modification through the effects of cultural interaction.

Ambassadors and Negotiations

At the end of the seventeenth century, war, peace, truce, and accommodation followed one after the other on the diplomatic stage of northeastern North America. Both among Native nations and between Amerindians and Europeans, the parties entered into negotiations in which each party attempted to advance its political, military, and economic interests. These talks were carried out by ambassadors who usually travelled by canoe on lakes and rivers to bring the "word" of their nation.

There is no clear indication that ambassadors always enjoyed diplomatic immunity in French-Iroquois negotiations. Even if this was often the case, there are examples to the contrary. In the summer of 1666, for example, Tracy, the commander of the Carignan-Salières Regiment, a veteran of the German and Spanish wars, had a Mohawk delegate to Quebec strangled and the rest of the delegation imprisoned.[20] Similarly, during the summer of 1687, some Iroquois delegates attending peace talks at Fort Frontenac were captured by the Marquis de Denonville, who had them sent to work on the Mediterranean galleys of the Sun King.[21] French diplomatic missions in Iroquoia could be equally risky. In 1690, for example, two peace delegates were tortured to death by the Onondagas.[22]

When it was necessary, in times of war, to send ambassadors to negotiate with enemy, the Native delegations customarily brought along a few prisoners to return so that the discussions might start off well. In 1697, for example, two Mohawk delegates went to Quebec taking with them "two young French ladies"; though irritated by the Mohawk's proposals, Frontenac "replied that he pardoned them nevertheless in consideration of the two captives."[23] On several occasions the Amerindians used representatives who were considered neutral to open or restart the negotiation process.[24] For example, Bacqueville de La Potherie described the case of an Oneida chief, Otacheté, "who found himself in the position of a mediator in peace talks between us [the French] and the Iroquois" in 1697,[25] and the case of Massias, "a La Montagne Iroquois ... who was a representative who went back and forth in all the negotiations" in 1699.[26]

In most of the negotiations between New France and the Five Nations, the role of mediator was played by Iroquois living in the colony's mission villages who were theoretically allies of the French but who, because of their links with Iroquoia, could travel without problems from Montreal to the villages of the League. There was also Oureouhare, the Cayuga sachem who survived the galleys of Louis XIV and returned to Canada in 1689. On several occasions, Oureouhare acted as Governor Frontenac's ambassador in his attempts to make peace with the Iroquois.[27] However – and the ambiguous case of Oureouhare illustrates this – it was not easy to draw the line between the role of mediation and that of espionage.[28] Secret relations and dealings had developed between the Iroquois in the mission villages and those in Iroquoia, enabling the Five Nations to be constantly informed of French military movements.[29]

Similarly, the Jesuits and the handful of other Frenchmen who had been adopted by the Iroquois all acted both as diplomats and as spies for the governor. Thus, the presence of missionaries in Iroquoia was considered very important by colonial authorities in both Quebec and Albany. The authorities in New York sent Protestant missionaries to the Five Nations not only for religious reasons, but also in support of their political strategy of gaining control and influence over the Iroquois.[30]

In addition, Native ambassadors who claimed to be acting on behalf of their nation often represented only a clan or a faction. They would subsequently have to convince all their compatriots in order to have their agreements ratified.[31] The political organization of the Amerindians of the northeast was based neither on absolute power nor on majority rule, but on consensus,[32] and no individual had to comply with a public decision that went against his or her wishes.

Finally, the hostage system provided a good means for keeping negotiations going and for judging the sincerity of delegates. In May 1694, for example, Frontenac stated to the Iroquois ambassadors who had come to negotiate in Quebec: "I ask that ... you leave me two of your people so that I can persuade the nations of the Pays d'en Haut that the proposals you have come to make to me are sincere."[33] Frontenac's suspiciousness can probably be explained by past wars, but it was also the result of a stereotypical view of the Iroquois as treacherous and untrustworthy. In 1697, receiving a delegation from four of the Five Nations, Frontenac refused to accept Otacheté as a hostage, regarding him as an Iroquois faithful to the French. This rejection led an Onondaga chief, Arratio, to offer himself as a prisoner and pledge of peace.[34] Similarly, in July 1700, out of six Iroquois delegates who came to Montreal to make serious promises of alliance, four remained as hostages.[35]

The System of International Conferences

The system of international conferences that brought together the Native peoples and the Europeans, two sovereign entities[36] and two cultures, for the purpose of mutual accommodation, was marked by a whole series of ritualized procedures whose form was at least as important as their substance; these procedures amply demonstrate the extent of European adaptation.[37]

Large-scale diplomatic meetings were preceded by invitations sent out several weeks, or even several months, in advance by the interested party or parties. In September 1700, for example, Governor Callière invited the various Native nations present in Montreal[38] to a peace conference to be held in August of the following year, and dispatched emissaries to the Great Lakes to invite the other allied nations as well.[39] The location for a council was always specified, and it was, of course, a very important issue, strategically as well as psychologically. In October 1693, for instance, the Oneida chief Tareha proposed in vain to Frontenac that he send French delegates to Albany to negotiate a general peace. The governor had no intention of negotiating such an agreement in any place other than New France.[40]

At the end of the seventeenth century, several sites were favoured for big international meetings: Montreal or Quebec when the French received Amerindian plenipotentiaries; Albany, the traditional setting for conferences between the Iroquois and New York; Michilimackinac, where the representatives of the Great Lakes nations met[41] and which could also accommodate French-Native meetings; and Onondaga, the capital of the Five Nations League, the site of negotiations both between Iroquois and Europeans, and between Iroquois and other Native nations. In 1695 the Huron chief Le Baron, who was hardly a supporter of the French alliance, stated outright to an officer posted in the west that Onondaga was the place "where all business must be concluded."[42]

Each party made preparations for the negotiations at home, with the speakers, on both the Amerindian and the European side, receiving their instructions there. La Potherie said of the Iroquois delegation that came to Quebec in May 1694: "The oration or the collars that this [Iroquois] ambassador pronounced was so much in conformity with what Father Milet, who had been held captive and had attended all their councils, had told Count Frontenac ... [it might] be said that no differences could be found."[43] Likewise, when Callière sent emissaries to Onondaga in June 1701, he gave them very precise instructions, including various speeches suited for all situations.[44]

The Native ambassadors were never picked at random. Among the Iroquois, they were the best orators and not always the hereditary chiefs. The same was apparently true among the Amerindians of the Great Lakes,[45] although the presence of prestigious leaders such as Onanguicé or Kondiaronk as delegates at major conferences in Montreal or even at Michilimackinac suggests that in the west the speakers were often important chiefs.[46] It is worth noting in this regard that chiefs in Native societies were in no sense the possessors of any kind of sovereignty, but at most were spokespersons. Thus, they had to have some talent for oratory. People who could use words skilfully were called upon to play a political and diplomatic role: words and power were closely connected.[47]

According to Iroquois custom, the hosts and visitors first met at the edge of the woods, a few kilometres from the place designated for the negotiations, to carry out part of the ritual protocol. Thus, in June 1701, when French delegates went to Onondaga, they were met beforehand a few leagues away, in Gannentaha, where the Iroquois welcomed them and invited them to rest. A little later, according to La Potherie, "Teganissorens, accompanied by 50 to 60 young people from Onondaga, and a quantity of women sent by the Elders to carry the baggage of the French ... came three leagues to our [French] ambassadors, whom he greeted according to custom with three strings of wampum ... With one, he dried their tears, the second cleared their throats, and the third wiped the braid stained with blood."[48] La Potherie was describing here the Amerindian reception ceremony[49] for their diplomatic partners, a ceremony that was preliminary to any talks and that included a ritual of condolences. When the delegates arrived at the site planned for the conference, they were usually welcomed with the sound of musket fire, as when the French arrived in Onondaga in July 1700[50] or the Iroquois in Montreal in September of the same year.[51]

The discussions did not start immediately. The delegates usually rested for two days before the conference began.[52] The conference itself was divided into a series of meetings held over several days or even several weeks. According to Amerindian custom, a party would only respond to a series of proposals the following day, or even two or three days later.[53] On the appointed day, the two parties placed themselves facing each other, and the talks began with the expression of condolences. In March 1699, for example, the Iroquois delegates who had come to Montreal mourned the death of Frontenac in front of Callière.[54] This ritual was a transposition to the diplomatic sphere of a ceremony essential to the political and social life of many of the Native nations of the northeast; this was the Condolence Council, which was devoted to mourning deceased chiefs and instating their successors. Here is a sign that the Euro-Americans, in their diplomatic relations with the Native peoples, were functioning within a framework that was fundamentally connected to Amerindian culture. Witness the behaviour of the Jesuit Father Bruyas, who, before making his proposals in Onondaga in August 1700, expressed "his regret at the loss by the Iroquois nation of several chiefs of merit."[55] The French had clearly learned that, to make agreements with the Native peoples, they had to participate in a ritual that lay at the heart of Native tradition. After the condolences, the main leaders smoked the peace pipe in turn in order to calm everyone and create feelings favourable to peace.[56]

The appointed speaker then took the floor with his essential collars, or belts, of wampum, which a French observer described as "the assurance of their word, and it seems that as eloquent as they are, they could not open their mouths if this collar did not appear before they spoke."[57] As the Baron de Lahontan explained: "Without the intervention of these Coliers, there's no business to be negotiated with the Savages."[58]

The wampum collars consisted of cylindrical beads made from marine shells,[59] polished, bored, and threaded in rows to form rectangular bands[60] or sometimes single strings.[61] The size of the wampum, its colour, and the symbols created by the alternation of white and purple beads were never random. A collar longer and wider than a single strand necessarily had greater symbolic value in negotiations. The colour white signified peace and life, black symbolized death, and red, the colour of blood, was a sign of war. For the Amerindians, wampum conveyed voice and word, and its purpose was, in a ritualized way, to affirm and validate the message transmitted.

After reciting the proposal that accompanied each collar, the speaker laid it down at the feet of the person addressed. If the wampum was accepted, it meant that the message would be taken into consideration and that there would probably be a positive answer, itself confirmed by another collar. But the wampum, and therefore the message, could be rejected immediately. In 1698, for example, Frontenac refused an Iroquois collar that asked him to return the hostages and prisoners that he held.[62]

In reality, it was not the wampum as such that was important to the Native peoples; rather it was its use and the process of exchanging gifts that resulted from it. It was therefore possible, in the absence of wampum, to use beaver pelts or other animal skins, tobacco, axes, clothing, or other goods. The Great Lakes nations, which had less wampum, appear to have used these things more frequently than the Atlantic nations or the Iroquois. Wampum, however, had the advantage of having a mnemonic function because of the symbols woven into it, and thus it acquired the value of a historical record. It was carefully preserved by the Native chiefs, and

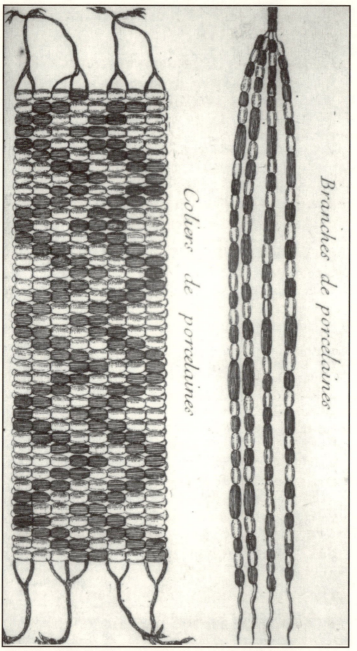

Wampum of the eighteenth century (From Bacqueville de La Potherie, *Histoire de l'Amérique septentrionale* [Paris: Jean-Luc Nion et François Didot, 1752], 1:334. Photograph: Marc Laberge, Vidéanthrop

historical tradition was maintained through oral transmission, for, as Lahontan wrote, "the savages have the best memory in the world."[63]

A seventeenth-century Jesuit said of these "savages": "These people, I believe, are the greatest orators of all the earth. They do nothing without it."[64] The Native peoples' skill with words was in evidence at diplomatic meetings.[65] The orators displayed a sense of theatricality, modulating their voices according to the subject and using gestures and metaphors[66] to develop their symbolism. The use of song, dance, or even mime was not rare, although these were subordinated to the spoken word. Charlevoix described the orators' performances as "somewhat like plays in which things that are very reasonable are expressed through rather comical gestures and manners."[67] Total silence was required while an orator was speaking, and only his companions could interrupt him, by shouting their approval.

Interpreters were essential figures at Euro-Amerindian conferences and even those among Native nations. In New France they were Jesuit missionaries, people connected to the administration of the posts or the fur trade, or coureurs de bois or voyageurs; all owed their linguistic abilities to their long contact with the Native people. The Native orators were concerned that their speeches should be correctly translated with all their rhetoric reproduced. Otreouti, a famous Onondaga chief representing the Iroquois at the La Famine meeting in September 1684 with Governor La Barre, told the French interpreter Le Moyne after finishing his speech: "Akouessan, take Heart, you are a Man of Sense; speak and explain my meaning; be sure you forget nothing, but declare all that thy Brethren and thy Friends represent to thy chief Onnontio, by the voice of the Grangula [Otreouti], who pays you all Honour and Respect, and invites you to accept of this Present of Beavers, and to assist at this Feast immediately."[68]

The conferences always ended with reciprocal gift giving, which had the value of a mutual commitment when a treaty was concluded, and with the noise and gaiety of a reconciliatory feast. All this was very costly for the colonies, especially when the diplomatic meetings were very large, as they were for the negotiation of the Treaty of Montreal in 1701.

The various elements that structured and adorned the protocol of the conferences were thus essentially of Amerindian origin,[69] although the Europeans also enriched the model of treaty

negotiation somewhat, if only with a musket salute or the introduction of alcohol to the feasts.

One of the ironies of European-Amerindian contact is that the
colonizers had to adapt, through the mechanisms of diplomatic protocol, to the rituals of people they considered "savages" or "barbarians" in order to negotiate agreements with them. In August
1690, during an important conference with the allied nations in
Montreal, Frontenac, a powdered, bewigged, elegantly dressed sex-
agenarian aristocrat, chanted the war song with a hatchet in his
hand and joined the Amerindians in their ceremonial dances. La
Potherie reported: "The cries and shouts Monsieur de Frontenac
was obliged to make to conform to their manners further increased
the Bacchic passion."[70] This is a striking example of European
adaptation, and it also illustrates Governor Frontenac's skill as a
diplomat and his ability to manipulate the Amerindians.

Similarly, Governor Callière said to the Iroquois ambassadors in
Montreal in September 1700, "I mourn the dead you have lost ...
and cleanse the earth that has been reddened with their blood."[71]
With these words, he was not only adhering to the Native ritual of
condolences, but also using the metaphors of Native orations.[72]
This capacity to play the other's game, to conform to a different
political culture, may in the long term be interpreted as a kind of
superiority on the part of the Europeans, who in imperialistic self-
interest adapted to the Native culture, the better to dominate. In the
short term, it was the diplomatic tradition of the Amerindians that
appeared to prevail.

2 Alliances and Strategies in the Late Seventeenth Century

Spurred by French and English imperialism, two major systems of alliances based on the fur trade were created in northeastern North America in the seventeenth century. It was a given of European diplomacy that any international (and, as in this case, bicultural and inter-ethnic) alliance be based fundamentally on specific advantages and even reciprocal concessions, in which each partner played its own game. Alliances are ambiguous in that they do not imply a perfect unity in action and thought on the part of their members. Thus, it is impossible to reduce diplomatic relations in northeastern North America in the seventeenth century to only two actors, since the multilateral alliances included several Native nations and indeed several colonies. For convenience, however, and without ignoring the factionalism that marked the Native peoples' political manoeuvring or the divisions that existed within the colonies, I will simplify the situation by speaking in terms of four players on the diplomatic chessboard of the negotiation of the Great Peace of Montreal: New France; New York; the Native peoples allied with the French, in particular the Great Lakes nations; and the Iroquois of the League.

THE NETWORKS OF ALLIANCES

The systems of alliances that were established in the seventeenth century were the result not only of European-Native contact, but also of the extension of the existing diplomatic networks, a sign that the Europeans were not their sole founders. In this sense, New France formed an additional branch among the multilateral Amerindian alliances. But it was an important branch, because the French governor, without having subjugated his partners, was nonetheless quickly given a central place in that system.[1]

Alliance and Power

From 1660 to 1700, the rival colonial powers of Europe attempted to build empires in North America in the name of two distinct principles presumed to justify and legalize territorial possessions: the "right of conquest" for the English and the "right of discovery" for the French.[2] In the ideology underlying this imperialism, the Native nations were seen as savage little tribes, lacking any form of organized government, that were destined to be saved through European conquest and assimilation.[3] On the basis of these theoretical arguments, which are nothing less than subjective, self-serving rationalizations, the Euro-Americans quickly came to consider the Native nations with whom they maintained relations as being completely under their sovereignty. According to the French and English view of the European-Amerindian alliance, Europeans had unequivocal authority over the Native peoples, who were generally reduced to the status of mere subjects either of His Majesty the King of England or of the Sun King. In this view, the Amerindian chiefs were rather like vassals owing military assistance and obedience to the colony in return for gifts and protection from external threats. To the authorities of New France, the Amerindians of the Great Lakes had a special status: there was no recognition of them as sovereign, but in the political tradition of the kingdom in relation to the provinces and other elements that composed it, they were placed, not under the yoke of the king, but under his "protection."[4]

To understand the historical nature of European-Amerindian relations, to identify the real relationships between the partners, we need to distinguish between theory and practice. It appears that the colonies and the Native nations collaborated within the networks of alliances. The French did not recognize the sovereignty of the Native nations, which did not possess states, but they negotiated with them in the same way that they negotiated in Europe, by signing proper treaties. This was a de facto recognition of the Native peoples' independence.[5]

The Amerindians, for their part, resisted the European discourse by regularly asserting their independence. In 1684, for example, an Iroquois chief told a delegate from New York: "Onontio [the French governor] has been my father for ten years and Corlar [the governor of New York] has been my brother for a long time, and that is because I accepted it: neither one nor the other is my master."[6] The relationships between allies were in no way relationships of dominance and submission. In the west, for example, French sovereignty extended only as far as the range of a musket from the forts.[7]

The Amerindian and European conceptions of alliance can be better understood by looking at the kinship terms used in the diplomatic sphere. Among the Native nations, people referred to each other metaphorically as grandfather, uncle, father, cousin, son, or nephew.[8] The colonial agents, whose political culture lent itself to such analogies,[9] in turn used the Native peoples' terminology. But the partners did not always have the same interpretation of the kinship terms they both used.

The metaphor of "brothers" structured the relations between the English and the Iroquois in the Covenant Chain. In the logic of both kinship systems, this term placed them on an equal footing. In 1688, however, the English governor of New York, Andros, tried to impose the father-and-children terminology on the Mohawks in the alliance and they immediately rejected it. Perhaps they wished to resist the hegemonic claims of the English or merely indicate to them that their "paternal" protection was not necessary. In contrast, the Amerindians of the Hudson River, in particular the Mahicans, had been calling the governor of New York their father since 1677. In other colonies, the Amerindians gave the English the status of "younger brothers" or "elder brothers," the latter endowing them with a certain symbolic superiority.[10]

The Iroquois sometimes used the metaphor of an uncle and his nephews to define the relationship between the French governor and certain of his allies in the mission villages.[11] This was not in any way a relationship of sovereign and subjects; in their kinship system, the uncle, whose moral authority was greater than that of the father, received respect for his protection of his nephew, and it was his role to advise him.

The French-Amerindian alliance, organized around the metaphor of a father and children, was more ambiguous than the English-Iroquois alliance.[12] The governor of New France, starting in the 1660s, called his Native allies and the Iroquois his "children," and insisted that they address him as "father."[13] This was one of the conditions required of the Five Nations for negotiating peace with the French.[14] Paternal authority, which was closely related to absolutism and Catholic dogma, was felt to give the governor coercive power over the Amerindians; Onontio established a relationship of authority over those peoples that were his "children," subordinating them to his will. However, the Native peoples did not share the Europeans' conception of paternal authority. Iroquoian society in particular was matrilineal, and cultural paternity did not coincide with biological paternity but was the prerogative of the maternal uncle; the father had no authority over his children. Whether or not the Algonquian nations of the Great Lakes were drawing on the Iroquoian matrilinear model in their dealings with the French,[15] the Great Lakes nations did not place any greater authority on the figure of the father. As the interpreter and coureur de bois Nicolas Perrot wrote, "The elders call the youths son and the youth call the elders father," adding, "A father would not dare use authority over his son, nor the chief over his soldier; he would ask him gently."[16] In fact, when the leaders of New France's allies called the governor their father, this was in no way a gesture of submission, but in their thinking a way of addressing a mediator and provider. The power of Onontio was thus associated with that of the chiefs in the Native societies of the northeast; his "orders" were merely suggestions, and his influence depended on his generosity, his power, and his ability to persuade. The Amerindians acknowledged that the French agents had a certain power – specifically, that of arbitration – but it was not of the coercive kind. As R. White writes, "The alliance, because it was largely Algonquian in form and spirit, demanded a father who mediated more often than he commanded, who forgave more often then he punished, and who gave more than he received."[17]

While there was a certain balance between the actors, this should not be seen as having overshadowed the power of colonialism. Behind individual subjective perceptions, there was an objective process of subordination of the Native peoples. Onontio, for example, took advantage of his position as arbitrator in the alliance to establish a colonial relationship with the Native peoples.[18]

The French-Amerindian Alliance

Origins and Development of the Alliance   The French-Amerindian alliance, as it developed under Champlain, was formed around the

Montagnais and the Algonquins from 1603 on, and then around the powerful Huron confederation starting in the years 1609 to 1615, on the basis of trade and joint military expeditions against the Iroquois.[19] The destruction of Huronia by the Five Nations in 1649–50 created a new situation. The surviving Hurons from the Great Lakes region came back together and joined with the Petuns, forming the Huron-Petun (or Tionontati) group, while the French ventured further into the west to rebuild the fur-trading network.[20]

The broadening of the alliance occurred between 1665 and 1680 through French expansion towards the Great Lakes. This expansion, first of trade, then of missionary activities, and, finally, with the arrival of the imperial authorities,[21] of political presence, involved the creation of a chain of economic and military posts[22] and the establishment of French-Amerindian alliances in the region of lakes Superior, Huron, and Michigan.[23] In addition to the Huron-Petuns, the main nations that became associated with the French were the Odawas, the Ojibwas (especially the Saulteurs), the Potawatomis, the Miamis, the Illinois, the Mascoutens, the Foxes, the Kickapoos, the Nipissings, the Winnebagos, and the Sauks.[24] Certain nations took leadership roles in these broad Native alliances, and it seems that the Odawas (the main trading partners of the French), the Potawatomis, and the Ojibwas actually held a hegemonic position along with the Huron-Petuns, who, because of their diplomatic tradition and the prestige of their past, acted as guardians of the "fire" of the alliance in Michilimackinac.[25] In 1695, finally, the French contracted an unstable alliance with the Dakota Sioux when a chief of theirs visited Montreal.[26]

Strengths and Weaknesses of the Alliance   The French-Amerindian alliance of the west had its strengths and its weaknesses. It was based on common interests but also on specific advantages for each actor. The French and the Native nations derived many benefits from their alliance economically and militarily, but also politically. For New France, alliances with the Amerindians were nothing less than the key to survival in North America. In 1699, referring to the possibility of a rupture in the friendship networks in the west, Intendant Champigny stated clearly, "The savages our friends will become our enemies, and the result will be the inevitable loss of the colony, which could never be sustained without them, and much less still if they were against us."[27]

The fur trade was not only the keystone of the system of French-Amerindian alliances; it also provided the basis for the existence of the colony on the St Lawrence, which was integrally linked to "King Beaver."[28] The Native peoples were essential suppliers of furs to New France both at the annual fair in Montreal and, even more in the 1680s, at the posts in the west.[29] The Odawas and the Potawatomis in particular made it possible for the French to obtain the best pelts, which were collected from the nations of the region northwest of the Great Lakes.[30]

In addition to the economic benefits of these alliances, there were obvious military advantages for the colony. The Jesuit fathers, who were clearly as well versed in the problems of empire as in religious affairs, said of the Native allies in 1692, "They are very useful in peacetime for their hunting, but particularly in war against our enemies, whom they alone can reach in the woods."[31] With their tradition as warriors, the Great Lakes nations, sometimes under the influence of French agents, contributed decisively to the weakening of the Iroquois Confederacy. In this effort, they constituted an auxiliary force that became essential to New France in the intercolonial rivalries of the late seventeenth and eighteenth centuries.[32] For example, some five hundred warriors from the Great Lakes nations took part in La Barre's expedition in 1684,[33] and more than four hundred of them participated when Denonville attacked and razed the Seneca villages in 1687.[34] The allies brought not only their "multitudes"[35] but also their ability to wage war in the woods, without which the French armies would never have managed to weaken the Iroquois as they did.[36]

If the Amerindians of the Great Lakes accepted – and even asked for – forts on their territories, it is because they benefited from their alliance with the French. Objectively or not, they saw the alliance as a means to enhance their power. They saw the French above all as absolutely essential trading partners. In exchange for furs, they obtained the whole range of European trading goods (firearms, pots, axes, knives, cloth, blankets, shirts, etc.). These goods were integrated into the Native way of life without really changing it, and without creating dependency in the strict sense, although a process leading towards it had clearly begun.[37]

Firearms, powder, and ammunition were particularly valued and sought after by the Amerindians,[38] and these military supplies were often distributed to them free,[39] as gifts.[40] According to Charlevoix, the Miamis and the Potawatomis had rifles as early as 1671.[41] Starting in the 1680s, to satisfy their Native allies, the French kept blacksmiths in the posts of the west to repair muskets and make balls.[42] At the great conference held in Montreal in 1701, the chief of the Miamis, Chichicatalo, said to Callière, "Father, we beseech you to have pity on us; we are unhappy since the French are no longer among us and in particular a blacksmith to mend our weapons and our axes."[43] The Amerindians used firearms in hunting but even more in waging war,[44] in order to impose their superiority in intertribal conflicts or at least to defend themselves against their enemies. This was particularly true for the nations allied with the French, especially the Hurons, who had experienced serious setbacks in their struggles against the Iroquois in the 1640s, in large part because of the lack of firearms.[45] At the end of the seventeenth century, the Native allies of New France were a better match for their enemies – the Five Nations and the Dakota Sioux.[46] In July 1695 an ambassador representing "twenty-two villages" of the latter "nation" went to Montreal to meet Governor Frontenac, to whom he appealed as a "father" for protection. The Sioux chief did not want to submit to a European colony, but intended rather to join the French alliance in order to benefit from it, as did the other nations. Therefore he asked first of all to be provided with "iron and ammunition."[47]

The presence of the French within the Native nations gave the latter many advantages. As La Potherie reported, "It was enough for a nation to possess Frenchmen to believe itself protected from the insults of its neighbours; they became Mediators in all disputes."[48] In July 1701 in Montreal, for example, the Foxes asked the governor if a Jesuit, a blacksmith, and "a few Frenchmen" (including Nicolas Perrot, who had considerable influence with the Amerindians of the Great Lakes) could be brought to them. If this wish was granted, said the chief of the Foxes, "the Sauteurs [Ojibwas] would not be bold enough to come and insult us."[49] Similarly, in 1673 the Illinois welcomed the arrival of the French,[50] whom they regarded as potential military allies against the Iroquois.[51] A last example is that of the Huron chief Kondiaronk, who, representing the nations of Michilimackinac in Montreal in 1682, asked Frontenac for French protection because the Iroquois continued to pose a military threat in the Great Lakes region. Significantly, he addressed Onontio as his "father," giving him the role of protector and provider.[52]

Clearly, there were economic and strategic bonds of interdependence between the French and their Amerindian allies. Denys Delâge notes two key links that were central to the system of French-Native alliances, beyond the fur trade: a shared resentment of the Iroquois and a shared fear of the expansionism of the British, who, because of their demographic superiority and in contrast to the French, had an antagonistic relationship with the first occupants of the land.[53]

The network of alliances between New France and the Great Lakes nations, although sustained by a broad range of interests, nevertheless remained a fragile economic and military construction. First of all, the Amerindians did not form a unified bloc; there were many tensions among the peoples in the Great Lakes region, and these sometimes degenerated into military clashes.[54] Such divisions ran counter to the trading and strategic interests of the French authorities, who were anxious to impose a "Pax Gallica" in the west, a necessary condition for trade. Furthermore, the Native allies did not hesitate to approach the Iroquois and the English on occasion.[55] They had more diplomatic leeway than the French in the context of imperial rivalries. In fact, at least in the short term, the French needed the alliance much more than the Great Lakes nations did. Thus, in 1690, following the success of Iroquois warriors in Lachine, near Montreal, the French alliance appeared to be in danger, as the nations of Michilimackinac were on the point of joining the political and trading network of the Iroquois and the English.[56] Furthermore, some groups – for example, the Foxes and the Mascoutens – by repeatedly robbing the French coureurs de bois, had placed themselves at the extreme limit of the alliance with the French.[57]

Other Allies of New France   New France's network of alliances was not limited to the Great Lakes nations. The French were also allied with the more closely knit union of the Wabanaki (or Abenaki) Confederacy and with the Algonquins, Montagnais, and other Amerindians settled in the colony's mission villages. The Wabanaki Confederacy was a multilateral alliance that included the Penobscots, the Mi'kmaqs, the Maliseets, and the Passamaquoddys.[58] Charlevoix regarded these nations as New France's "best allies."[59] Their military activity against New England during and after the war of the League of Augsburg (1688–97) provided a valuable bulwark for the French in Acadia.[60] It was because the Abenakis were under great pressure from the threat of the British colonies that they allied with the French,[61] although they did not hesitate to start talks with the English when they felt abandoned by the French.[62] As for the Algonquins and the Montagnais, they had been allied with the French since the beginning of the seventeenth century. The former were more active in the war against the Iroquois and seemed more attached to their alliance with the French.[63]

Finally, there were allied Amerindian villages within the colony on the St Lawrence that had been established in the second half of the seventeenth century. These *réductions*, based on those in Paraguay, were established jointly by the civil and religious authorities. The French called their residents *domiciliés* because they had settled permanently on the St Lawrence and were part of colonial society. They were Christian converts who were originally from Georgian Bay (Hurons), New England (Abenakis), or Iroquoia, who had all come to "plant their villages" near the French settlements. The Hurons settled near the town of Quebec in 1650, following the destruction of their confederation by the Iroquois, and established themselves permanently at Lorette (Wendake) in 1697. Some of the Abenakis, fleeing the threat of the English colonists, sought refuge with the French in the late 1670s and established two villages on the St Lawrence, St François (Odanak) and Bécancour (Wôlinak). The Iroquois converts, who were mainly Mohawks and Oneidas, migrated to the Montreal region starting in 1667, encouraged by the missionaries living among them and by the civil authorities, who wanted to use their villages as a buffer zone against enemy attacks. In doing so, they were breaking with the League, in keeping with the Amerindians' secessionist tradition, and joining the French alliance.

The region was not new to the Iroquois; documents indicate that the Mohawks had hunting territories around Montreal well before the establishment of the réductions and perhaps as far back as the late sixteenth century. The exodus became very large and contributed to the demographic weakening of the Iroquois League. The reasons for these migrations were varied; they were sometimes related to conversion, but they sometimes involved social concerns (a desire to escape the scourge of alcoholism) or political, or even economic, aims (to take part in the so-called smuggling between

Huron couple, c. 1750–75. Anonymous watercolour, Ville de Montréal, Gestion de documents et archives, Philéas Gagnon Collection, BM7, 42500 (034-02-04-01).

The garments and accessories worn by this Huron man and woman show a blend of traditional aboriginal clothing such as leggings and moccasins along with European items obtained as gifts or through trade – glass beads, silver earrings, armbands and bracelets, wool blankets, and linen shirts.

Montreal and Albany). Two communities were established: Sault St Louis (Kahnawake), two leagues south of Montreal; and La Montagne, a Sulpician mission located at what is now the intersection of Atwater and Sherbrooke streets in Montreal, which in addition to Iroquois included Hurons, Nipissings, and Algonquins.

The majority of the Iroquois converts were actually prisoners adopted by the Five Nations, and more than twenty different nations were represented in the Montreal-area réductions. The mission villagers were valuable military auxiliaries for the colony, especially between 1684 and 1696, a period during which they took part in many raids against the Five Nations, teaching the French the art of combat in the heart of the forest. Under the guidance of the missionaries, they all practised a syncretic Christianity, and despite the process of subjugation, they remained de facto autonomous allies of the French. Colonial power was not exercised fully in the mission villages; the villagers were not subject to French justice, paid no seigneurial dues, and were not conscripted into the militia.[64]

Furthermore, the mission villagers gradually established political ties among themselves and created a network of alliances of their own. This network, known as the Seven Fires and whose existence is documented under the British regime (after 1760), may date back to the French regime. There are indications that Kahnawake (Sault St Louis), the capital of this federation, was already a centre of diplomacy in the networks of alliances of the northeast in the early eighteenth century. There the Iroquois from the mission villages met their brothers from the League, but also delegates from the Great Lakes and Atlantic nations. In 1705 some Abenakis told chiefs from Kahnawake, "You are my elder brother and the centre to which comes all the news under the ground from Orange [Albany] and from the Iroquois and from the most distant nations; you always have your ears open, let me know what you learn."[65] It is not possible to say conclusively that the political federation of the Seven Fires already existed in this period or that Kahnawake played a central diplomatic role, but it is clear that the Iroquois from the mission villages, taking advantage of Montreal's strategic position, acted as intermediaries in the international networks. They certainly did so during the negotiations for the Great Peace of 1701. Their diplomatic role, which was essential for those negotiations, had been enhanced as a result of the peace agreement concluded between them and the Iroquois of the League at the end of 1696.[66]

The Covenant Chain

The English-Iroquois diplomatic network, known as the Covenant Chain, was a multilateral alliance that included both English colonies and Native nations. Founded in Albany in 1677,[67] was a pact of friendship whose origins went back to the earliest treaties negotiated between the Dutch colonists and the Amerindians of the Hudson in the first half of the seventeenth century. Initially, in 1618, the pact was symbolized by a rope,[68] and then, in 1643, when New Netherland formed an alliance with the Mohawks, by an iron chain. The English replaced the Dutch in New York in 1664, and the chain, renewed, now included the Iroquois Five Nations.[69] Finally, through two peace treaties negotiated in Albany in 1677, the chain became silver,[70] thus inaugurating the Covenant Chain, strictly speaking.[71]

The colonies concerned were placed under the general supervision of New York, and the Iroquois held a dominant role among the nations of the alliance.[72] Their proximity to Albany also gave the Mohawks a key role in the Covenant Chain, as they were the New York settlement's closest allies.[73]

Like the French-Amerindian network, the English-Iroquois alliance was based on mutual economic benefits. The Iroquois, in particular, could obtain European products cheaply.[74] For the English, from a geostrategic point of view, the Five Nations formed a valuable "barrier between the ... French and their Indians, and His Majesty's Plantations as Far as Virginia and Maryland."[75] Along with the Amerindians of the Hudson Valley – primarily Mahicans – they also constituted important military allies for New York in the War of the League of Augsburg.[76] The Iroquois alliance was also an excellent springboard for the English to use to penetrate into the Great Lakes region, which had been claimed by New France.[77] With the Five Nations as enemies, the English would have no hope of forming an alliance with the nations of the west.

The geographic proximity of the partners, the relative unity of the Iroquois League, and the low prices of the goods in Albany probably gave the Covenant Chain a more solid foundation than that of the French-Amerindian coalition. However, the two allies did not have the same conception of the chain that bound them metaphorically. The English regarded the Iroquois as their subjects, whereas the Iroquois saw the alliance as an association of equals in which each partner was free to act according to its own strategies.[78]

THE STRATEGIES OF THE PARTIES

It is difficult to speak of common strategies on the part of the Native peoples. There were dissensions within the leagues, nations, and villages that made it almost impossible for them to establish a united policy. The absence of coercion meant that each person, each family, each clan could act freely. War in particular, far from being the preserve of any authority, was very often an individual matter, and young warriors who wanted to distinguish themselves in combat could break up the negotiation of alliances by the elders. The Iroquois Confederacy, the most highly centralized alliance, was itself weakened by factional tensions.[79] Such dissension did not only afflict the Native nations; the French and the English were also divided. In New France, for example, the missionaries and merchants did not always see their relations with the Amerindians in the same way, and the administrators did not control the activities of the coureurs de bois.[80]

To simplify matters, however, I will speak of the main strategies of all the parties in the Great Peace of Montreal. They all endeavoured, first and foremost, to maintain their alliances, but they also wanted to keep the option of extending them or at least of establishing economic relations with a member of another political network. It was certainly difficult for an Amerindian nation to deal with two enemy colonies without problems; it was still more delicate for a European power to have excellent relations with two nations that were at war.[81]

The Strategies of the French

By about 1700, the little colony established by Champlain on the St Lawrence River at the beginning of the seventeenth century had begun to look like the hub of an "empire." The activities of the explorers, coureurs de bois, missionaries, and other agents of New France in the regions of the Great Lakes and the Mississippi had made it possible for the French to build a network of influence in the west, in spite of orders from Jean-Baptiste Colbert, the minister of marine, that colonization efforts should be concentrated on the St Lawrence.[82] It was primarily the fur trade that motivated this expansion westward, and in order to keep control of trade, the French had to maintain their alliances with the Amerindians. They had to first of all block all English or Iroquois efforts to get the nations of the west to join the Covenant Chain.[83] A break-up of their political alliances with the Great Lakes nations would have resulted in the end of the French colony. As the Jesuit historian Charlevoix remarked, "If these people ever joined with the Iroquois and the English, a single campaign would suffice to oblige all the French to leave Canada."[84] French imperial policy in the west thus consisted in preventing any such rapprochement by encouraging wars between the allied nations and the Iroquois.[85] In this effort, New France also had to work to ease the conflicts among its allies and even those between its allies and the enemy Sioux nation, since this would facilitate French trade in the Great Lakes region.[86]

This policy of keeping the conflict alive between the Five Nations and the nations of the west was consistent with the French military strategy of wearing down the Iroquois Confederacy to force it to make peace.[87] Accordingly, with or without their allies of the Great Lakes, the French organized military expeditions against the Iroquois villages.[88] This allowed them to demonstrate their military power to the Great Lakes nations, who always tended to ally themselves with the strongest party.[89] In 1689, with war between the French and the English imminent, Callière and Denonville, to defeat the Iroquois, even prepared a plan to conquer New York. Such a victory would not only have refuted England's claims of sovereignty over Iroquoia, but would also have cut off the supply of weapons and ammunition to the Five Nations from their English and Dutch allies.[90]

Still, while the French had an interest in weakening the Iroquois, it was not in their interest to destroy them completely. The strategic paradox lay in the fact that the Five Nations, while remaining dangerous enemies, were a geopolitical cornerstone of the French trading empire in North America. Callière was very explicit on this point when he told the minister of marine, in 1694, that they had to leave the Iroquois "strong enough that the fear that our Odawas may have of them still serves as a barrier to prevent them from going over to the English to seek a good market for their merchandise."[91] What was at stake in this policy was revealed in the negotiations of 1701.

The Strategies of the Nations in the West

The Great Lakes nations that were allied with the French did not always work together. There were both tensions between nations and

political dissension within them. These divisions may have reflected
the different diplomatic approaches of the nations of the west, but
since these nations were probably aware that they constituted a network of shared interests against external threats, it is still possible
to speak of common strategies.

The Great Lakes nations (Odawas, Potawatomis, Sauks, Miamis,
Huron-Petuns, etc.) that were most often at war with the Iroquois
at the end of the seventeenth century could appreciate both the material advantages of alliance with the French and Onontio's military
aid, although they sometimes found this aid insufficient. While the
French were afraid of losing their alliance with these nations, the reverse was also true: the Great Lakes nations wanted at all costs that
a separate peace between the Iroquois League and New France be
avoided.[92] Their desire to wage war against the Five Nations did
not readily accommodate the occasional peace efforts towards the
Iroquois of the French governors.

A diplomatic coup by the Huron-Petun chief Kondiaronk in the
fall of 1688 illustrates this strategy of the Great Lakes nations. With
a hundred warriors, Kondiaronk started out from Michilimackinac
to make a raid against the Iroquois. When he arrived at Fort
Frontenac, he was surprised to learn that Denonville was negotiating a peace with the Iroquois and that some Onondaga delegates
were expected in Montreal at any moment. Pretending to return to
Michilimackinac as advised by the commander of the fort, Kondiaronk decided to intercept the Iroquois delegation in order to foil any
rapprochement between the French and the Iroquois. He set up an
ambush for the Onondaga ambassadors at La Famine, on the other
side of Lake Ontario, and after capturing them, he convinced them
that he had acted on the authority of Denonville. When Teganissorens, who represented the Iroquois delegates, told him what he
knew already, Kondiaronk feigned surprise and anger, and released
his prisoners, telling them: "Go, my brothers, I unbind you and
send you back to your people, though we are at war with you. It is
the Governor of the French who made me take an action so base
that I will never get over it unless your Five Nations take just revenge." New France's hopes for peace with the Iroquois were thus
temporarily shattered, and the war began again in earnest, to the
satisfaction of the Hurons and their allies.[93]

While the nations of the west had an interest in prolonging hostilities between the French and the Iroquois, they, too, could be
tempted by a diplomatic rapprochement with the Five Nations and

thus with the Covenant Chain network of alliances. This can be explained both by English-Iroquois political overtures and by the economic and military deficiencies of New France. The nations of the west were attracted by the English market in Albany, where they could obtain more goods for their pelts than in Montreal,[94] an attraction that intensified when the French were unable to absorb all the fur production of their Native allies.[95] Thus, at the end of the seventeenth century, certain groups were wavering between two strategies: either to work towards a pan-Amerindian coalition that would bring together the Great Lakes nations and the Iroquois or to play the traditional card of the French alliance against the Five Nations. This dilemma was reflected in the emergence of two factions among the Hurons of Michilimackinac around 1695. One faction, which favoured the French, was led by Kondiaronk;[96] the other, which favoured a reversal of alliances, was led by a man the French called Le Baron.[97] The strategy of rapprochement with the Iroquois – which was also the strategy of some Odawa chiefs in Michilimackinac – had the advantage of providing access to the Albany market, but it implied the end of the alliance with the French. In addition, this rapprochement was difficult for peoples with no coercive power or centralized government. The leaders in the west were unable at this time to contain the endemic guerrilla warfare between their peoples and the Five Nations, an enmity related to the quest for prestige by young warriors.

The allies of Onontio also did not look kindly on the increasingly distant expeditions of the French coureurs de bois, who were going far beyond Michilimackinac and Green Bay to trade with the Assiniboines and the Sioux in order to obtain pelts at the source and thus at lower cost. Through this trade, the Sioux were being supplied with firearms.[98] Since about 1660, possibly as a result of the dispersions of the Native nations caused by the Iroquois Wars,[99] a war had been going on between these Sioux and the Odawas, Huron-Petuns, Foxes, Potawatomis, Miamis, and other allies of New France.[100] French expansion in the early 1690s thus constituted a military threat to these groups. Champigny even reported to the French court in 1697: "[T]he Miami savages having this year made war against the Sioux, many Frenchmen who found themselves in the area declared themselves in favour of the latter [Sioux] against the others [Miamis] and killed a few of them [Miamis]. It is to be hoped that the Miamis ... do not take the opportunity to unite with the Iroquois."[101] The French alliance was thus weakened, and the coureurs de bois and voyageurs – who often acted without the approval of the colonial authorities – were no longer safe in the territories of the allied nations,[102] particularly when they travelled through the country of the Foxes, where robberies were frequent.[103] In 1695 the Foxes, as well as the Mascoutens, who were permanently at war with the Sioux, were even reported to be on the point of joining the English-Iroquois alliance to protect themselves from their Sioux neighbours and enemies.[104] The nations of the west were all the more tempted to do so because they did not appreciate the failure of the French to take military action against the Iroquois.[105] Tensions were also high between the French and the Miamis in 1697 because of French trading with the Sioux. All these allied groups were in fact divided. In trading with the Sioux, the French were failing to respect the code of the alliance, but the Native allies were hesitant to leave Onontio's family.[106]

The Strategies of New York

Of the English colonies established on the Atlantic seaboard of North America in the seventeenth century, New York was the most involved in diplomatic or military relations with the Iroquois League, the nations of the west, and New France. The centre of Native affairs was Albany, and it was there that the English governor organized diplomatic meetings with the Iroquois or other Native nations.[107] Through these periodic conferences, New York sought to maintain control over the Five Nations, or at the very least to preserve its alliance with them. This alliance was indeed absolutely essential to it in the imperial rivalry with the French.[108] It was in the interest of the English to encourage the Iroquois to fight against New France in time of war,[109] and to permanently prevent the slightest rapprochement between the French and the Five Nations.[110]

New York had major economic and imperial ambitions with respect to the Great Lakes. It had to have access, directly or indirectly, to the furs in the west, since at the end of the seventeenth century the Iroquois were no longer good suppliers. For this reason, the English sought to trade with the nations belonging to the French system of alliances in order to induce them to join the Covenant Chain,[111] hoping thus to bring them into Albany's economic, and therefore political, fold. In 1685 and 1686, Governor Dongan, a strong proponent of expansionism, sent two trade expeditions to Michilimackinac with the assistance of French deserters and a few Seneca warriors. Charlevoix reported that they were very well received by the Hurons and the Odawas, who found the English prices very tempting.[112] This was at least true of the first expedition, but the second one was intercepted by the French.[113] The position of the Iroquois League with respect to this English expansionism remained ambiguous, however. While some Senecas had taken part in the trade expeditions organized by New York, the Iroquois did not necessarily view all these expeditions positively. Above all, they were not prepared to let the Amerindians from the west cross their territory to trade in Albany.[114]

The Strategies of the Iroquois League

The Iroquois played a decisive role in northeastern North America in the seventeenth century. Their geographic position south and east of Lake Ontario, from the Genesee River to Lake Champlain, gave them a central, and therefore strategic, position in the diplomatic and trade networks. They were situated both between New France and the English colonies, and between the English colonies and the Great Lakes nations. Moreover, through raids, they could easily block communications on the Ottawa River between the Great Lakes and the French colony.[115]

In the seventeenth century, five Iroquois nations were joined together in a confederacy whose origins may date back to the fifteenth century. The League was structured metaphorically as a longhouse: from east to west, there were, first, the Mohawks, the "keepers of the eastern door"; then the Oneidas, the "younger brothers" of the Mohawks; then the Onondagas, the keepers of the wampum collars of the "public treasury" and organizers of the councils of the League; then the Cayugas, the "younger brothers" of the Senecas; and finally the Senecas, the "keepers of the western door" of the Iroquois longhouse.[116] The confederacy was very often divided, and in fact each nation defined its own strategies insofar as it was able.[117] The Mohawks in particular, because of their special relationship with New York, had a much more difficult relationship with the French than the four nations situated further west, although all of them were frequently at war with New France.

The Iroquois were united by common strategic interests. They had to replenish the population of the League by taking prisoners, but they could not have too many enemies at one time. This explains why, beginning in the 1690s especially, they tried to reach a rapprochement with the Great Lakes nations and isolate New France.[118] This policy was accompanied by a diplomatic offensive to induce the Iroquois in the réductions to become their allies right under Onontio's nose.[119] In the 1690s, the famous Onondaga diplomat Teganissorens developed a typical Iroquois strategy of balance between the two competing empires. It involved guaranteeing the Five Nations their power and independence,[120] and it was this strategy that allowed the Iroquois to get out of the impasse of war in 1700–1701.

3 Wars and Peace in the Seventeenth Century

The Great Peace of Montreal marked the close of a major chapter in Canadian history. It largely ended two thirds of a century of what historians have called the "Iroquois Wars." These wars were among Native nations, but they also frequently involved the European colonies, New France, and New Netherland (which became New York).

WARS

War was at the heart of Native culture. Father Lafitau said of the Iroquois: "The men ... are properly born only for great things, especially for warfare," which they see as "a necessary exercise." The Baron de Lahontan also spoke of the inherent bellicosity of Native societies. "The greatest Passion of the Savages," he wrote, "consists in the Implacable Hatred they bear to their Enemies." War was carried out all the more readily because it expressed the relatively horizontal nature of social relations, the decentralization of power in Native communities. "Each one is master of his actions," wrote Father Charlevoix, and Louvigny, a French officer, noted that "an individual is capable of making war and of involving his nation in it."[1]

The conflicts between the Iroquois and the Hurons, Algonquins, Montagnais, and French began in the early seventeenth century,[2] but they only reached significant proportions towards the end of the 1630s. The Five Nations finally asserted their supremacy, victoriously fighting the Huron confederation (1649–50) and various other Iroquoian nations: the Petuns were defeated in 1649, the Neutrals in 1651, and the Eries in 1654.[3] In these conflicts, the Iroquois warriors had the advantage of their geographic position (which enabled them to receive material support from the Dutch) as well as the psychological and technological superiority of firearms. In addition, unlike the Hurons, they had not been weakened by divisions between converts and traditionalists as a result of the evangelizing work of the Jesuit fathers.[4]

Interpretations of the Iroquois Wars until now have often been based on the rationalistic work by G.T. Hunt, *The Wars of the Iroquois*. According to Hunt, the goal of the Five Nations in attacking their Iroquoian neighbours to the north and west in the 1640s was control of the fur trade: they wanted to gain access to English goods by acting as middlemen with the nations of the northwest, or at least by plundering their furs, since the supply of beaver in Iroquoia was no longer sufficient.[5] This economistic view of Native warfare was taken up by many writers, partisans of the term *beaver wars*. Without necessarily endorsing the middleman interpretation, these researchers emphasize the economic aspect of war; they see the quest for furs, which is related to dependence on European goods, as having driven the Iroquois to conquer new territories.[6] Some ethnohistorians, while not always rejecting this economic interpretation, have tried to link war to other factors: the quest for prestige, honour, blood feuds, the religious dimension of sacrifice seen as a fertility rite, etc.[7] Finally, D.K. Richter, whose analysis has been elaborated upon by anthropologist R. Viau, sees war among the Iroquois as a mourning ritual and as a means to capture enemies to replace the dead.[8]

The Amerindian wars of the seventeenth century were fundamentally wars of capture, which are different from vendettas. Iroquois warfare functioned as a huge matrix, a system for replacing, assimilating, and reproducing, according to the principle of filiation. This conception of war did exist among the Algonquians of the Great Lakes (Odawas, Ojibwas, Potawatomis, etc.), but it was among the Iroquois that it was expressed most radically, given the matrilineal nature of their society. In Iroquois society, descent was transmitted through the female line, and individuals thus belonged to their mother's family. While it was men who made war, it was

War (From *Mémoires de l'Amérique septentrionale, ou la suite des voyages de Mr le Baron de Lahontan* [La Haye: Chez les Frères l'Honoré, Marchands Libraires, 1703], 2:185. National Archives of Canada, C-99243.)

women, or rather mothers, who were at the centre of the sociological mechanism governing it – filiation. It was on the initiative of a clan mother that a war party was usually constituted: she presented a wampum collar to some young warriors and urged them to bring her back prisoners or, failing that, scalps, "to appease the Soul of her Husband, her Son, or her Close Relation"[9] and replace him. War, according to R. Viau, was a way of conquering death, of appeasing the deceased and preventing their souls from coming back to torment the living. In paying homage to the dead and giving them compensation if not rebirth through predation and capture, war led to the regeneration of the social fabric and the spiritual well-being of the group. If they were not integrated physically (tortured and eaten), prisoners were integrated socially through the mechanism of adoption. They were symbolically brought back to life, as if reborn. The Iroquois placed the priority on the adoption of children, who were easier to assimilate, but also of women, in order to increase their collective fertility.[10]

Most prisoners, according to Charlevoix, were in fact adopted and integrated into lineages – and in such great numbers that in the 1660s the Iroquois League consisted of two-thirds prisoners.[11] Governor Denonville stated in 1685: "Most to be feared is the Iroquois, who is the most powerful ... through the number of slaves this nation takes every day among its neighbours by abducting their children at a young age and naturalizing them."[12] The intensity of the wars, especially around 1650, surpassed anything the peoples of the region had previously experienced. They were no mere exercises with a handful of combatants, but spectacular clashes leading to the destruction of whole villages and the capture or killing of thousands of people. The institution of war – and its underlying structure of mourning and childbirth – was intensified by two situational factors: first, the epidemics of European origin – as well as, paradoxically, the wars themselves, which resulted in major losses – led the warriors to capture more and more enemies to make up the demographic deficit; and second, the desire to trade pelts for muskets with their English and Dutch allies, together with the need to feed their families, perhaps led the Iroquois to broaden their territorial base to support their hunting activities. W.J. Eccles, a proponent of the demographic explanation, however, rejects the idea that the Iroquois sought to increase their hunting territory north of Lake Ontario: "They certainly did not establish themselves there, in present day southern Ontario, to hunt since there was nothing left to hunt, save perhaps squirrels and racoons – no deer, beaver, otter, etc."[13] Thus, he refutes the recent theories of Brandão and Starna, for whom the possibility of hunting in the "territories north and west of Lakes Erie and Ontario" was at the heart of Iroquois strategies in the second half of the seventeenth century.[14] It is difficult to resolve this question. What is certain is that Native warfare gradually changed in nature during the seventeenth and eighteenth centuries. Capture as the basis of the social bond remained its cultural engine, but it increasingly involved the economic and geopolitical stakes that governed the North American colonial arena.

The Iroquois raids continued in the west after the dispersion of the Hurons and their Iroquoian and Algonquian neighbours. They were also directed against the French colony on the St Lawrence, whose very existence appears to have been threatened at the beginning of the 1660s. Louis XIV responded to the worried entreaties of the colonists, and in 1665 the Carignan-Salières Regiment, made up of twelve hundred men, landed at the town of Quebec with the mission of invading Iroquoia. Two military expeditions were organized against the Mohawks. The first, in January 1666, was a failure, but in the second, in September, the French burned down many enemy villages. In 1667 the Mohawks, and also the Oneidas, were thus induced to make peace with the French as the other Iroquois nations had done during the two previous years.[15]

The maintenance of the peace was favoured in the following decade by the fact that the Five Nations were waging wars against the Mahicans in the east and the Susquehannocks in the south. But once these fronts were quiet, at the end of the 1670s, the Iroquois – who had become staunch allies of the English with the formation of the Covenant Chain in 1677 – again turned their attention towards their enemies in the west. In 1678 they attacked the Illinois and the Miamis, with whom Cavelier de La Salle had made an alliance a few months earlier.[16] I do not share the view of F. Jennings that this war was related to the fur trade. The Iroquois were certainly irritated by the fact that the French were arming their Illinois enemies, but they did not favour a policy of expansion westward (which would have taken them quite far away); rather, their raids were in the tradition of wars of capture.[17] In addition, according to J.A. Brandão, in the 1680s they felt the need to react to the French policy of encirclement, which translated into the creation of increasing numbers of posts (in particular, Fort Frontenac) on the doorstep of Iroquoia and the expansion of the French-Amerindian alliance. "Onnontio, your fyre shall burn no more at Cadracqui [Fort Frontenac], it should never be kindled again,"[18] said an Iroquois orator in 1695, when Governor Frontenac was on the point of re-establishing the fort, which had been abandoned in 1689. The League, writes Brandão, "seemed determined ... to extinguish the french 'fyres' in North America."[19]

Anxious to preserve their economic and political interests in the west, the French leaders had decided to take military action against the Five Nations. Governor La Barre, in 1684, and then Denonville, his successor, in 1687, sent French-Amerindian expeditions against the Senecas. The first failed miserably, forcing La Barre to negotiate a humiliating peace treaty with the Iroquois. The second destroyed four villages that had been deserted by their inhabitants. The conflict spread to the colony in subsequent years, in the context of the War of the League of Augsburg (1688–97). The Iroquois attack on Lachine in 1689 marked the renewal of hostilities. Frontenac, who had succeeded Denonville, attempted to resume the diplomatic dialogue, but he too finally had to resort to force, attacking the Mohawks in 1693 and then the Onondagas and the Oneidas in 1696 and urging his allies in the Pays d'en Haut to harass the Iroquois.[20]

SEPARATE AND GENERAL PEACE AGREEMENTS

From 1609 to 1700 – the date of the peace treaty preliminary to the Great Peace of 1701 – wars were interspersed with periods of negotiation leading to peace treaties that were not always very lasting. The Great Peace of Montreal, as we will see, was negotiated with some difficulty, largely because the French wanted to make it a general peace that would include the Five Nations as well as the allied nations. It was not the first treaty of this kind, but in the course of the century, the strategic jockeying of the various parties, and sometimes the pressure of a particular situation, had generally led to the conclusion of separate peace treaties.

Separate Peace Agreements

These separate peace agreements might include both Native nations and European colonies, but they might also exclude the Europeans.

Throughout the seventeenth century, in addition to treaties between the French and the Iroquois, there were agreements or truces negotiated separately between the Five Nations and the Great Lakes nations.

Negotiations did not necessarily result in treaties. The intervention of a third party could disrupt the negotiation process. In 1635, for example, the Mohawks tried to conclude a separate agreement with the Hurons, but the French successfully opposed it.[21] Similarly, as we have seen, in 1688 Kondiaronk ruined the separate negotiations between the French and the Iroquois. Twice, however, New France was induced to conclude simple bilateral treaties with the Iroquois, in effect abandoning its Amerindian allies. The first time was in 1653, during a conference held in Montreal, at which the Five Nations persuaded the French to agree to remain neutral in the event of conflict between the Iroquois on one side and the Algonquins and Montagnais on the other.[22] The second time was in 1684, during La Barre's failed expedition against the Senecas, when what was supposed to have been a glorious military victory for the French was transformed into a resounding diplomatic failure. At La Famine, his army weakened by an epidemic, La Barre (as mentioned above) was forced to agree to a peace treaty with the Iroquois, which allowed the Five Nations to continue their raids against the Illinois, allies of the French, and even against the Miamis.[23] It was well understood at that time among the members of the French-Native alliance that any negotiations had to be inclusive.[24] La Barre's bending of this convention could only make the nations of the west suspicious of their French ally. Groups from the Great Lakes, as we will see, also held separate talks with the Iroquois, often in order to recover captives.

General Peace Agreements

From the perspective of the Great Peace of Montreal, I mean by "general peace agreements" those treaties concluded between the French, their allies, and the Iroquois. There were many attempts to achieve such treaties in the seventeenth century. As A. Beaulieu has shown, in the 1630s Champlain hoped to establish trade and diplomatic ties with the four western nations of the Iroquois League. In the 1650s as well, several attempts were made to build an alliance between the French and these four nations. However, plans

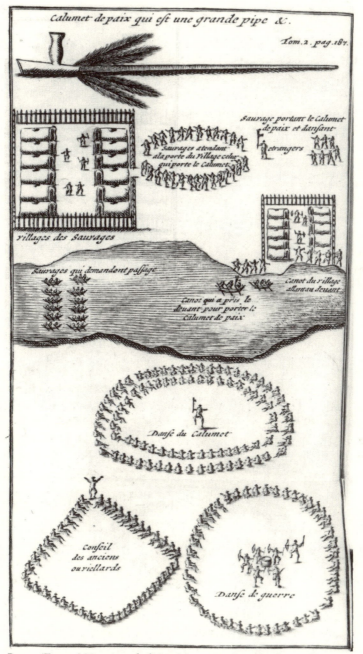

Peace (From *Mémoires de l'Amérique septentrionale, ou la suite des voyages de Mr le Baron de Lahontan* [La Haye: Chez les Frères l'Honoré, Marchands Libraires, 1703], 2:101. National Archives of Canada, c-99244.)

for a French-Iroquois alliance failed, essentially for two reasons: first, because of divisions among the Iroquois, the French were unable to make peace with the whole confederacy; and second, while the Iroquois wanted to make peace with New France, they refused to do so with its Native allies.[25] A general peace, therefore, was particularly difficult to arrange.

The peace treaty concluded with the Mohawks at Trois-Rivières in 1645 by Governor Montmagny, for example, was a sham; the four western nations of the League did not take part in it, and among the Hurons, Algonquins, Montagnais, and Attikameks, only the baptized Amerindians were covered.[26] Furthermore, this peace, which was really nothing more than a truce, was broken by the Mohawks the following year.[27] Of the treaties negotiated in the seventeenth century, those signed from 1665 to 1667 with the Five Nations were the ones most like the treaties of 1700–1701, since they involved New France, its allies, and all the nations of the Iroquois League.[28] Two comments must be made, however. It appears that no representatives of the nations allied with the French were in Quebec for the negotiation of the final treaty in 1667; and secondly, this peace, which was broken about a decade later, was less lasting than the peace of 1701.

In 1641 the French refused to conclude a separate treaty with three Iroquois nations because they were afraid of jeopardizing their network of alliances.[29] At the end of the century, the situation was similar. The entire French discourse with the Great Lakes nations consisted of repeating to them that the colony would never make peace with the Iroquois without including them, and that this would be in the interest of the Great Lakes nations. In fact, the French were seeking to ensure the survival of their colony, since the failure to include the nations of the west in a peace treaty with the Iroquois would probably have led to the disintegration of New France's alliances with the Native peoples.[30] There remained the problem of the almost constant refusal by the Iroquois – until 1700 – to include the Great Lakes nations in a peace treaty with the French. The Five Nations were in fact divided. For some Iroquois, swept along by the momentum of war, peace with the nations of the west was simply not a possibility in the immediate future; others preferred to persuade the Great Lakes nations to join the Covenant Chain and thus, without the French knowing, to seek a separate peace.[31]

THE FAILURE OF FRENCH-IROQUOIS
NEGOTIATIONS, 1688–1695

In looking at French-Iroquois peace negotiations at the end of the seventeenth century, we can identify a first series of events preliminary to the phase of the years 1697–1701.

After the conference at La Famine in 1684, which had taken place under specific circumstances, four years went by before the resumption of talks. Between 1688 and 1695, there were three disjointed attempts to negotiate peace in the North American context of the War of the League of Augsburg. On both sides, the negotiations were motivated by the losses of the war. Although the conflict with the Iroquois may have been related to French strategic interests in the west – the maintenance of a French-Native alliance based on war – it was an obstacle to the economic and demographic development of the colony.[32] Peace with the Five Nations was necessary, and from 1688 to 1695, Denonville and especially Frontenac strove for it without success.

In June 1688, eleven months after Denonville's expedition against the Seneca villages, a delegation of Onondagas, Oneidas, and Cayugas arrived in Montreal, led by Otreouti, who asked to talk peace. The French agreed, and a precarious truce was concluded. It was hoped that this would be the starting point for a more general peace that would include the Mohawks and the Senecas, but as we have seen, Kondiaronk put a stop to these negotiations.[33] It seems, in any event, that these talks could not have led to "planting the Tree of Peace," since the Iroquois had set as a condition the return to America of the Cayuga and Oneida ambassadors who had been deported to Marseille in 1687.[34] We may also assume that it was partly because of this deportation – disgraceful in their eyes – that fifteen hundred Iroquois raided Lachine in August 1689, killing or capturing some one hundred French, including about fifteen civilians.[35]

Frontenac, back in New France in the autumn of 1689,[36] wanted to start the talks up again immediately. In order to do so, he had brought back from France some Iroquois prisoners,[37] including Ourehouare, the Cayuga sachem, and he sent four of them to Onondaga to invite the Five Nations to come to Montreal to negotiate peace – but without success. The four emissaries came back with the Iroquois refusal in March 1690. Meanwhile, during a council held in Onondaga, the Mohawks, who were allied with the English, and the Senecas, who were in negotiations with the Odawas, forcefully rejected any peace process with the French. The Iroquois also refused to hold any talks as long as all their prisoners were not returned to them.[38] Frontenac nonetheless decided to send a second delegation to Onondaga in April, made up of Iroquois prisoners and a few Frenchmen; in spite of the eight collars prepared by Ourehouare (who lived in the town of Quebec near the governor), peace was rejected once again. The Iroquois captured three French delegates and had the others tell their governor that they were by no means his "children" but rather the "brothers" of the English.[39] The majority of the League members at this time were hostile to any peace with the French.[40]

The last attempt was the negotiations held from June 1693 to October 1694 or even April 1695, which were a kind of dress rehearsal for the talks of 1700–1701. They began in June 1693 with the arrival in Quebec of Tareha, a pro-French Oneida chief who was anxious to conclude a peace but was by no means representative of the Iroquois Confederacy. He promised to return at the end of the summer with delegates from each of the Five Nations.[41] Returning on 28 September, he informed Frontenac that the four other nations refused to negotiate a treaty with the French, and invited him, without success, to come to Albany to negotiate a general peace.[42] On 17 May 1694, however, ten delegates of the League arrived in Montreal, led by Teganissorens, who represented the neutralist pole of Iroquois politics. At a major conference that began on 23 May, Teganissorens expressed a desire to conclude a peace with his "brothers" from Sault St Louis and La Montagne. Frontenac, for his part, requested the return of "all the prisoners you may have in your villages, that is, men, women or children, both French and Savages who lived among us, and all the other Nations of the Pays d'en Haut who are our Allies, whose interests are as dear as my own, without excluding any of them." In the presence of a few chiefs from the Great Lakes, another meeting was set for the end of August.[43]

The conference held in Montreal in September 1694 brought together French officers, ambassadors of the allied peoples (Huron-Petuns, Odawas, Miamis, Illinois, Algonquins, Abenakis, and Iroquois from the mission villages), and Cayuga and Seneca delegates, accompanied by thirteen French prisoners. Frontenac, however, rejected most of the Iroquois wampum collars, since the Five Nations still refused to include the nations of the west in a general peace. The Huron chief Kondiaronk, responding to the governor's diplomacy, said to the Iroquois delegates: "I have listened to your words, Goyogouen [Cayugas] and Tsonnontouan [Senecas], it is good that you have come to meet our Father Onontio ... he is willing to see the Iroquois here again, provided that they bring him back his nephews who are prisoners among them, French, Hurons, Outaouaks [Odawas], and his other Allies, so I exhort you with this collar, you Goyogouen and Tsonnontouan, to give spirit to the three other Iroquois nations." Peace seemed to be far from a reality. Frontenac even invited his allies in the west to redouble their attacks against the Iroquois.[44] The following month, Tareha arrived in Quebec leading an Oneida delegation. He brought back with him six prisoners, including Father Milet, who had been captured in 1689, and carried out the ritual of condolence, presenting three strings of wampum. But the governor answered: "My tears cannot be Entirely Dried as long as I do not see all my Children and nephews near me, ... my throat will still be burdened, until I am no longer obliged to cry out so much for their return, and my ears can only be unblocked by the sound of the thanks that they will give me in freedom." The peace process stumbled over the thorny question of prisoners, an issue that would poison the negotiations until 1701.[45] In April 1695 the talks were ended for a time "by a last message from the Iroquois, who a few days later started the war again."[46]

Although they were already weakened, the Five Nations still had enough room to manoeuvre to reject Frontenac's proposals. At the same time, they were carrying on negotiations with groups in the west in hopes of establishing their own peace.[47] We will see in Part Two the extent of this Iroquois diplomatic overture, a tactic that was part of the feverish diplomatic dance that took place at the end of the seventeenth century.

Negotiations on All Fronts, 1697–1701

The intense negotiations that preceded the Great Peace of 1701 involved the French, the English in New York, the Iroquois of the League, and the various allies of New France, in particular the Amerindians of the Great Lakes and the Iroquois in the mission villages. They took place at four principal sites: Onondaga, Michilimackinac, Albany, and Montreal, where the peace agreement was finally concluded.

4   Iroquois Delegations and Colonial Rivalries

During the years 1697–99, there was a phase of negotiations that directly involved the Five Nations and either New France or New York. The quest for peace by the Iroquois, starting in 1697, was the result of their obvious exhaustion; it was complicated, however, by divisions within their confederation. The Five Nations thus entered these talks in a weakened position, but as we will see, they were nonetheless able to promote their own interests and were not restricted merely to responding to colonial pressures.

THE IROQUOIS' MOTIVES FOR SEEKING PEACE, 1697

It was during the winter of 1696–97 that the intense negotiations began that were to lead, four years later, to the Great Peace of Montreal. At least at first, this process was completely independent of the conflict between the French and the English in the War of the League of Augsburg, since news of the Treaty of Ryswick (30 September 1697) only reached the shores of New York – and then Iroquoia – in December 1697, and the authorities in the town of Quebec only learned of it in February 1698.[1] This clearly shows that while the launching of the peace talks was a consequence of New France's diplomatic and military effort, it was in a sense the Iroquois who were the driving force. We can thus say that the Great Peace of Montreal was also the result of the Iroquois' desire for peace.[2]

This desire for peace was a result of the exhaustion of the confederation. In 1694 the Onondaga chief Sadekarnaktie lamented to representatives of New York: "The Grease is melted from our flesh and drops on our neighbours who are grown fatt and live at ease while we become lean. They flourish and we decrease."[3] The numbers speak for themselves. According to a report from Albany, the Iroquois Confederacy had 2,550 warriors in 1689 and only 1,230 nine years later, a reduction of more than half. In nine years of war, the number of Mohawk warriors was reported to have dropped from 270 to 110,[4] of Oneidas from 180 to 70, of Onondagas from 500 to 250, of Cayugas from 300 to 200, and of Senecas from 1,300 to 600.[5] In comparison, the number of Iroquois warriors was estimated at 2,050 by Denonville in 1685, at 1,400 "at most" by Bellomont in 1697, at 1,200 by Callière in 1701, and at 1,500 by Bacqueville de La Potherie at the beginning of the eighteenth century.[6] This decline in population of the Iroquois Confederacy was countered, however, throughout the seventeenth century by the massive adoption of prisoners of war; this practice was still current in the 1680s.[7] But in the following decade, while the Five Nations continued their raids, they lost the supremacy they had had in the 1650s over the nations of the west.

There are many factors behind the population decline of the Iroquois, but given the lack of sufficiently precise sources, it is impossible to determine the relative importance of each one. There is no doubt, in any case, that war, epidemics, and emigration were the major causes of the weakening of the Five Nations at the end of the seventeenth century.

War, indisputably, was the primary factor. In June 1693 a Mohawk orator told Fletcher, the governor of New York: "We are a mean poor people and have lost all by the Enemy."[8] The enemy in this case was the French and their settled allies, the Algonquins and the Abenakis, who were carrying on an exhausting war of harassment against the Iroquois.[9] In addition to little raids organized against the Iroquois warrior/hunters,[10] major expeditions were mounted against the villages of the League. In 1687 Denonville's army laid waste to the large Seneca villages (from which most of the population had fled),[11] and there were expeditions against the Mohawks in 1693 and against the Onondagas and the Oneidas in 1696. The first one, that of 1693, was decisive: "Since that time," wrote La Potherie, "this nation of aniés [Mohawks] has become

Iroquois allant a la Decouverte

Iroquois warrior, late eighteenth century. Engraved by J. Larocque, from Jacques Grasset de Saint-Sauveur, *Encyclopédie des voyages ...* vol. 2: *Amérique* (Paris, 1796). National Archives of Canada, C-003165.
This Iroquois warrior is depicted holding a ball-headed club in one hand and wampum strings in the other. He also carries an iron axe and a trade gun adorned with a scalp.

the smallest of the five Iroquois nations, and it is now the one that causes us the least concern."[12] The 625 men (soldiers, militiamen, Amerindian allies) who attacked the Mohawks by surprise destroyed three villages and killed or captured many people.[13] During the expedition of 1696, the French-Amerindian army, two thousand strong – under the nominal command of Frontenac, who at seventy-four years of age had to be carried through the woods in an armchair – pursued the same ritual of destruction in Onondaga territory, where the enemy had fled, and then in Oneida territory.[14] It was the repetitive nature of these military operations that was hard on the Iroquois; while the direct loss of human lives was small, the destruction of food stocks and the devastation of the corn fields contributed to the weakening of their economy and, consequently, to their demographic decline.[15]

It was not only in the east that the Five Nations were put to the test during the years 1690–96. On their western frontier, the Great Lakes nations that were allied with the French (the Illinois, Miamis, Odawas, Potawatomis, etc.) were also waging "a hard war" against the Iroquois[16] and bringing back to their villages "large numbers of scalps."[17] The Senecas, in particular, experienced constant harassment; La Potherie stated: "All these parties of our allies hampered the Iroquois greatly. The Tsonnontouans [Senecas], who were within easier reach of their enemies' attacks, were forced to abandon their villages because of the great losses of their warriors, and they joined with the Goyogouins [Cayugas]."[18] The years 1691–93 were especially catastrophic for the Iroquois; according to Charlevoix, they lost more than four hundred men.[19] Hostilities continued from 1694 to 1696. Frontenac and Champigny reported to the court in 1694 that four or five hundred Iroquois had been killed or captured by the Illinois alone.[20] In 1696 a group of Odawas and Potawatomis defeated a party of Iroquois, bringing back to Michilimackinac "thirty scalps" and thirty-two prisoners.[21] Frontenac, in 1692, reported to the minister of marine: "All the nations of the Pays d'en Haut ... had more than eight hundred men in different small parties that every day were at the doors of the villages of the Iroquois or harassed them on their hunts, which harmed them greatly."[22] Beyond the human losses, this war in the west disrupted the economic activities of the Five Nations. It became impossible for the Iroquois to use certain hunting territories located around Lake Erie or even near Fort Frontenac. The safest area in which they could hunt was "towards the land of the Andastes [Susquehannocks]," that is, to the south-east.[23] According to R. Aquila, "the Iroquois were unable to go on regular hunts, since they had to remain in Iroquoia to protect their families and villages from the enemy."[24]

On the whole, the practically permanent state of war in the west (despite attempts at separate negotiations between the Iroquois and the Great Lakes nations), to a large extent stimulated by agents of New France, seems to have been an important cause of the weakening of the Five Nations. But in 1697 this factor had not yet induced the Iroquois to present a united front in seeking peace with the French and their allies. It would be decisive in doing so in 1700.

The Five Nations were weakened not only by war, but also by emigration towards the réductions of New France. In the 1690s this emigration contributed greatly to their demographic deficit, in particular for the Mohawks and the Oneidas. For the Iroquois as a whole, the result was tragic. The English, too, found it alarming: in 1700 Robert Livingston, the secretary of Indian affairs in New York, noted bitterly that two-thirds of the Mohawks were living "in Canada."[25] In addition, residents of Iroquoia, in particular the Senecas, had fled south to the Susquehanna River Valley.[26]

Concerning the Mohawks, Father Bruyas reported to Frontenac in 1691: "Because of disease ... and the loss of many braves, they lost their taste for a war which they had engaged in only of necessity."[27] Throughout the seventeenth century, the Five Nations, like the rest of the Native population of northeastern North America, were devastated by disease. From 1634 to 1640, for example, they lost half their population to smallpox.[28] In the summer of 1679, disease ravaged the Iroquois villages.[29] In 1690 smallpox was said to have "killed four hundred Iroquois and one hundred Mahingans [Mahicans],"[30] and in the summer of 1696, the epidemic again struck the Iroquois territories, in particular that of the Senecas.[31]

Alcohol is also put forward by some writers as a factor in the decline of the Iroquois population. Introduced by the Europeans, it was the more easily distributed in Native societies because they were disintegrating as a result of the actions (intentional or not) of the Europeans. It is certain that the violence and mortality caused by excessive alcohol consumption contributed to the demographic weakening of the Iroquois,[32] but this was clearly a secondary factor.

All in all, a variety of factors account for the truly catastrophic decline of the Iroquois population, a decline that necessarily influenced

the political evolution of the Five Nations and favoured their enter-
ing a peace process with the members of the French-Native alliance.
A final explanatory factor concerns English-Iroquois relations.
Extremely important allies of New York in the war against the
French that began in 1689, the Iroquois often stressed to the colonial
authorities in Albany the inadequacy of military action by the English, their inability to provide troops (except in the years 1690–91)
or even just to supply the Iroquois with arms and ammunition.[33]
This situation – combined with the separate peace concluded between the French and English in 1697 – could only lead the Five Nations to take an independent course of action, and thus to negotiate
separately with the French, as they had already done in 1694.

DIVISIONS AMONG THE IROQUOIS

It took more than three years after the Treaty of Ryswick for the
Peace of Montreal to be negotiated. The delay was due in large part
to the complex diplomatic manoeuvring of the Five Nations, fuelled
by internal divisions and contradictions. The Iroquois, whose exhaustion in the 1690s I have already mentioned, wanted to negotiate a peace with the French, but they were also anxious to preserve
their alliance with New York. At the same time, they followed their
central political principle, which was to maintain their independence in relation to the colonial powers.[34] Their relations with the
Great Lakes nations also presented various possibilities: peace, and
thus alliance, or war. And if they chose peace, should it be a separate peace or a general peace under the auspices of New France?[35]
Prisoners were another problem, as their return was a prerequisite
to the negotiation of any peace for the French and their allies. How
was this to be achieved without creating dissatisfaction in Iroquois
families?[36] Finally, the sachems were not always able to control the
young warriors, who were quick to organize raids to prove their
courage, even if it meant disrupting the peace process.[37] Because of
the very structure of Iroquois society, a society without a state,[38] all
these questions, all these problems, could lead only to tensions
within the League and, even more damaging, to serious political
and diplomatic divisions.

As we have seen, although the Iroquois Confederacy was a cohe-
sive, organized unit, it was often divided on issues of external relations, and each of the Five Nations had its own strategies that could

take precedence over the interests of the League. In the first half of the seventeenth century, the Mohawks established a hegemonic position among the Iroquois because of their special relationship as middlemen between the Dutch and the four western Iroquois nations, but after the treaty of 1653 strong tensions developed between the Mohawks and those four nations. For the latter, peace had created opportunities for trade with the French and thus the possibility of their no longer being dependent on the Mohawks to obtain European goods. When the Mohawks became aware of this danger, they tried to use force to counter the positive relations that were being established between the French and the Onondagas.[39] These divisions still existed during the years leading up to the negotiation of the Great Peace of Montreal. During these years, the French, observing that the Mohawks were the Iroquois who most resisted the peace process,[40] planned a new military expedition against the Mohawks soon after the conclusion of the Treaty of Ryswick.[41]

The diplomatic jockeying of the various Iroquois nations may be explained both by their desire to preserve particular interests (for the Mohawks, to preserve their special relationship with New York) and by external military pressures. In 1694 the two Iroquois nations most interested in negotiating peace with the French were the two western-most nations, the Senecas and the Cayugas. While it is extremely tempting to attribute this to their desire to put a stop, through the French, to raids by the Great Lakes nations,[42] there were other factors at play.

The divisions among the Iroquois were not only among the nations of the confederacy; there were also tensions within the nations themselves and, even more, in the clans and villages. The Amerindian nations of northeastern North America, unlike the European nations, did not have the structures of state and bureaucracy, centralized institutions possessing coercive power. Thus, among the Iroquois (as among the Algonquians), political power was distributed among local chiefs, sachems, war chiefs, and simple orators, who tried at their level, through their prestige, their powers of persuasion, or the giving of gifts,[43] to create a consensus. Only rarely were all the chiefs in agreement, and the internal political life of the Iroquois was dominated by factional manoeuvring.

Such factions probably existed during "prehistoric" times,[44] expressed in rivalries among families, but the serious divisions, the major contradictions, that undermined Native societies developed only after contact. The case of the Iroquois is a good example. They were allied with the English, but the English tried to dominate them, and English demographic pressure quickly led to the expropriation of Native territory on the Atlantic coast and finally constituted a threat to the Five Nations themselves.[45] The ambiguous nature of the English alliance tended to give rise to opposing political positions within the League. In addition, with the massive absorption of prisoners of war,[46] the social fabric of the Iroquois had become very cosmopolitan at the end of the seventeenth century. Iroquois society no longer had the homogeneity it had had in the past; tensions existed between "natives" and prisoners, tensions the missionaries happily exploited and exacerbated.[47] Jesuit activity was intense among the Five Nations after the peace of 1667, and strong divisions quickly developed, with converts on one side and traditionalists on the other, as had been the case with the Hurons two decades earlier.[48] These divisions had repercussions within the clans, dissolving the kinship relationships that had defined Iroquois political structures.[49] As a result, traditional disagreements were all the more difficult to resolve.[50] The religious polarization created by the Jesuits quickly became political: the "Christian" factions became "pro-French," and the traditionalist factions, "pro-English."[51] At the very end of the seventeenth century, the Mohawks tended to favour a close alliance with New York; the faction among them favourable to the French had become very small, if not non-existent, the Christian converts having emigrated to the Canadian réductions.[52] The pro-French factions within the four other nations, which had been silent during the 1680s, emerged in force in the negotiation of the peace of 1701, in particular among the Senecas and the Onondagas.[53]

Whether polarized around Montreal or Albany, no faction was able to impose its views decisively in the councils. As a result, the political system became deadlocked and the confederacy had enormous difficulty promoting unified action.[54] Ultimately, the Iroquois could only try for a compromise, which crystallized in the last years of the seventeenth century in the formation of a middle faction that promoted a policy of neutrality.[55]

The political disagreements among the clans, villages, and nations of the League only complicated negotiations between the Iroquois and Montreal, Albany, and Michilimackinac. These divisions led to the problem of how representative the Iroquois delegations were. In 1693, for example, the Oneida chief Tareha came to Montreal to discuss peace, but he spoke only for a few houses of his nation. The same thing occurred four years later. Thus, at the end of the seventeenth century, French policy was entirely focused on the effort to convince the Five Nations Confederacy as a whole to sign a peace treaty in Montreal, while Iroquois policy was entirely focused on the effort to accommodate the various factions within the confederacy and create a diplomatic consensus.

This brief examination of Iroquois factionalism would not be complete without a glance at the very penetrating analysis of Bacqueville de La Potherie, who, no doubt informed by Nicolas Perrot, said of the Iroquoian peoples, "When they carry out some remarkable undertaking against a nation that they fear ... they seem to form two parties, the one agrees and the other opposes it: if the first party succeeds in its plans, the other approves and supports what has been done: if its intentions are thwarted, it joins the other party; so that they always attain their goal."[56] Seen in this light, the division into factions is not a sign of political weakness but rather a method of increasing the room to manoeuvre. However, it is not clear that the Five Nations in the early eighteenth century were capable of such a subtle strategy.

THREE-WAY NEGOTIATIONS: IROQUOIS, FRENCH, AND ENGLISH, 1697–1699

The peace negotiations went through three stages between 1697 and 1699: the year 1697, first of all, before the announcement of the Treaty of Ryswick; then the first months of 1698, when French-English diplomatic sparring for "sovereignty" over the Iroquois intensified; and finally, the period from the spring of 1698 to the fall of 1699, when the separate negotiations between the French and the Iroquois seemed to have reached an impasse.

The First Timid Steps towards Peace, 1697

The first French-Iroquois talks took place in 1697 while the Amerindians of the west were conducting raids against the Five Nations, before the French-English peace.[57] The Oneidas were the first to begin negotiating, and then the four western Iroquois nations negotiated together independently of the Mohawks.

Although Frontenac's expedition against the Onondagas and the Oneidas in August 1696 was not decisive in military terms, it undoubtedly contributed directly to getting negotiations started. From the next winter on, a desire for peace seemed to spread from certain Iroquois villages.[58] On 11 January 1697, an Iroquois from Sault St Louis informed the colonial authorities in Montreal that some Oneidas were about to arrive, in keeping with the promise they had made to Frontenac the previous summer (during the campaign of destruction against Iroquois villages) "to come settle on his lands."[59] Thirty-three Oneidas arrived at Montreal on 5 February. They were, of course, not the plenipotentiaries of the Iroquois League, since the Mohawks and Onondagas had been opposed to this delegation. In addition, their (apparent) desire to settle in the colony indicated that they did not even speak on behalf of their nation but, like Tareha four years earlier, represented pro-French factions.[60] Callière, then governor of Montreal, received them favourably, and on Frontenac's recommendation sent Otacheté, an Oneida sachem living in Sault St Louis and the chief of the band, with "a collar to respond to the one they had brought to tell the rest of the people of his nation that they would be welcome."[61]

A few days later (on 16 February), two Mohawks arrived in Montreal accompanied by two captive French women, and from there they were taken to Quebec to meet Onontio. On behalf of their nation they asked the governor if he wanted peace and thereby the resumption of trade between Montreal and Albany. It is unclear whether these delegates were seeking an immediate agreement[62] or whether they had simply come to obtain information on the state of affairs in the French colony and to recover some prisoners.[63] In any case, Frontenac rejected their collars and warned them that in the future "no Iroquois should venture to appear before him but in entire submission to his will." The two Iroquois were even held prisoner in Quebec for the whole winter.[64] In short, the state of war continued.

Nevertheless, it is certain that the French fervently wanted to put an end to the hostilities and thus free the colony from the military and economic constraints of the war with the Iroquois. The diplomatic effort conceived by the general staff of New France was also a response to the new strategic situation that arose as a result of the separate peace of 1696 between the Iroquois of the League and the settled Iroquois, a peace that, among other things, deprived Frontenac of the military cooperation of his allies from Sault St Louis and La Montagne in any French raids against the Five Nations.[65] The French strategists wanted to use a general peace as a springboard to consolidate their alliance with the Great Lakes nations, which the current state of trade – the glut of furs on the market – had put in jeopardy.[66] The fact remains that Onontio found the diplomacy of the Iroquois League too timid in 1697, since it did not fit into his own peace plans. The representatives of the Sun King were eager to conclude a peace treaty with the Iroquois, of course, but only on their terms. Frontenac wanted first of all to make an arrangement with the entire Iroquois Confederacy, that is, with delegates of each of the Five Nations, including the Mohawks.[67] This arrangement, moreover, was to be reached independently of the English.

The second objective of the French was that peace with the Iroquois should be part of a general peace that would include their allies in the Great Lakes region.[68] This would not only confirm the French-Amerindian alliance, but also short-circuit any separate peace between the Iroquois and the Great Lakes nations. The exchange of prisoners was the third demand of the French. This procedure, which was traditional for Europeans in peace negotiations, was complicated by the distinctive nature of Amerindian societies. In these societies, unless they were put to death, prisoners, Native or otherwise, were adopted by families to replace their dead, acquiring all the rights and duties of the deceased. They thus became full members of the nations that had captured them. As the officer Lamothe Cadillac wrote, "Strangers are adopted as children of the house, as brothers, sons-in-law, or other relatives." Clearly, it would never have been easy to give them up.[69] In the Native societies of northeastern North America, releasing prisoners was equivalent to losing one's relatives.[70] The chiefs, moreover, did not have the authority to oblige families to give up prisoners.[71] These difficulties were aggravated by the tendency of non-Native prisoners to prefer Amerindian life to European ways.[72]

In the winter of 1697, the Iroquois were far from unanimous in their acceptance of all these French demands. In the following summer, however, the negotiations moved forward. At the instigation of

Teganissorens, the Onondagas now seemed to support the Oneidas' diplomatic efforts.[73] Despite the opposition of English and Mohawk delegates – the latter of whom objected to the imprisonment of two of their compatriots in Quebec – the Onondagas and the Oneidas resumed negotiations with the French in August 1697, through Otacheté.[74] Accompanied by "a little Frenchman" and carrying four wampum collars, Otacheté spoke of peace on behalf of the Five Iroquois Nations. This, of course, did not fool the French, who were well aware that Otacheté represented neither the Mohawks nor the Senecas and Cayugas.[75] Furthermore, only one prisoner was brought back; there seemed to be no question of returning others; and no mention was made of the Great Lakes nations. In short, Otacheté's mandate might only have been to keep the "fire" of the negotiations going[76] or perhaps even to prevent the disaster of another French invasion.[77] Frontenac gave him until the end of September to bring back to the colony the Oneidas who, according to him, were supposed to have settled there, and to obtain the participation of representatives of the other four Iroquois nations.[78]

Otacheté returned to Montreal and then to Quebec in November of that same year. He was accompanied by two Oneidas and, more importantly, two Onondaga chiefs, including the sachem Arratio (Aradgi?). Arratio acted as orator for the delegation before Frontenac and, speaking on behalf of the four western Iroquois nations, expressed a desire to build a solid peace with the French and to forget the "nasty business of the past."[79] This conference was a perfect illustration of the nature of the French-Iroquois diplomatic process with respect to the Mohawks. The Mohawks, who were pro-English, seem to be have been pushed aside by the other four nations of the League.[80] Frontenac, in a position of strength, informed the Oneida and Onondaga emissaries of his dissatisfaction. The Five Nations were, in fact, not fully represented, and there were no Cayuga or Seneca plenipotentiaries to prove that these two tribes were involved in the peace process. Furthermore, Arratio had not brought any prisoners with him, and there was still no discussion concerning the Great Lakes nations. Since it was in the interest of the French to keep the negotiations going, Frontenac let these ambassadors return to their nations, keeping a hostage, Arratio, as a pledge of peace.[81]

The peace process was thus set in motion, although there were still many obstacles to be overcome. A new element, however, was that, beginning in the winter of 1697–98, the negotiations were taking place in the diplomatic context of the peace following the Treaty of Ryswick.

Implications of the Treaty of Ryswick

In January 1698 a delegation from Albany arrived in Montreal to inform the French that a peace treaty had been signed in Europe the preceding autumn.[82] This truce, negotiated by the European empires, greatly complicated the diplomatic relations of the various parties, and the separate French-Iroquois talks continued in a context of increased colonial rivalry over the status of Iroquoia.[83]

With the Treaty of Ryswick, the Iroquois lost the purely theoretical advantage of English military support. In particular, they no longer had the benefit of the constant threat of an attack on Canada by the combined forces of New York and New England; with this threat gone, the French would now have more confidence to mount a new expedition against the Iroquois.[84] The English, too, now had to deal with a changed landscape. New York's long-standing effort to prevent any peace between the French and the Iroquois thus became much more difficult. To be consistent with their claim of sovereignty over Iroquoia, the English had to prevent their Iroquois allies from continuing to wage war against New France. In their view, since the Treaty of Ryswick had established peace between the subjects of the English Crown and those of the Sun King, the Iroquois had to make peace with New France and to do so through the efforts of the English.[85] The French, on the other hand, wanted to make peace with the Iroquois independently of the Treaty of Ryswick and, if necessary, to speed the process through military threats.[86]

As it had proven impossible for the Iroquois to reach a peace agreement with the nations of the west, there were two possible paths for Iroquois diplomacy: that of a separate peace with the French at the risk of breaking the Covenant Chain, or that of a peace agreement negotiated under the auspices of New York according to the English understanding of the Treaty of Ryswick – an agreement that would also include the Great Lakes nations – at the risk of jeopardizing their independence.[87]

The European peace treaty of 1697 led, in both the mother country[88] and the colonies, to a series of sterile diplomatic struggles concerning who supposedly had sovereignty over the Iroquois. English delegates, with a score of French prisoners, arrived in Quebec in June 1698 carrying a letter from Governor Bellomont of New York[89] to Frontenac.[90] The letter asked the French to return their English and Iroquois prisoners in exchange for French prisoners in Albany and Iroquoia.[91] Frontenac was well aware that such a transaction would imply a recognition on his part of British sovereignty over the Five Nations. He therefore answered Bellomont by saying that he was about to conclude a separate peace with the Iroquois independently of the Treaty of Ryswick, but that he would be willing to return the English prisoners to him. Moreover, he claimed French sovereignty over the Five Nations, arguing that the Jesuits had been active in Iroquoia for a very long time and that the Iroquois addressed him as "father."[92] In fact, the Five Nations, although weakened, were still politically independent from both the French and the English. According to Charlevoix, the Mohawks declared to the representatives of New York at a conference in the summer of 1698 that "they were masters of their lands; that they had been settled there long before the English had come."[93]

French-Iroquois Negotiations and English Diplomatic Manoeuvring, 1698–1699

From the spring of 1698 to the fall of 1699, the negotiations between the French and the Iroquois were inconclusive. While delegations representing the Five Nations frequently went to Albany to parley, the Iroquois diplomats only very irregularly travelled down the St Lawrence to Montreal and those who did so were far from the plenipotentiaries of the League, as if it was only possible for the Iroquois to maintain a weak "fire" in the negotiations.

In the spring of 1698, the famous Onondaga war chief La Chaudière Noire (Black Kettle) appeared at Fort Frontenac and informed the French that a decision had been made by the League to go to Montreal in June to discuss peace. But he added that the Iroquois also intended to resume their war against the Odawas "to avenge the death of more than one hundred of their people that they had killed." The French policy of including allies from the west in any "Iroquois peace" thus seemed again to have been rejected by the Five Nations.[94] The war with the allies of New France reduced to nothing the promises – the hopes? – of the Onondaga chief, whose party was shortly after intercepted and defeated by a party of Algonquins. La Chaudière Noire and some thirty other Iroquois perished in the ambush. This terrible blow seems to have stunned the Five Nations and kept them from sending a delegation to Montreal as planned.[95]

In July, however, while Frontenac was holding a conference with some Odawa delegates, Tegayesté, an Iroquois from Sault St Louis, arrived in Montreal, carrying a wampum collar from the Onondagas. This ambassador declared to Onontio that as a result of the attack by the Algonquin warriors in the spring, the nation of La Chaudière Noire was in mourning; he then proposed an exchange of prisoners, but without mentioning the fate of the Amerindian prisoners held in Iroquoia. Tegayesté was also reported to have told Frontenac in front of the delegates of the Great Lakes nations "that the Iroquois had appeared to him to be resolved to make peace with us [the French], but that he did not believe them inclined to do so with our allies." The governor rejected the Iroquois collar and, taking advantage of the presence of the delegates of the Great Lakes nations, strongly reaffirmed his intention to include them in a peace agreement with the Five Nations. This was in the interest of both partners in the French-Amerindian alliance, and Frontenac threatened the Iroquois with their combined fire.[96] Once again, the importance of alliances in French colonial policy was evident, as Frontenac clearly hoped that through his discourse he might both reassure his allies and push the Iroquois League towards peace.

At the very time when Frontenac was negotiating with Tegayesté and the ambassadors of the Great Lakes nations, Governor Bellomont was holding a conference in Albany with delegates of the Five Nations to persuade them to stop their separate negotiations with the French. He told the Iroquois ambassadors that under the Treaty of Ryswick it was up to the English to carry out an exchange of prisoners, since the general peace also included the Great Lakes nations. The sachems replied that they were surprised, if it were really the case that a French-English peace agreement covered all the Native peoples, that ninety-four of their people had recently been killed on the western frontier. They pretended to accept the principle of giving up their prisoners to the English, but did not specify any date, which gave them room to manoeuvre in order to negotiate separately with the French. While saying that they agreed not to negotiate independently any more, the Iroquois delegates did not bother to inform the governor of Tegayesté's mission to Montreal. The sachems were thus playing a subtle double game of compromise designed to avoid offending either of the two European powers while they settled the internal divisions in Iroquoia.[97]

Onontio's recent threat to invade their villages with his allies, however, led the Iroquois to moderate their policy. In August, while Bellomont was telling Quebec that any French attack on the Five Nations would lead to retaliation by the forces of New York, the Iroquois were holding council in their capital, Onondaga, in the presence of English delegates. The sachems decided to take back to Montreal any French prisoners who wanted to go, and to have them accompanied by emissaries from Albany.[98] In fact, New York had not approved this procedure, fearing that despite the presence of their delegates it could lead to a separate arrangement between the Iroquois and the French. The Iroquois resolution, which excluded the nations of the west from the peace process – and therefore would not have satisfied the French – remained a dead letter.

In September the French had still had no news from the Iroquois when the brother of Tegayesté arrived in Montreal with three French prisoners, bearing a message from the Onondagas saying that delegates of the four western Iroquois nations would soon arrive with other prisoners. The purpose of this delegation was probably to prepare the French for the possibility of united decisions within the League.[99] In October, in any case, English influence among the Five Nations seems to have been restored, and the diplomats from Albany were able to dissuade the delegates from the four western Iroquois nations from going to Montreal. To accomplish this, they had to lie to the sachems, saying that the Iroquois prisoners would be returned to them by the French, through Albany.[100]

After the pause of 1698, however, the French-Iroquois negotiation process began again in 1699. In January the Onondaga sachem Ohonsiowanne and the Oneida sachem Otacheté went to Montreal, where they met with Le Moyne de Maricourt, a French officer who had special influence among the Iroquois, having been adopted by the Onondagas. He told them that the French had no intention of releasing prisoners as long as there were no delegates from the Five Nations in Montreal to sign a peace agreement independently of the English. The following month, Teganissorens informed New York that the three central nations of the League were going to send delegates to Montreal to negotiate peace.[101]

Bringing eight belts and four strings of wampum, as well as three French prisoners, three Iroquois sachems arrived in Montreal in March 1699. They were Ohonsiowanne and Tsonhuastsuan (for the Onondagas) and Otacheté (for the Oneidas). On 8 March they addressed Governor Callière[102] on behalf of the Five Nations,[103] asking for peace, an end to military raids by the Great Lakes nations, and an exchange of prisoners to take place in Albany, "where the great business of peace will come to an end."[104] The Iroquois, who had planted a Tree of Peace at Albany "as soon as the Hatchet-makers [Europeans] arrived," wanted to hold peace negotiations there and to include the nations of the west in the Covenant Chain. But the French did not agree with this method of achieving peace.[105]

Callière answered the Iroquois ambassadors a few days later, saying that there would be no peace concluded except in Montreal, that French officers would then be dispatched to Iroquoia to recover the "young Frenchmen and allied savages," and, in addition, that peace could be negotiated only "jointly with all the allies."[106] The governor granted them a sixty-day truce, but he spoke only for his settled allies and the Algonquins, not the nations of the west, which allowed him to maintain pressure on the Five Nations.[107] To encourage negotiations, Callière freed Arratio and four other Iroquois, and a meeting was set up for the following June.[108]

The Iroquois delegates still had to convince their compatriots and to counter the influence of the English and their own internal divisions. During a council held in Onondaga in April 1699, the sachems announced that a delegation would be sent to Montreal in accordance with Callière's proposals, despite pressure from the New York diplomats. In June, however, Teganissorens told Albany that this would not occur, and the English promised that Iroquois prisoners would be released, even claiming that some had already been freed.[109]

However, separate negotiations between the French and the Iroquois, which New France wanted, soon began again as a result of new raids by the allied nations against the Senecas in the summer of 1699. In mid-September, while sachems from the four western nations of the League were meeting with delegates of New York in Albany and asking them, in keeping with the English understanding of the Treaty of Ryswick, to stop these raids, a delegation of Onondagas (represented by Ohonsiowanne and Tsonhuastsuan) went to

Montreal to meet with Callière. Through Massias, an Iroquois from La Montagne, they asked for an exchange of prisoners and that Maricourt come to Iroquoia to make sure that the French prisoners went. They especially asked Callière to put a stop to the raids by his allies in the west.[110]

The French governor answered them two days later. He deplored the absence of delegates from the three other Iroquois nations and refused to allow Maricourt to leave, since "the season [was] too advanced." He apparently had heard nothing about the war in the west, and he raised the spectre of a French-English alliance to pressure the Iroquois to conclude a peace agreement with him on his terms.[111]

While nothing conclusive came out of this conference, it was becoming more and more evident that the importance of the Great Lakes nations in the military and diplomatic arena at the end of the seventeenth century was increasing. For the Iroquois, relations with these nations had two sides: a negative one of war and a positive one of separate negotiations towards an alliance.

5 Accommodation and Confrontation in the West

To fully understand the treaty of 1701, we have to look at Amerindian activity in the Great Lakes region. There, the Iroquois and the nations allied with the French engaged in military jockeying and diplomatic manoeuvring that influenced the peace process and the development of the French-Amerindian alliance.

ATTEMPTED ALLIANCES BETWEEN THE IROQUOIS AND THE GREAT LAKES NATIONS

In the late seventeenth century, the Iroquois made diplomatic overtures towards the nations of the Great Lakes region, traditionally linked to New France's network of alliances, to try to persuade them to join their alliance with Albany. These negotiations, which were hindered by French diplomatic action and the Amerindians' ready resort to war, would become most intense in 1700, at the very time when, in Montreal, the Iroquois, were working towards a general peace with the French and the Great Lakes nations.

Attempts at Rapprochement before 1696

The idea of an alliance between the Native nations of the west and the Iroquois did not originate at the end of the seventeenth century. The Hurons, in particular, had made repeated overtures to the Five

Nations. In the 1640s, paradoxically in the context of the fall of Huronia, the two Amerindian groups had discussed the possibility of alliance.[1] The history of Huron-Iroquois relations during the second half of the seventeenth century is characterized by a sometimes very rapid alternation between fighting and truces, the latter often serving as an opportunity to recover prisoners. The apparent complexity of the diplomatic scene was also the result of the interplay of factions and of the fact that any faction – or even any individual – could organize a raid against a group with whom their nation was negotiating peace. Thus, an intertribal alliance was not necessarily collective in nature.[2]

Similarly, between 1670 and 1700 the Five Nations had no long-term, coherent strategy regarding relations with the Great Lakes nations. Their policy on alliance was not maintained continuously and did not apply to all the nations of the west. It was interrupted by the periodic resurgence of wars of capture, such as the campaigns against the Illinois and the Miamis around 1680. The strategy of rapprochement with the nations of the west (primarily a Seneca strategy) was probably related to Iroquois conflicts in other theatres, such as the one with the Susquehannocks in the mid-1670s, but also, finally, to the military decline of the League. In addition, an alliance with the nations of the west would perhaps have allowed the Five Nations, with British support, to short-circuit the Native political alliances of New France and to expand the Covenant Chain towards the west.[3] As one Iroquois was quoted as saying, making peace with the nations that are in "allyance with the French of Canida ... will strengthen us and weaken the enemij."[4]

A. Beaulieu and M. Lavoie have argued that the Five Nations' refusal to allow all the western tribes to be included in the French peace process has to be understood in the light of the Iroquois message of peace. According to Iroquois oral tradition, the League was founded by Hiawatha and the peacemaker Deganawidah to put an end to the continuous cycle of warfare and death among the Five Nations. Thus, according to Beaulieu and Lavoie, the political goal of the Iroquois in the seventeenth century was to gather and assimilate all the nations (including the European colonies) under their Tree of Peace, which would ideally be planted at Onondaga and whose roots would extend in all directions. "The Tree," as W.N. Fenton explains, "has long needles ... which grow as the confederacy prospers ... Peoples attracted by the smoke spy the tree and follow its roots to the trunk. If they accept the principles of the Great Law, they may enter the Longhouse [the confederation] as props to strengthen it." The Iroquois would therefore certainly have preferred that a general peace agreement be concluded in their capital rather than in Montreal, because, as Beaulieu and Lavoie say, they would have provided shelter to many nations and would thus have represented the centre of the world.[5] The Five Nations' diplomatic offensive in the west could have resulted in a general peace, but one that would have been under their hegemony, which most members of the French-Amerindian alliance rejected.

French sources report a number of rapprochements between the Iroquois and the Great Lakes nations. These accounts are often overly alarmist, as their purpose was to get the mother country to react, but if the negotiations caused such concern, it was also because they were a threat to the French-Amerindian alliance. According to Charlevoix, in 1670 "the Iroquois had sent gifts to the Outaouais [Odawas] to persuade them to bring them their pelts, which they wanted to trade with the English in New York."[6] In 1676 some Senecas went to Michilimackinac with gifts for the Hurons.[7] In 1686–87 the Senecas were again close to forming an alliance with the Odawas and the Hurons of Michilimackinac. Two English trade expeditions sponsored by Dongan, the new governor of New York, and guided by renegade coureurs de bois and Senecas, actually got to Michilimackinac. The local Amerindians welcomed them warmly, both because the English offered them trade goods at low prices and because they had brought back captives in return for safe conduct.[8] Three years later, shortly after the Lachine raid, the French alliance with the Great Lakes nations appeared to be threatened by alliance negotiations between the Odawas and the Iroquois, who were exchanging wampum belts and smoking "red stone peace pipes."[9] But the Michilimackinac Odawas finally withdrew under pressure from the French and the pro-French factions in their ranks.[10]

The talks nevertheless began again in the following years. While negotiations were under way in Quebec in 1694, Iroquois delegates were sent to Michilimackinac to arrange a separate peace by convincing the Odawas and others that a peace had been concluded between the Five Nations and New France.[11] Fear on the part of the western nations of a separate peace between the Iroquois and the French, together with French military inaction, spurred negotiations between the Iroquois, the Huron-Petuns, and the Odawas around 1695–96. "They all felt an urgent need to join with the Iroquois," wrote La Potherie with respect to the allies in the west.[12] The weakness of the French-Amerindian alliance lay in the fact that the French lacked the economic means to back up their political expansion into the west; because their ability to sell furs – the linchpin of the alliance – fluctuated constantly, the allied nations were tempted to look towards the Covenant Chain.[13] However, the raids organized by pro-French war chiefs and, especially, Frontenac's expedition against the Onondagas and the Oneidas in 1696 enabled the French to restore their alliance. The war between the Amerindians of the Great Lakes region and the Iroquois even intensified in the following years.[14]

For the nations of the west, the risk in allying themselves with the Iroquois and the English was that they would be leaving the "cabin" of Onontio, who provided them with many gifts and substantial military support. In the long term, moreover, the western Amerindians were generally well aware of the danger of British colonization. Thus, political tradition pulled the Great Lakes nations back towards New France, and therefore away from the Iroquois.

Divisions among the Allies of the Great Lakes Region

The nations of the French alliance, as we have already noted, were sometimes in conflict with one another.[15] What is more, some of them – or perhaps only factions within them – occasionally showed defiance of Onontio. The degree of the fragility of the alliance could be measured by the extent of the rapprochement of the nations of the west with the Five Nations. For the Amerindians of the Great Lakes, it was a question of having to constantly weigh the options – whether to preserve the French alliance or to form an alliance with the English and the Iroquois. Many of the Great Lakes groups had not established a consensus on this question and therefore had the utmost difficulty arriving at a clear policy.[16] The attraction of the Albany market,[17] the prospect of peace with the Five Nations,[18] the fear of a separate French-Iroquois peace, the problems posed by the development of closer trade links between the French and the Sioux and, after 1696–97, by French withdrawal from their posts in the West, all contributed greatly to weakening their alliance with the French and favouring rapprochement with the Iroquois.

The Iroquois did not make a general overture to all the Great Lakes nations.[19] Some of those nations were in fact more disposed to make war than peace with the Five Nations. The Illinois, in particular, but also the Potawatomis, the Sauks, and the Ojibwas were on strained diplomatic terms with the Iroquois in the late seventeenth century. This was not the case with the Foxes[20] and less so with the Hurons and the Odawas, nations that were nonetheless central to the French alliance. Frontenac reported that in the winter of 1695 the Iroquois had "a number of secret discussions with the Odawas and the Hurons, while at the same time they sent a big war party against the Miamis with the intention of destroying them, or of forcing them to declare themselves against us [the French]."[21] The Michilimackinac Hurons (or Huron-Petuns), even though they were at the heart of the French alliance network, were, according to French observers, the driving force behind the movement in favour of alliance with the Iroquois. According to La Potherie, in the summer of 1695 the Odawas and other allies, with the exception of the Hurons, put the Iroquois country to fire and sword.[22] Nicolas Perrot reported that in 1689 the Hurons of Michilimackinac proposed "to destroy the Odawa nations" with the assistance of the Iroquois. "It is well known," he wrote, "that the Hurons have always sought to destroy the nations of the Pays d'en Haut, and that they were never strongly attached to the French; but they did not dare to declare it openly. When they made war on the Iroquois, it was only in appearance, for they were basically at peace with them."[23] To be more precise, the Hurons were sometimes at war and sometimes at peace with the Iroquois. It seems that they also had difficulty seeing eye-to-eye with certain Algonquian groups, particularly the Odawas. But, at the risk of belabouring the point, it must be stressed that the Huron-Petun nation was not unanimously receptive to Iroquois overtures, any more than the four Odawa nations were. Only certain groups were receptive; among the Hurons, for example, as we have seen, there was a pro-French faction led by Kondiaronk and a pro-Iroquois faction headed by Chief Le Baron.[24]

*Negotiations between the Iroquois
and the Amerindians of the West, 1697–1700*

In 1697 "thirty families" of the Great Lakes Hurons, led by Le Baron, were reported to have come to settle near Albany.[25] Bacqueville de La

Potherie even reported that in the following year Huron-Petun and Seneca warriors "struck a blow in the fields of Michilimackinac."[26] These Hurons had probably joined the Iroquois League, which Kondiaronk refused to do.

From 1697 to 1699, the war between Onontio's allies and the Iroquois intensified, temporarily interrupting negotiations.[27] But in 1700 the Iroquois renewed peace and alliance negotiations on the basis of trade with Albany. In June of that year, Callière held a conference in Montreal with some Odawa delegates whom he accused of holding separate negotiations with the Iroquois: "I have also learned that you sent back [to the Iroquois] with wampum belts a few of the prisoners you had taken from them, in order to negotiate with them without my participation." He maintained that these talks jeopardized the peace process as he saw it – that is, as being under his not Amerindian, supervision.[28] In June, five delegates from the Great Lakes nations (including Mississaugas) approached Onondaga on behalf of sixteen villages of "three several nations, who are very strong and numerous." Their intention was, by planting "a tree of peace," "to make a firm league with the Five Nations and Corlaer," to "open a path for all people, quite to Corlaer's house," to "have free liberty of trade," and to share the "hunting places" with the Iroquois.[29] Most of the nations of the west, however, favoured war with the Five Nations at this time. The Iroquois could not end these conflicts without French intervention.

THE FRENCH AND THE PAYS D'EN HAUT

Although the French-Amerindian alliance in the Great Lakes had been weakened by the closing of many posts in 1696–97, the French strove to keep the wars going between their allies and the Iroquois in order to force the latter to make peace.

The Problem of French Withdrawal from the Posts in the West

The commercial basis of any alliance between the French and the western nations was that New France would buy the furs of these nations in order to retain their friendship. However, by the 1690s the French market had become saturated and could no longer absorb the enormous quantities of pelts that poured out of the west each year.[30]

About 1695–96 the colony faced a serious economic crisis, and the authorities in the home country decide to act. Minister of marine Pontchartrain was convinced that the overabundance of beaver pelts on the market was due to the existence of the military posts in the west and to excessive trading by the coureurs de bois. Therefore, it was decided at Versailles in May 1696 to abandon all posts in the Great Lakes region except for Fort St Louis (Peoria), to cancel all trading permits,[31] and to restrict fur trading to the centre of the colony.[32] This decision prompted a flood of reports to the French court from Quebec and Montreal, all stressing the importance of the French presence in the west. If the posts were abandoned, it was argued, not only would the trade be "lost," but so, too, would be "the whole colony, [since] all our allied savages, through alliances with the English and the Iroquois, would become, like them, our enemies."[33] In short, while economics required abandoning the west, political considerations dictated the maintenance of a military, if not a commercial, presence there. Therefore the minister of marine decided on a less restrictive policy, allowing the colony to keep Fort Frontenac, Fort St Joseph des Miamis, and the post at Michilimackinac.[34] The French were still forbidden, however, to trade in the Great Lakes region.[35]

The maintenance of the missions and a few posts was a minor matter compared to the problem posed by the cessation of trade relations in the west. Instead of coming to trade their furs in Montreal at low prices, the Amerindians of the Great Lakes were now more tempted to take them to Albany;[36] the suppression of trading permits, the interruption of trade, and the return to the colony of French officers had deprived the Amerindians of their usual sources of supplies, including the essential gifts.[37] In Montreal, in 1697, the Potawatomi chief Onanguicé declared to Frontenac: "Since we lack powder and shot and all the other necessities that you used to send us, how do you expect us to make do, our father? Will most of our women, who have only one beaver pelt or two, send them to Montreal to obtain their little necessities? Will they entrust them to drunkards, who will drink them and bring them back nothing? … You will see us no more, my father, I say to you, if the French abandon us, this is the last time that we will come talk to you."[38] This speech from a chief who, according to La Potherie, had enormous influence in the diplomatic network of the Great Lakes nations,[39] says a great deal about the extreme fragility of the French system of alliances around 1697. Nonetheless, Onanguicé, like Kondiaronk, eventually opted to maintain his friendship with the French. Although he was an avowed enemy of the Iroquois, he even contributed to the success of the Great Peace of Montreal.

War Diplomacy

There were two main obstacles to an alliance of the Iroquois and the nations of the west: on the one hand, internal divisions within both the Iroquois Confederacy and the league of the Great Lakes nations, and the resulting inclination of many groups to make war; and on the other hand, the capacity of the French to sabotage the slightest faltering steps towards such an alliance. As Governor Denonville explained in 1688, "Since I have been in this country, all we have been able to do was to divert our Savages from establishing ties with the Iroquois in order to engage in trade."[40]

At the same time as they were negotiating peace with the Iroquois, the French were doing their utmost to keep their existing Native alliances intact.[41] This constant diplomatic action by New France with regard to the allied nations was carried out either in the colony in the presence of the governor when Amerindian ambassadors came from the Great Lakes,[42] or in the Great Lakes posts through officers or missionaries.[43] In each nation, as J. Clifton and, later, R. White have shown, the alliance depended on the chiefs.[44] For example, Callière wrote in 1696 that Frontenac had asked Lamothe Cadillac, commander at Michilimackinac, to prevent any separate accommodation between the allies and the Iroquois "by means of our most loyal savages."[45] Through repeated gift giving and constant efforts to maintain the loyalty of influential chiefs, the French endeavoured to prevent the Great Lakes nations and the Five Nations from concluding any separate agreement, hoping instead to negotiate a general peace in Montreal.[46] For New France, the allied nations had to be included in any French-Iroquois peace if the French-Amerindian alliance was to be maintained, and the colonial agents thus constantly asserted the necessity of a general peace in their meetings both with delegates of the nations of the west[47] and with those of the Five Nations.[48] However, the only way that the French could maintain their alliances in the west was by encouraging warfare between the Iroquois and the Great Lakes nations. To this end, Frontenac, followed by Callière until 1700, sought to induce New France's allies to fight the Five Nations.[49] This policy was also intended to force the Five Nations to conclude a general peace. It was both a flaw and a paradox of French policy that to force the Iroquois to make peace they had to get them in a stranglehold by inciting the allies to fight them. This hardly created the conditions for a general peace. Moreover, there was a risk that a separate peace between the Iroquois and the nations of the west would weaken the French colony.[50]

In order to concentrate the military forces of their allies against the Iroquois, the French constantly sought to divert them from their military ventures against the Sioux or, further to the south, the Quapaw (or Akansas).[51] They also had to calm disputes among the allied nations and ensure that they did not divide their forces. At the July 1698 conference, Frontenac thus sought to prevent the Kiskakons and the Sable Odawas (two of the Odawa nations) from leaving Michilimackinac as they had proposed to do.[52] The following year, in Montreal, after informing the allied ambassadors of "the state of affairs with the Iroquois," Callière asked them not to attack the Sioux, and promised to punish any Frenchman who dared to supply weapons to them.[53] French diplomatic action in the west would become more clearly defined with the mission of Father Enjalran and Le Gardeur de Courtemanche, in the winter of 1700–1701.

Frontenac did not hesitate to use blackmail to induce his allies to make war against the Iroquois. For example, at the August 1695 conference he declared to them, "I could accept him [the Iroquois] as a friend, but I do not want to do it because you would be destroyed if I made Peace with him without including you in it."[54] It should not be concluded, however, that the war between the Iroquois and the Great Lakes nations was a mere creation of French imperialism.

"TOSS THE HATCHET TO THE SKY": THE IMPACT OF WAR

Their losses to the western nations were one of the main reasons the Iroquois sought to make peace in 1697. Three years later, those losses had become the deciding factor.

During a conference at Michilimackinac in 1695, the French commander Lamothe Cadillac said to the chiefs of the Great Lakes nations: "Let us think once again not only of making war, but of continuing it until the common enemy [the Iroquois] is entirely destroyed. Since it began, your villages have grown bigger, your cabins have filled with children and with beautiful youth."[55] These words are doubly interesting: they highlight the military difficulties of the Five Nations, but also the cultural basis of First Nations warfare, the taking of prisoners. The Great Lakes peoples, like the Iroquois, adopted those prisoners that they did not kill.[56] On many occasions at the end of the seventeenth century, the Native allies of New France had chosen not to "bury the hatchet" against the Five Nations but rather to "toss the hatchet to the sky," or to make war.

Traditional historiography has tended, on the one hand, to depict the Iroquois of the seventeenth and eighteenth centuries as the major diplomatic and military force among the Amerindian nations of the northeast and, on the other, to attribute their decline, and therefore the peace of 1701, to the French military expeditions of 1687, 1693, and particularly 1696.[57] It seems clear, in the light of French and English sources but also of Native oral traditions, that the Great Lakes nations played a far greater role than the French in the Iroquois defeat.

Baron de Lahontan, who had firsthand experience of the Iroquois Wars in the 1680s,[58] said, "I lay this down for an uncontested Truth, that we [the French] are not able to destroy the *Iroquese* by our selves."[59] and a little later, "Since we cannot destroy the *Iroquese* with our single forces, we are necessarily oblig'd to have recourse to the Savages that are our allies."[60] This idea that the French did not have the capacity to defeat the Five Nations militarily is also implicit in Charlevoix's observation, after Frontenac's expedition of 1696, that the Iroquois were "dazed rather than subjugated."[61] In 1698 Frontenac and Champigny were concerned about a possible Anglo-Iroquois attack, "in which case," they said, "the [French] troops that are stationed here [in the colony] would certainly be too weak." They further commented that "[even] in view of the weakened state of the enemies, we believe that our forces in their present state would be insufficient to continue the war if we were obliged to, without relying on our allies."[62] Bacqueville de La Potherie, finally, stated outright: "[F]or ultimately, as soon as these nations [of the Great Lakes] cease to defend our interests, it will be a catastrophe for Canada. They are our support and shield; it is they who curb the Iroquois in all the hunting parties they are obliged to make outside their territory for subsistence. Indeed, they go further, bringing fire and sword into the centre of their [Iroquois] territory."[63]

Frontenac's expedition in 1696, while it enabled the French to devastate the Onondaga and Oneida villages, resulted in only one Iroquois fatality.[64] The same year, a raid by the Odawas and Potawatomis resulted in at least fifty, and perhaps as many as seventy, deaths and the capture of more than thirty prisoners among the Senecas.[65] The war in the west was also a decisive factor between 1697 and 1700, since the French were no longer making military expeditions, unlike their allies from the Great Lakes or even some Algonquins. In 1698 the latter defeated about thirty Onondaga warriors led by La Chaudière Noire at the eastern end of Lake Ontario.[66] According to Charlevoix, it was this attack that finally persuaded the Iroquois to accept a general peace.[67] In short, the wars among the Native peoples wore down the Five Nations much more than the French expeditions did.

At the beginning of the 1660s, Iroquois supremacy – an example is their triumph over the Hurons around 1650 – had started to waver. In 1662 the Iroquois suffered a major defeat by the Ojibwas, Odawas, and Nipissings near Lake Superior. Perrot even stated, "They say the Iroquois have not dared go near Lake Superior since that time."[68] According to Ojibwa oral tradition, as reported in the nineteenth century by G. Copway and W. Warren – and also according to the oral tradition of the Huron-Petuns and even that of the Iroquois – at the end of the seventeenth century the Five Nations suffered terrible military setbacks in warfare against the combined forces of the Ojibwas, Odawas, Potawatomis, Huron-Petuns, and their allies, and were pushed out of the area that is now Ontario.[69] J.A. Brandão and W.A. Starna consider these oral traditions "unconfirmed by the documentary record."[70] It is certainly difficult to take these nineteenth-century accounts at face value. They are, like European sources, biased, ethnocentric documents that give us a distorted "memory" of the past. While the Great Lakes Amerindians certainly had a tendency to idealize their past exploits and to remember mainly their victories at war[71] analysis of the French and English sources provides relatively satisfactory support for the thesis based on Ojibwa oral tradition.

In 1697, according to one of the authors of the *Jesuit Relations*, the Odawas, Potawatomis, Sauks, and Huron-Petuns caused the deaths of more than a hundred Senecas in some five months.[72] In the summer a war party led by Chief Kondiaronk defeated fifty-five Iroquois in a canoe battle on Lake Erie.[73] At the end of the year, the

Huron-Petuns killed twenty Iroquois warriors who were about to launch a raid against the Odawas.[74] In the first six months of 1698, Bellomont counted ninety-four violent deaths in the Iroquois ranks.[75] The military threat to the Five Nations was becoming more and more alarming, even in the view of the English, and in April 1699 Bellomont said, with some exaggeration, that the allies of the French were on the point of totally destroying the Iroquois.[76] At the conference of September 1699 in Montreal, the Iroquois orator pleaded to Callière: "I beseech you, my father, make your allies stop coming into our territory every day and breaking our heads."[77] At the same time, Onondaga sachems asked the English in Albany, "how to behave ourselves in this Extreamity, for wee can endure it noe longer."[78]

The bloodletting continued the following year. In the spring, twenty-eight Iroquois were defeated by the Odawas near the strait of Lake St Clair and Lake Erie.[79] A French officer counted another forty-two Iroquois deaths in the west.[80] La Potherie reported to the minister of marine in August 1700 that in the course of the year the Iroquois had lost fifty-eight men at the hands of the Miamis.[81] Charlevoix, finally, reported that the Iroquois complained to Callière in July 1700 that they had lost a hundred and fifty men in their war against the Odawas, Illinois, and Miamis, probably within less than a year.[82] In August 1700, when the neutralist faction of the Iroquois was acquiring a decisive influence, a sachem informed Bellomont that "the Dowaganhaes or Far Nations have now kill'd many of our people att their hunting."[83]

Deprived of all English military support, the Iroquois had to resign themselves to peace with the French on Onontio's conditions. Their raids against the Amerindians in the west continued to the end of the 1690s, but without any real success.[84] In the winter of 1698, Bellomont counted fourteen hundred warriors among the Iroquois,[85] but by the summer of 1700, this figure had perhaps fallen to eleven hundred, a decrease of almost 20 per cent in the number of men of fighting age. The estimate of three hundred people in the ranks of the League killed during this period is not exaggerated. The war in the west was without question traumatic for the Iroquois.[86] The nations allied with the French, although engaged in open conflict with the Sioux at the same time, inflicted defeats on the Iroquois that would hasten the peace process in 1700–1701.

6 On the Path to Montreal, 1700–1701

The peace negotiations between the French and the Iroquois took a decisive turn in 1700–1701. Pressured by the disasters of the war in the west, inclined to follow a course of action independent of New York, and taking advantage of their rapprochement with the Christian Iroquois of Montreal, the Five Nations, under the influence of the pro-French and neutral factions, resolved in 1700 to resume talks with New France. Although they were obliged to accept peace terms dictated by the French and their allies in these negotiations, the Iroquois nevertheless succeeded in asserting their own interests, which were later recognized in the Montreal agreements of 1701. Meanwhile, the French-English diplomatic duel continued; so did the war in the west, but not for long, as the combined pressure of the French and of Amerindian factions, in particular among the Huron-Petuns, brought the hostilities to an end, creating the conditions for a general peace.

THE IROQUOIS DECISION TO MAKE PEACE: MARCH TO JULY 1700

There were three factions in Iroquois political life at the very end of the seventeenth century. First of all, there were the pro-French, led by the Onondaga Aradgi, and the Senecas Aouenano and Tonatakout. They were determined to accept French conditions for peace even if it meant breaking the chain that bound them to New

York. At the other extreme, the pro-English faction, represented by
the Onondaga chief Sadekarnaktie, was extremely hostile towards
New France and wanted to maintain the alliance with the English;
in 1700 they still rejected the idea of capitulation to the French. In
the middle were the proponents of neutrality, led by the Onondaga
sachem Teganissorens, who wanted to guarantee the political independence of the Iroquois League through a strategy of balance between the two competing empires.[1] In reality, it was not a question
of being pro-French or pro-English, but of managing the interests
of the League in the best way possible by more or less espousing
the strategies of the colonial players. Should they accept the French
terms for peace? Should the nations of the west be included in a
general peace? These questions divided the League and its constitu-
ent nations. The Cayugas and the Onondagas seem to have been
torn, while the Oneidas, not to mention the Mohawks, continued
to reject Callière's proposals. Only the Senecas, exhausted by the
war, seemed prepared to respond positively to the French
demands.[2]

On 12 March 1700, two Iroquois delegates went to Montreal to
meet Onontio and keep the negotiations alive. Both emissaries
favoured peace but by no means represented their entire confederacy.[3] The main orator promised the French governor that delegates
from each Iroquois nation would go to Montreal in the coming
June. Callière, who also asked that the Senecas cease hostilities in
the west, accepted the proposal, and the date was set for "straw-
berry time." For these two delegates, there remained the rather delicate problem of convincing their compatriots to actually come to
Montreal in the summer. In the spring of 1700, a consensus had not
yet been reached among the Iroquois, some of whom still refused to
conclude a treaty with New France.[4]

A partial consensus among the Five Nations would be established
during the summer. On 18 July 1700 an Iroquois delegation arrived
as agreed in Montreal and met with Callière in a conference that
would prove to be a turning point in the peace process. This delegation, however, still did not represent the Five Nations. It consisted
of six delegates – four Senecas (Tonatakout, Aouenano, Tsonhuastsuan, and Toarenguenion) and two Onondagas (Aradgi and Ohonsiowanne) – who claimed to be acting in the name of the four
western nations of the League but who in fact represented only the
faction within these nations that was determined to accept the

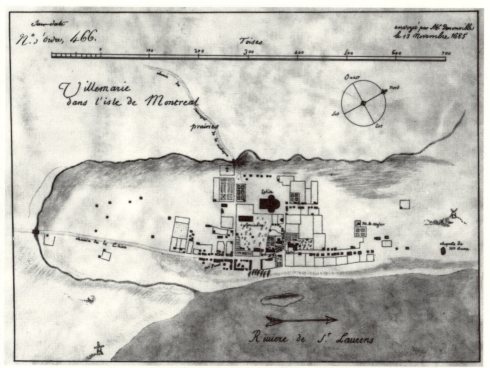

Map of "Villemarie on the Island of Montreal – sent by Mr. Denonville on November 1685," drawn by Robert de Villeneuve (National Archives of Canada H3/340.)

French terms. Neither the Cayugas nor the Oneidas seemed ready to accept this policy,[5] and even certain Seneca and Onondaga sachems remained unconvinced.[6]

The debates began a few days after the arrival of the Iroquois ambassadors, in the presence of delegates of the Algonquins, Iroquois from the Sault and La Montagne, and, in the final days, Hurons from Lorette and Abenakis. Tonatakout, the Iroquois orator, presented eight wampum belts and three wampum strings, one by one, asking the nations of the west to suspend hostilities and promising to make a general exchange of prisoners that would include returning both French prisoners and those from the nations of the west, "without there remaining any." To accomplish this, he asked Onontio to delegate three Frenchmen, Maricourt, Chabert de Joncaire, and Father Bruyas, to accompany them to Iroquoia.

Callière responded to the Iroquois ambassadors two days later with six wampum belts. He refused to recognize Tonatakout's mandate and showed his dissatisfaction that no Cayuga or Oneida delegates had come to Montreal,[7] but he accepted the request to send three French ambassadors to Onondaga, on condition that he retain four of the six Iroquois delegates as hostages. He scheduled the next meeting for the end of August in Montreal and demanded that representatives of the four western nations attend.[8]

For the first time, therefore, the Iroquois seemed to be on the point of giving in to French demands and accepting the inclusion of the Great Lakes nations in general peace negotiations in Montreal. The war in the west was bearing fruit for New France. For the Five Nations, it was now a question of working to bring the factions together.

THE ONONDAGA CONFERENCE, AUGUST 1700

The quest for consensus, spearheaded by the neutral faction led by Teganissorens, gained decisive momentum during the Onondaga conference in August 1700. While the initiative had at first been left to the group favouring the French, which had sent delegations to Montreal in March and July 1700, it subsequently passed to the neutral faction, which was propelled to the forefront by the temporary transfer of the diplomatic theatre from Montreal to the Iroquois capital. Aouenano's humiliating policy of capitulation was then replaced by a policy of restoring the Iroquois League and maintaining diplomatic openness towards the Great Lakes nations.[9]

It was not an arbitrary choice when the Seneca and Onondaga ambassadors asked that Father Bruyas, Joncaire, and Maricourt be the ones to accompany them to Iroquoia as representatives of the French. The Senecas had adopted Joncaire as a son,[10] Maricourt was also considered a full member of the Onondaga nation, and Father Bruyas had served as a missionary to the Oneidas and the Mohawks.[11] All three were thus respected and influential figures, "cultural brokers who would be instrumental in bringing the Five Nations to terms with the French."[12]

When they arrived in Iroquoia, the welcome that met the French plenipotentiaries was indeed enthusiastic. In Gannentaha, which the party reached on 4 August, an elder declared: "Now we no longer doubt the uprightness and sincerity in the heart of our father, Onontio, who sent us the Black Robe [Bruyas] and our son Joncaire. Our land will become beautiful; you will be witnesses to the faith of all our warriors when you enter our village."[13]

On 10 August, when the Seneca, Cayuga, Oneida, and even Mohawk[14] sachems had arrived in the Iroquois capital, the League Council could finally take place, in the presence of the three French ambassadors. Father Bruyas presented Callière's proposals, which he had already put forward in Montreal three weeks earlier, and also requested the right to establish a new Jesuit mission in Onondaga. The situation, however, had changed in relation to the July conference in Montreal, both because the negotiations were taking place in Onondaga and because it was no longer the pro-French Tonatakout who was leading the debate, but Teganissorens, the leader of the neutral faction.[15] In addition, when Bellomont learned that a French delegation had been sent to Onondaga, he quickly dispatched a young interpreter, John B. Van Eps, to the Iroquois capital, to attempt to break up the French-Iroquois negotiations. But the English officer, lacking tact, forbade the sachems, in the name of Bellomont, to hold council with the French and ordered them to go to Albany in "ten or twelve days."[16] This imperious tone, a real challenge to Iroquois sovereignty, shocked the League Council. They closed ranks around Teganissorens,[17] who replied to the New York ambassador: "What does my brother Corlard mean, how should I understand him? While peace has been made in Europe, it seems he is still singing war. Why does he forbid us to listen to the voice of our father Onontio?"[18] During the final session, Teganissorens said in the presence of Bruyas, Maricourt, and Van Eps that delegates from each nation would go to Montreal. He told Van Eps: "You will say to my brother Corlard that I will go down to Montreal where my father Onontio has lit the fire of peace. I will also go to Orange [Albany]; my brother calls me, and so that there is nothing you do not know, here is the wampum belt that I will carry to my father Onontio."[19]

The League Council did not fully agree to the capitulation orchestrated by the faction favourable to the French. The words of Teganissorens showed clearly that the League had no intention of breaking the Covenant Chain.[20] As W.N. Fenton explains, "Iroquois policy was to keep the path open to Albany and maintain the chain, yet to hold the English at arm's length."[21] The French delegation of August 1700 nonetheless achieved a resounding success. The Iroquois wholeheartedly supported the conclusion of a peace agreement with the French and their allies independently of New York, thus rejecting any form of English sovereignty over Iroquoia.

However, there was still the problem of prisoners. During the first few days after their arrival, Bruyas, Maricourt, and Joncaire met with French prisoners adopted into Iroquois families and encouraged them to return to the colony.[22] On 11 August Joncaire left Onondaga and went to the villages of the Cayugas and the Senecas for the same purpose.[23] La Potherie reported: "There were several Frenchmen who avoided him so as not to be obliged to go down to Montreal. The savage life is so pleasant and so tranquil, whatever fondness one might have for his fatherland, that nothing could make them change their minds and return home."[24] It should be noted, however, that while many French prisoners did indeed remain in Iroquoia, this was also because the families that had adopted them refused to let them go, even using force to keep them. In all, the French delegates managed to bring back only thirteen French prisoners,[25] and no prisoners from the nations of the west were returned by the Iroquois families. This was not at all in keeping with Callière's plans, for he hoped to bring these nations together in a peace treaty under his auspices.

The nations of the League had not yet all agreed to carry out separate negotiations with the French. Besides the Mohawks, the Oneidas balked at sending a delegate to Montreal and only sent one wampum belt.[26] In light of the Onondaga conference, and in preparation for the one scheduled in Montreal, they had to redefine the Covenant Chain with the English, both because the alliance with New York was economically essential to them and because they had to take into account the pro-English faction. At the end of August, therefore, fifty sachems from the Five Nations – accompanied by more than one hundred and fifty women and children – went to Albany. Sadekarnaktie, acting as orator, told the governor that if the English helped the Five Nations to counter military pressure from the Great Lakes nations, they would no longer have any dealings with the French.[27] In short, the Iroquois justified their negotiations with New France by the inability of New York to fulfil the military aspect of the Covenant Chain.[28] Under the influence of Teganissorens, the Five Nations thus moved more and more towards an independent, neutral course of action.

THE PEACE OF SEPTEMBER 1700

With the peace of September 1700, preliminary to the Great Peace of Montreal, the wars that had raged intermittently since 1609 between the French and the Iroquois came to an end. This treaty, which also inaugurated a peace process between the Five Nations and the Native peoples of the west, was concluded at the Montreal conference held between 3 and 9 September, with Callière presiding and many Native delegates in attendance.[29]

Nineteen Iroquois sachems arrived in Montreal on 31 August, accompanied by Bruyas, Joncaire, and Maricourt. These Iroquois leaders were Seneca, Cayuga, and Onondaga chiefs, but they spoke also for the Oneidas. When they entered the town, they "were greeted with salvos of artillery."[30] Some representatives of New France's allies were already there, namely the La Montagne and Sault Iroquois and the Abenakis. Ambassadors from the nations of Michilimackinac would arrive a few days later, after the Iroquois had delivered their proposals.[31] There were also Huron-Petun delegates, led by Kondiaronk, and delegates of the four Odawa nations,[32] represented by Koutaoiliboe, seconded by Kinongé and Kileouiskingié.[33]

The conference began three days after the arrival of the Iroquois ambassadors, and a Seneca orator opened the debates. Fundamentally new to the peace process was that the Seneca orator was no longer speaking on behalf of the pro-French faction, but in the name of most of the Iroquois, and he was taking a position of neutrality.[34] Central to his proposals was that all the Great Lakes nations be included in a peace treaty. "The last time we came here," he declared, "we planted the Tree of Peace; now we are spreading the roots to reach as far as the nations of the upper country so that the tree will be solidly planted. We are also adding leaves to it so that we can do good business in the shade. Perhaps the people of the upper country will cut some roots from this big tree, but that will not be our fault."[35]

Supporting each of his proposals with a wampum belt, the orator then turned his attention to the release of the thirteen French prisoners and insisted that Callière return to the Iroquois "all prisoners held by the Great Lakes nations and by the savages of this region [the Iroquois of Montreal]."[36] The Seneca delegate finished his speech by asking the French governor to allow the Iroquois to sell their furs at Fort Frontenac and at the same price as they would obtain in Montreal.[37]

Callière, in spite of the edict of 1696, which had prohibited trading outside the colony, agreed to this trade request. In the presence of the Iroquois, the Huron-Petuns, and the Odawas, he promised to be the chief guarantor of the general peace and, according to the French-Amerindian tradition of alliance, assumed a role as referee and mediator in the event of conflict among the Native nations, in particular between an Iroquois party and a party from an allied nation. If a nation violated the peace, he said, the party attacked should not in any way counterattack, but should call upon Onontio, who would see to obtaining reparation and, if need be, use force, joining with the injured party to punish the recalcitrant attacker.[38] This stipulation could only delight the Iroquois, but it did not settle the peace definitively. Callière continued by asking for the return of all prisoners, both French and Amerindian, still in Iroquoia, and set a date in August of the following year for the exchange of prisoners in the presence of Iroquois delegates and delegates of all the nations of the west.

Few ambassadors from the Great Lakes attended the conference in September 1700, but those present were of considerable importance, given the diplomatic weight of the Huron-Petuns and the Odawas. Kondiaronk and Koutaoiliboe certainly did not represent all their compatriots, but rather their own factions. It goes without saying that they wanted peace as much as the Iroquois and the

French. The Huron-Petun leader, the first of New France's allies to speak, declared: "Onontio ... takes the hatchets of all the nations; for myself, I throw mine at his feet. Who would be bold enough to go against his will, he who is our father here? I do not at all doubt that the people of the upper country will follow what he wishes; it is up to you, the Iroquois nations, to do so too."[39] Kondiaronk continued a little later, saying to the Iroquois ambassadors: "I am surprised that your brother Corlar treats you so inhumanely, you who have been so loyal to him. You lost most of your warriors in this war by supporting his party. Your villages have been burned ... He should not threaten you as he has just done while you are seeking peace and tranquillity."[40] Like all present, Kondiaronk wanted peace, and he would use his influence to extend it to all the nations of the alliance.

On 8 September each Native representative signed the various articles on which they all agreed, and even the signatures of the Oneidas and the Mohawks appear among the thirteen Native pictograms on the peace treaty.[41] This treaty was a clear success for the French: it meant peace, at last, with the Iroquois, and above all it had come about in spite of diplomatic pressure from New York.[42] English claims to sovereignty over Iroquoia had been demolished. Callière argued that it was important to take advantage of this situation to ensure Iroquois neutrality between the two colonies, leaving them "freedom in spiritual matters, in the certitude that they will prefer our Missionaries over the Ministers of the English."[43]

For New France, another positive aspect of this peace with the Iroquois was that the way was opened for the construction of a fort on the river between Lake Erie and Lake St Clair.[44] This project was the idea of Lamothe Cadillac, the colourful French officer who had been commander of the Michilimackinac post from 1694 to 1696. Cadillac intended to found a French colony at Detroit and make it a gathering place for all the nations of the west. Such a settlement, he argued, would enable New France to curb English expansion in the Great Lakes, to secure greater control over Iroquois activities in the west, and to exert a predominant influence over the allied nations. Although Callière and Champigny initially opposed Cadillac's plan, which they believed would risk disturbing the Five Nations in their hunting grounds and might even encourage trade between the Amerindians of the west and the Iroquois, it was nonetheless approved by Versailles.[45] All that remained was to convince the

Great Lakes nations and especially the Iroquois not to take offence at the construction of the fort.

The Iroquois also scored points with the treaty of 1700. Peace in the west was well on the way, and the possibility of trading at Fort Frontenac would allow them to escape economic dependence on Albany. In addition, the French were implicitly allowing them to maintain their commercial and even religious ties with the English. However, they had been ordered to bring back their other prisoners, and since not all the Great Lakes nations had been included in this treaty, military pressure persisted in the west.[46]

The Huron-Petuns and Odawas present at this conference still had to transform the precarious truce into a general peace. As a result, the eleven months preceding the great conference of the summer of 1701 were marked by intense diplomatic activity.

DIPLOMATIC MANOEUVRING IN THE WEST

Governor Callière and the chiefs of the western nations present in Montreal in September 1700, particularly Kondiaronk, wanted the peace treaty signed at that conference to include all the nations of the French-Amerindian alliance. Callière therefore dispatched two ambassadors, Le Gardeur de Courtemanche, soldier and diplomat, and the Jesuit father Jean Enjalran, to make preparations in the west for the 1701 meeting. Their mission was threefold: first, to go to "all the nations of the Great Lakes" to inform them about the agreements of September and have them "accept and sign them"; second, to convince the allied chiefs to go to Montreal "at the beginning of August" 1701, accompanied by all their Iroquois prisoners, for a general exchange of prisoners;[47] and finally, a traditional policy element, to attempt to put a stop to the wars still going on between the Odawas, Miamis, and others, on one side, and the Sioux, on the other.[48] While this French diplomatic mission was under way, Kondiaronk and Koutaoiliboe, who had returned to Michilimackinac after the Montreal peace conference, were also attempting to induce the various allied nations to promise to come to Montreal to negotiate with the Iroquois.[49]

The two French ambassadors left Montreal immediately after the signing of the treaty of September 1700. Callière had had them

Aboriginal man of the Outaouaks nation, c. 1700.
Sketch attributed to Louis Nicolas. From the *Codex
Canadiensis*, Gilcrease Museum, Tulsa, Arizona,
4726.7.

The tattooed man in this sketch is wearing head and
arm bands made of wampum beads and carrying a
calumet.

"loaded with wampum collars to attach ... [his] words according to the custom of the savages."[50] They reached Michilimackinac on 30 October, probably in the company of Kondiaronk and the other Huron-Petun and Odawa chiefs. There were hardly any Native people in the "capital" of the Great Lakes at the time, most having left for their hunting grounds. Father Enjalran stayed there to await the return of the various Michilimackinac chiefs and negotiate with the Odawas and the Huron-Petuns together with Kondiaronk. Meanwhile, Courtemanche undertook the delicate task of touring Amerindian encampments all around Lake Michigan, reviewing the nations allied with New France. He went first to St Joseph River, southeast of Lake Michigan, where from 29 December to 22 March he met mainly with Miamis, but also with Potawatomis, Sauks, Foxes, Mahicans (Loups), and Huron-Petuns.[51] He continued his voyage southward and from 8 to 14 April parleyed with representatives of the six Illinois nations.[52] He continued on to meet with the Ouiatenons, reaching Chicagou (Chicago) on 29 April. Then he visited the Mascoutens and on 14 May arrived in the Green Bay region, the territory of the Winnebagos, Potawatomis, Sauks, Menominees, Foxes, and Kickapoos. His mission accomplished, Courtemanche finally returned to Michilimackinac on 2 June, and shortly thereafter to Montreal, accompanied by the allied delegations.[53]

Mission accomplished? Certainly, but not without major difficulties and not without local support from various Amerindian leaders. Most of the Great Lakes nations were still at war with the Iroquois during the winter of 1700–1701. Courtemanche observed that this was at least the case for the Potawatomis, Sauks, Miamis, Illinois, and Mascoutens.[54] However, it seems that the news he brought of peace restrained most of the warriors of the allied nations from pursuing their war against the Iroquois. On no condition did the nations allied with New France want to be excluded from a treaty of such importance. Their future in the house of Onontio was at stake, and after all, nothing would prevent them from resuming the war later.

While the desire for a general peace seems to have prevailed among the nations of the west, some persistent hesitation reveals the internal tensions dividing these nations. From time to time, factions objected to sending ambassadors to Montreal to conclude the treaty planned by Callière and certain Native chiefs.[55] Within each nation, obtaining consensus was tricky. Their difficulties can be explained principally by a circumstance that could have undone the diplomatic efforts of Onontio and Kondiaronk. There were rumours in the west, in the spring of 1701, of an epidemic in Montreal.[56] Events would prove that these rumours were well founded and were in no way a pretext for the western nations to avoid concluding the peace treaty, since the very lives of their ambassadors were at stake. Therefore, a refusal to go to the conference should not necessarily be interpreted as a reflection of political dissension within the alliance. On the contrary, going to Montreal in spite of the rumours of disease was proof of extraordinary determination on the part of the Native delegates.

Some nations, then, such as the Illinois, the Gokapatagans (Kickapoos), and some of the Mississaugas, balked at taking part.[57] The hesitation, and even more the refusal, of certain nations or factions to support the peace strategy also reflected various motivations above and beyond fear of the epidemic. The Illinois, who at this time were no longer under threat from the Iroquois and who had other enemies, perhaps considered this voyage unimportant.[58] The desire on the part of some to continue the war against the Five Nations was probably another obstacle to peace.[59] Certain Odawa groups, finally, had already concluded a separate peace with the Iroquois, and their strategy of alliance with the Covenant Chain naturally implied the rejection of a pro-French diplomatic approach.[60]

But the main problem appears to have been that the nations of the west were reluctant to give up the Iroquois prisoners whom they had adopted and "naturalized."[61] For many nations, this was the most signifiant impediment to a consensus in favour of peace. Onanguicé, in particular, a Potawatomi chief who enjoyed a great deal of influence in the Great Lakes region, was opposed to the allied nations' returning all their Iroquois prisoners.[62] La Potherie reported that the chief "had frightened away, indeed, many Nations who accepted his interpretation too easily. Moreover, he foresaw with a great deal of understanding all the unfortunate consequences that could come from the excessive good faith of those who wanted to return all the Prisoners all at once, because knowing the character of the Iroquois which is so two-faced, it was not difficult to believe that they would themselves be duped."[63] Onanguicé's fear, as we will see, was well founded. However, at Kondiaronk's insistence, he finally agreed to go to Montreal and to bring all his prisoners back there. Kondiaronk stated on 1 August 1701 before Callière: "Onanguicé explained that we were moving too quickly to bring back all the Iroquois prisoners. The Nations felt strongly that this was so. I made him the present of a kettle and a gun to urge him to follow me to Montreal, assuring him that there was more reason to be content than he thought. He therefore decided to come."[64]

Clearly, Kondiaronk played a pivotal role in building the peace of 1701. It is likely that without him the mission of Courtemanche and Enjalran would have been much more difficult. At a conference held in Michilimackinac in the spring of 1701,[65] Kondiaronk, more than Enjalran no doubt, told "all the nations of the Lakes" what had occurred in Montreal in September 1700 and endeavoured to convince them to go there in August with all their Iroquois prisoners.[66] Through discussion and gifts, he finally succeeded in creating a semblance of consensus among all the allies meeting together in Michilimackinac. Other chiefs worked to support Kondiaronk's policy, including Quarante Sols, the chief of the Hurons of St Joseph River, who announced to Callière on 1 August 1701, "I have also personally helped the Miamis and their prisoners who did not have the use of canoes, and I have made gifts to those who had prisoners to urge them to return them."[67]

What motivated this policy? Was it the desire to preserve and even consolidate the French political alliance and, beyond that, to maintain the whole network of alliances built around the Odawas, the Huron-Petuns, and Onontio? That is likely, but no doubt there was more to it than that.[68] It was a matter of recovering prisoners, preventing the conclusion of a separate French-Iroquois treaty, and, perhaps, through a peace settlement with the Five Nations, promoting trade with the English in Albany.

FINAL PREPARATIONS, WINTER–SPRING 1701

A Fragile Peace

In the period immediately after the peace agreement of September 1700, the west was more than a theatre of negotiations. The following month, in fact, Odawas who had not attended the conference surprised a Seneca hunting party, killing several men and capturing the chief.[69] The incident showed the fragility of the truce concluded in Montreal, but also of the treaty negotiated between the Iroquois and certain groups in the west in June 1700. The ambush could only encourage the Iroquois to opt for general peace negotiations in Montreal, happening as it did at a time when their relations with New York had deteriorated somewhat. The Onondagas, for example, were blocking the construction of an English fort on their territory and were opposed to New York's sending a trading expedition to Michilimackinac. The neutral camp was thus reinforced to the detriment of the faction favourable to the English, and a consensus gradually developed around Teganissorens.[70]

In March 1701 two Onondaga ambassadors went to the town of Quebec, and through Massias, a La Montagne Iroquois, they complained to Onontio that the Odawas had violated the cease-fire. These delegates were complying with the arbitration clause introduced by Callière at the conference in September 1700, which they had all the more reason to use in that they were unable to counterattack. Massias acknowledged this implicitly when he stated that the Algonquins, the Nipissings, and even the Crees were using the hunting grounds around Fort Frontenac,[71] a sign that New France's allies were exerting military pressure on Iroquoia everywhere. Callière reassured them and promised to try to have the Seneca chief captured by the Odawas returned to them. Before the two ambassadors left, the governor reminded them of the meeting in August.[72]

Teganissorens in Montreal, May 1701

It was probably not long afterwards that the Iroquois got wind of Cadillac's plan for Detroit and became alarmed. A French fort at such a strategic location might hamper their freedom of movement in the west and, like Fort Frontenac, constitute a military threat to Iroquoia.[73] It was primarily for this reason that Teganissorens, accompanied by other chiefs, including Aradgi,[74] went to Montreal in May 1701. The Onondaga chief, speaking to Callière, claimed that the French had no right to build at Detroit and insisted that they delay construction of the fort at least until the conference in August. He also asked for reparation for the attack by the Odawas the preceding fall and clarification of the rumour about an imminent resurgence of hostilities between the French and the English. Finally, he asked that the peace be enforced in the west and that the Iroquois be able to hunt there without fear of attack, a request that was all the more urgent in that the Senecas had been the target of a new enemy raid early that spring.[75]

On the question of the war in the west, Callière adjourned the debate until the conference scheduled for August. He tried to reassure Teganissorens regarding Detroit, presenting this settlement as a means of guaranteeing peace in the west and as a supply centre for the Iroquois. Finally, Callière described to the Onondaga chief his plan to ensure the neutrality of the Five Nations in the eventuality of a new French-English war. "This will be the means," he said, "to preserve the peace with us and all our allies, and to keep the route open for you to come here ... to obtain whatever trade goods you want." Nothing could have satisfied Teganissorens more that this prospect of neutrality.[76]

French and English Ambassadors in Onondaga, June 1701

It was in Onondaga at the end of June that the last of the preliminary negotiations took place before the big conference of August 1701. Shortly after the departure of Teganissorens, Callière delegated Bruyas, Maricourt, Joncaire, La Chauvignerie, and a score of other Frenchmen to conduct these negotiations.[77] The English also sent a few ambassadors to the Iroquois capital to try to obstruct the French plans and to invite the Five Nations to a conference planned for the following month in Albany.[78]

Citing the issue of the Spanish succession and the probability of a new intercolonial war in the near future, the French insisted on committing the Five Nations to neutrality. They also asked the Iroquois for permission to send Jesuits into their villages. The English delegates, as would be expected, expressed opposition to these plans. Teganissorens now found himself in a very delicate situation, mainly because of the religious question, since divisions within the League Council were again creating cracks in the fragile consensus he had established. Criticizing the inability of the English to provide the League with military support against the French-Amerindian allies, the Onondaga leader indicated that it was for this reason that he wished to continue separate negotiations with New France.[79] Three days later, he announced the decisions of the League Council, which revealed the neutralist leaning of its policy. On the problem of the missionaries, Teganissorens said that the Iroquois would receive a minister or a Jesuit from either the English or French, whichever sold their goods at the better price, and thus put off the question until later, to the great displeasure of the English.[80] Above all, he added in the same vein of compromise, some delegates should go to Montreal and others to Albany, while he himself would remain in Onondaga to symbolize Iroquois neutrality.[81] He then declared his desire for alliance with both European powers: "I hold my Father by one hand, and my brother Corlard by the other one – who would dare attack me? – I value them both equally and do not want to ever be separated from them."[82] According to A. Beaulieu and M. Lavoie, the Iroquois wanted to stay at the centre of the political arena and, even more, at the centre of the world.[83]

Since the Iroquois had agreed to release their prisoners, Maricourt asked if he could take back as many as possible, at least from among the French prisoners; he seemed to have little concern for Native prisoners from the west. Despite the use of some force, he managed to gather only six women and a child, prisoners who, according to D.K. Richter, were "more vulnerable to assimilation" and "who had no desire to return to Canada."[84] Teganissorens admitted to Maricourt, presenting "a wampum belt of an extraordinary size," that "Elders like him were not complete masters of the slaves, who, once adopted into families, were out of their jurisdiction."[85] The following day, he asked Maricourt why the Iroquois should return prisoners who did not want to be returned when the French did not force the Mohawks living near Montreal to go back to Iroquoia.[86] Joncaire, for his part, returned from Seneca and Cayuga territory with a few prisoners.[87]

While the thorny problem of prisoners remained unresolved at the end of this conference in Onondaga, the Iroquois had nonetheless affirmed their willingness to accept the French terms and to commit themselves to policies of balance and neutrality in the future. Delegates of each of the Five Nations therefore prepared to go to Montreal, like the delegates from the Great Lakes. The way finally seemed clear, and the Tree of Peace rose majestically on the horizon.[88]

PART THREE

The Montreal Conference, Summer 1701

The long round of negotiations that had begun in the winter of 1697 culminated in the conference in Montreal in late July and early August 1701. This spectacular conference, which brought together some forty nations, led to agreements that in part determined the diplomatic history of northeastern North America in the eighteenth century.

7 Montreal, Capital of Peace: 21 July to 7 August 1701

In the summer of 1701, Montreal was the political centre of northeastern America. In an atmosphere of exuberance and reconciliation, Native people and Frenchmen exchanged goods and gifts, displayed wampum belts, smoked the peace pipe, and danced and feasted to establish a lasting alliance. The small colonial town became the hub of the kind of cross-cultural encounter that, beyond the process of conquest, has characterized the experience of the New World.

FORTY SOVEREIGN NATIONS

On 4 August the representatives of forty distinct nations put their signatures on the Treaty of Montreal. Of these nations, only one was European: France, in whose name the colonial authorities of Canada were acting. The thirty-eight or thirty-nine other nations were from the vast area extending from Acadia to the eastern edge of the Great Plains.

The French

Louis Hector de Callière, as governor general, was the head of New France, but he was directly answerable to the king, of whom he was the mere representative, the ambassador in a sense. It was in the name of Louis XIV, and thus of France, that the administrators of

e. 7. 1701.
Joint a la lettre de M. le Chr.
de Callieres
Recueil des traitez de paix
Iroquois

Ratification De la Paix

faitte au mois de septembre Dernier, entre La Colonie de
Canada, Les Sauuages Ses alliez, et les iroquois dans vne
assemblée generalle des chefs de chacune de ces nations
Conuoquée par monsieur le Cheualier de Callieres
gouuerneur et Lieutenant general pour le Roy en la
nouuelle france,

A Montreal le quatrième aoust 1701

Comme il ny auoit icy L'année Derniere que Des
deputez des hurons et des outaouacs lorsque ie fis la paix
auec les Iroquois pour moy et tous mes alliez, ie iugeay qu'il
estoit necessaire d'enuoyer le Sieur de Courtemanche,
Et le R. P. Anjalran, chéz toutes les autres nations mes
alliez, qui estoient absents pour leur apprendre ce qui
s'estoit passé, et les inuiter a descendre des Chefs de
chacune auec les prisonniers iroquois qu'ils auoient affin
D'écouter tous ensemble ma parolle.

J'ay vne extreme ioye de voir icy presentement tous mes
enfans assemblez, vous hurons, outaouacs du Sable,
Kiskakons, outaouacs Sinago, nation de la fourche,
Sauteurs, poutéeatamis, Sakis, puants, folles auoines, venards
maskoutins, Miamis, Ilinois, amikois, nepissingues, algonquins
temiskamingues, Cristinaux, gens des terres, Kikapoux, gens
du saule, dela montagne, Abenakis, et vous nations iroquoise,
et que m'ayant remis les vns, et les autres vos interets
entre les mains ie puisse vous faire viure tous En
tranquilité, ie ratiffie dont auiourd'huy la paix que nous
auons faitte au mois d'aoust dernier voulant qu'il ne Soit
plus parlé detous les coups faits pendant la guerre, et
Je me Saisy de nouueau detouttes vos haches, et detous vos
autres instruments de guerre, que ie mets auec les miens
dans vne fosse Sy proffonde que personne ne puisse les
reprendre, pour troubler la tranquilité que ie restablis
parmy mes Enfans, en vous recommandant lorsque vous
vous rencontrerez de vous traiter Comme freres, et devous
accomoder ensemble pour la chasse, de maniere qu'il n'arriue

The treaty signed in Montreal on 4 August 1701 (Archives nationales de
France, Fonds de colonies, CIIA, vol. 19, folios 41–44. Photographs from
the National Archives of Canada.)

aucune Brouillerie des vns auec les autres, et pour que cette
paix ne puisse estre troubléé, ie repete ce que i'ay desja Dit
dans le traité que nous auons fait, que s'il arriuoit que
quelqu'vn de mes enfans en frapast vn autre, celuy qui aura
esté frapé ne se vangera point, ny par luy ny par aucun
de sa part, mais il viendra me trouuer pour que ie luy en
fasse faire raison, vous declarant que si l'offençant
refusoit d'en faire vne satisfaction raisonnable, ie me ioindra
auec mes autres alliez à l'offensé pour l'y contraindr
ce que ie ne croit pas qui puisse arriuer, par l'obeissance
que me doiuent mes enfans qui se ressouuiendront de ce que
nous arrestons presentement ensembles, et pour qu'ils ne
puissent l'oublier, j'attache mes parolles aux colliers que
ie vais donner a chacune de vos nations affin que les
anciens les fassent executer par leurs jeunes gens, ie vous
inuite tous a fumer dans ce calumet de paix ou ie comence
le premier, et a manger de la viande et du bouillon que
ie vous fais preparer pour que i'aye comme vn bon pere
la satisfaction de voir tous mes enfans reunis,
Je garderay ce calumet qui m'a esté presenté par les
miamis affin que ie puisse vous faire fumer quand
vous viendrez me voir,

    Apres que toutes les nations cy dessus eurent entendu
    ce que monsieur le Cheualier de Callieres leur dit, ils
    repondirent comme il suit,

Le Chef des Kiskakons

Je n'ay pas voulu manquer mon pere ayant sçû que vous
me demandiez les prisonniers des Iroquois, a vous les amener
en voila quatre que ie vous presente pour en faire ce qu'il
vous plaira, c'est auec cette porcelaine que ie les ay deliez,
et voicy vn calumet que ie presente aux iroquois pour fum
ensembles quand nous nous rencontrerons, ie me rejouy de
ce que vous auez vny la terre qui estoit bouluersée, et ie
~~raiiiiy~~ souscrit volontiers a tout ce que vous auez fait,

Les Iroquois,

Vous voila assemblez nostre pere comme vous l'auez
souhaitté, vous plantates l'année derniere vn arbre de paix

42

Et vous y mîtes des racines et des feuilles pour que nous y fussions
a l'abry, nous esperons presentement que tout le monde entend —
ce que vous dites, qu'on ne touchera point a cet arbre, pour nous
nous vous asseurons, par ces quatre colliers que nous suivrons —
tout ce que vous aurez reglé; nous vous presentons deux prisoñrs
que voicy et nous vous rendrons les autres que nous avons, Nous
esperons aussy presentement que les portes sont ouvertes pour
la paix, qu'on nous renvoyera le reste des nostres,

Les hurons,

Nous voila icy comme vous l'avez demandé, nous vous presentons
douze prisonniers, dont cinq veulent retourner avec nous, pour
les sept autres vous en ferez ce qu'il vous plaira, nous Vous —
remercions dela paix que vous nous avez procurée et nous —
la ratifions avec ioye,

Jean le blanc outaouac du Sable,

Je vous ay obey mon pere aussy tost que vous m'avez demandé
en vous ramenant deux prisonniers dont vous estes le maistre,
quand vous m'avez commandé d'aller ala guerre ie l'ay fait,
et a present que vous me le deffendez iy obey, ie vous demande
mon pere par ce collier que les iroquois rellient mon corps —
qui est chéz eux, et qu'il me le renvoyent (C'est adire les gens
de sa nation)

Sangouessy outaouac Sinago,

Je n'ay pas voulu manquer a vos ordres mon pere quoique ie —
n'aye point de prisonniers, Cependant voila une femme et un
enfant que i'ay racheptés et vous ferez ce qu'il vous plaira;
et voila un calumet que ie donne aux iroquois pour fumer come
freres quand nous nous rencontrerons,

Chichicatalo, Chef des Miamis

Je vous ay obey mon pere en vous ramenant 8 prisonniers Iroquois
pour en faire ce qu'il vous plaira, Si i'avois eu des Canots, ie vous
en aurois amené dauantage, quoy que ie ne voye point icy des —
miens qui sont chéz les iroquois, ie vous rameneray ce qui m'en
reste, Si vous le souhaitté, ou ie leur ouvriray les portes pour qu'ils
s'en retournent,

Onanguissé pour les Sakis,

Je ne fais qu'un mesme corps avec vous mon Pere, voila Un —
prisonnier Iroquois que i'avois fait a la guerre, Souffrez qu'en vous
le presentant ie luy donne un calumet pour emporter chéz les
Iroquois et fumer quand nous nous rencontrerons, ie vous remercie

De ce que vous eclairez le Soleil qui estoit obscure depuis la guerre

Onanguisset Chef des Potrouatamis,

Ie ne vous seray point vn long discours mon pere, ie n'ay plus que
deux prisonniers que ie mets a vos deux costez pour en faire cequ'il
vous plaira, voila vn calumet que ie vous presente pour que vous
le gardiéz, ou que vous le donniéz a ces deux prisonniers afin
qu'ils fument dedans chéz eux, ie Suis tousiours prest a vous
obeir iusqu'a la mort,

Misgensa Chef Outagamis,

Ie n'ay point de prisonniers a vous rendre mon pere, mais ie
vous remercie du beau jour que vous donnéz a toute la Terre
par la paix, pour moy ie ne perdray iamais cette Clarté,

Les Maskoutins

Ie ne vous amene point d'Esclaue iroquois par ce que ie n'ay pas
esté en party contre eux depuis quelque tems, m'estant amusé a
faire la guerre a d'autres nations, mais ie Suis venu pour vous obeir
et vous remercier de la paix que vous nous procuréz,

Les folles auoines.

Ie Suis seullement venu mon pere pour vous obeir et
embrasser la paix que auéz faite entre les Iroquois et nous,

Les Sauteurs et les Puants

Ie vous aurois amené mon pere des Esclaues iroquois Sy-
Ien auois eu, voulant vous obeir en ce que vous m'ordonnéz,
ie vous remercie de la clarté que vous nous donnéz et ie Souaitte
qu'elle dure,

Les Nepissingues

Ie n'ay pas voulu manquer a me rendre icy comme les autres
pour ecouster vostre voix, i'auois vn prisonnier iroquois
l'année passée que ie vous ay rendu, voila vn calumet que
ie vous presente pour le donner aux iroquois Si vous le Souaité-
affin de fumer ensembles quand nous nous rencontrerons,

Les Algonquins

Ie n'ay point de prisonniers a vous rendre mon pere, l'algonquin
est vn de vos enfans qui a tousiours esté a vous, et qui y Sera
tant qu'il viura, ie prie le maistre de la vie que ce que vous
faites aujourd'huy Dure,

La Mikois

N'ayant point d'autre volonté que la vostre j'obey a ce que
vous venéz de faire,

43

L'Abenakis,

Quoy que ie parle des Derniers ie ne suis pas moins auous
mon pere, vous sçauez que ie vous ay tousiours esté attaché
ie n'ay plus de haches vous l'auez mise dans vne fosse l'année
derniere et ie ne la reprendray que quand vous me l'ordonnerés

Les Gens Du Sault

Vous n'ignorez pas vous autres Iroquois que nous ne
soyons attachez a nostre pere nous qui demeurons auec luy
et qui sommes dans son sein, vous nous enuoyaste vn collier
il y a trois ans pour nous inuiter a vous procurer la paix
nous vous en enuoyasmes vn, en reponse, nous vous donnon
encorre celuy cy pour vous dire que nous y auons trauaillé,
nous ne demandons pas mieux qu'elle soit de Durée faite
aussy devostre Coste ce qu'il faut pour Cela,

Des Gens dela Montagne

Vous auez faib assembler icy nostre pere toutes Les
Nations pour faire vn amas de haches et les mettre
dans la terre, auec la vostre, pour moy qui n'en auois pas
d'autre, ie me rejouy de ce que vous faites auiourd'huy, et
J'inuite Les Iroquois a nous regarder comme leurs freres

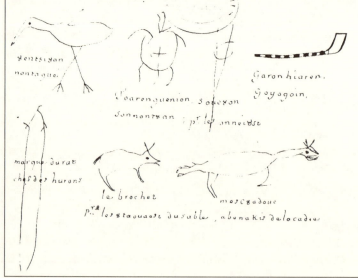

Tentsigan
nontagne.

Oarenguenion Sadekon
Sonnontan pt les onneiost

Garonhiaron.
Goyogoin.

marque du rat
chef des hurons

le brochet

moscgadouc

pte les staouaest du sable, abenakis delocadies

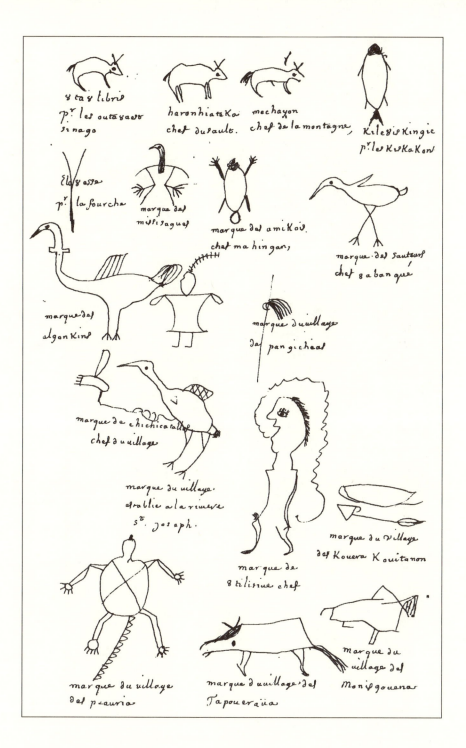

8 tas tibris
pr les outagaus
sinago

haronhiateka
chef du sault.

mechayon
chef de la montagne,

Kilegis kingie
pr les KisKaKons

Els 8 esse
pr la fourche

marque des
milisagues

marque des amikois
chef ma hingan;

marque des sauteurs
chef gabangué

marque des
algonkins

marque du village
des pangicheas

marque de chichicatalo
chef d'un village

marque du village
establie a la riviere
st joseph.

marque de
8 tilisiue chef

marque du village
des Koueva Kouitanon

marque du village
des psauria

marque d'uvillage des
Tapoueraua

marque du
village des
Monisgouenas

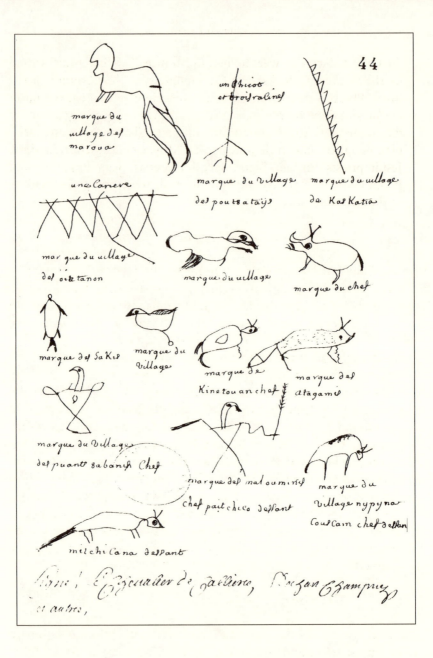

44

Signé, L'Escuadier de galliers, Bozan Champmez
et autres,

the Canadian colony were acting. In Montreal, Callière was assisted by the intendant, Bochart de Champigny, and the governor of the town, Philippe de Rigaud de Vaudreuil. He was also backed up in the negotiations by the most skilful and experienced diplomats in the colony, veritable Native affairs officers: Nicolas Perrot in particular, but also Chabert de Joncaire, Le Moyne de Maricourt, and the Jesuit priests Vincent Bigot, Jacques Bruyas, Jean Enjalran, and Julien Garnier.[1] Ten key individuals in all represented the interests of the Sun King.

The Iroquois of the League

The French delegates sent to Onondaga by Callière in June 1701 returned to Montreal on 21 July accompanied by two hundred Iroquois.[2] The Mohawks, who had said that they would attend the conference, were not in the delegation. However, four Mohawk ambassadors arrived in Montreal "several days after the departure" of the delegates, and they accepted "the same conditions as the others."[3]

As planned, Teganissorens was not part of the Iroquois delegation, nor of the one sent to Albany slightly earlier.[4] At the head of the Onondaga, Seneca, Oneida, and Cayuga delegation in Montreal were the three Seneca leaders Tekanoet, Aouenano, and Tonatakout,[5] who acted as orators, as well as the Onondaga sachem Ohonsiowanne, the Seneca chief Toarenguenion, the Cayuga delegate Garonhiaron, and the Oneida delegate Soueouon, who signed the treaty for their respective nations.[6] The aim of these ambassadors, who were from the pro-French faction, was to promote the policy of neutrality developed by Teganissorens within the League Council.[7]

The Great Lakes Nations

The delegation of the Great Lakes nations, which formed a flotilla of almost two hundred canoes,[8] arrived in Montreal on 22 July.[9] The delegates numbered between seven and eight hundred[10] and apparently represented thirty distinct nations, all allied with the French. There are unfortunately problems of identification, but on the basis of the signatures and the speech made by Callière on

6 August, we can nevertheless identify twenty-eight[11] of them. The nations were (in alphabetical order):

- The Amikwas, or Beaver nation, represented by Mahingan. In the debates, the Odawas spoke for them.[12]
- The Crees, or at least one of their bands from the area northwest of Lake Superior (pictograph unidentified).
- The Foxes (or Outagamis), represented by Noro and Misk-ouensa.[13]
- The "Gens des terres" ("inlanders"), which may be a band related to the Crees (pictograph unidentified).
- The Huron-Petuns (Tionontatis), represented by Kondiaronk, Houatsaranti, and Quarante Sols, the latter acting specifically for the Hurons of the St Joseph River.[14] These chiefs had created a consensus within their nation, which had abandoned the pro-English ideas of Le Baron. The signature of Kondiaronk appears on the treaty of 4 August, although it was probably made on his behalf by another Huron-Petun chief or a French scribe, since Kondiaronk had died on 2 August, a victim of the epidemic.[15]
- The Illinois, who were divided into several groups:[16] Kaskakias, Peorias, Tapouaros, Maroas, Coiracoentanons, and Moingwenas. In fact, no Illinois ambassador reached Montreal. Those who had expressed the desire to attend after the conference in Michilimackinac in May 1701 either died along the way (or at least their chief died) or preferred to return home rather than face the epidemic that had already claimed many Native people. The Potawatomi chief Onanguicé was responsible for representing them,[17] and he may also have signed for them, unless the French exceeded the mandate given them by the Illinois, who, according to Kondiaronk, were reluctant to take part in the conference.[18] It is more likely that the Illinois' pictographs on the treaty were collected by Courtemanche during his diplomatic mission to the Great Lakes and then reproduced on the treaty in Montreal.
- The Kickapoos, according to Kondiaronk, did not send any delegates to the conference.[19] This nation is nevertheless quoted twice in the minutes of the treaty negotiations[20] (pictograph not identified).
- The Mascoutens, represented by Kiskatapi[21] (pictograph not identified).
- The Menominees (or Folles Avoines), represented by Paintage.[22]

- The Miamis of the St Joseph River, as well as the Piankashaws and the Ouiatenons, both Miami nations, all represented by Chichicatalo.[23]
- The Mississaugas, whose chief was represented by Onanguicé on 4 August.[24]
- The Nipissings, represented by Onaganiouitak[25] (pictograph not identified).
- The Odawas, who were divided into four subgroups: the Sable Odawas, represented by Outoutagan, alias Jean Le Blanc, chief and orator, and by Kinongé, or Le Brochet, who signed the treaty; the Kiskakons (or Culs Coupez), represented by Hassaki, chief and orator,[26] and by Kileouiskingié, signatory of the treaty; the Sinago Odawas, represented by Chingouessi, chief and orator,[27] and by Outaliboi, who made the symbol of his nation on the treaty; and, finally, the Nassawaketons, or Odawas of the Fork, represented by Elaouesse, orator and signatory.[28]
- The Ojibwas (Saulteurs), represented by Ouabangué.[29]
- The Potawatomis, represented by Onanguicé, seconded by Ouenemek.[30]
- The Sauks, represented by Coluby[31] and sometimes by the Potawatomi chief Onanguicé.[32]
- The Timiskamings, from the lake of the same name (pictograph not identified).
- The Winnebagos (Puants, Otchagras).[33]

There were obviously leaders among all these ambassadors from the Great Lakes. Certain chiefs, through their talent as orators and their ability to persuade others, but also because of the political prestige of their nations, were pre-eminent in the league of the Great Lakes nations. Three figures can be identified as wielding enormous influence among the western peoples in the context of the peace of 1701. They represented the three central native nations of the French-Amerindian alliance (the Huron-Petuns, Odawas, and Potawatomis). First of all, there was Kondiaronk, on whom Callière relied particularly for the success of his policy of general peace;[34] on 23 July this Huron-Petun chief spoke on behalf of all the allied nations.[35] Then there was Outoutagan, the chief of the Sable Odawas; he spoke on 25 July for the Ojibwas and the four Odawa nations,[36] on 2 August for more than ten different nations,[37] and on 6 August for all the nations of the alliance.[38] The third great orator was Onanguicé; in addition to the Potawatomis, he represented the Sauks and most of the Illinois nations, and on 6 August he made a speech on behalf of all the nations of the west.[39]

The Amerindians were quite concerned about respect for title and hierarchical rank within the alliance. Thus, on 6 August, when Callière held the final session for his allies, the Huron-Petun chief Quarante Sols was "scandalized" that Outoutagan, the Odawa leader, presumed to make a speech on behalf of all the nations "without having asked the specific opinion of the Hurons."[40] The order of speeches and signatures on the treaty gives some measure of the prestige of the various actors in the nations of the alliance, and once more the pre-eminence of the Huron-Petuns and the Odawas is evident.

New France's Other Allies

Besides the French, the Iroquois of the League, and some thirty Great Lakes nations, the following nations also attended the conference of August 1701:

- The Algonquins, represented by the chief who, more than three years before, had defeated the hunting party of the Onondaga chief La Chaudière Noire.[41]
- The Abenakis, represented by Haouatchouath and Meskouadoue (the latter had already signed the treaty of September 1700). These delegates probably spoke for the whole Wabanaki Confederacy, namely the Penobscots, Passamaquoddys, Maliseets, and Mi'kmaqs, all traditional allies of the French.[42]
- Finally, the Iroquois who were settled in the vicinity of Montreal, which included those from Sault St Louis (Kahnawake), whose orator was called L'Aigle (The Eagle), and those from La Montagne, who were led by Tsahouanhos.[43]

The Absentees

Certain Native groups did not take part in the conference, although they belonged to the French alliance. The absence of the Montagnais was not surprising; although they were traditional allies of the

French, they had been only peripherally affected by the Iroquois Wars of the second half of the seventeenth century and had not taken part in the peace negotiations with the Five Nations. The absence of the Hurons of Lorette is more surprising. They had participated with the French in military expeditions to Iroquoia and were not excluded from peace negotiations with the Five Nations. For instance, they were present in Montreal in July 1700 – like the Algonquins, the Abenakis, and the Iroquois of Sault St Louis and La Montagne – for an important conference with ambassadors from the League.[44] It is possible that they were represented by other groups in 1701. Kondiaronk could have spoken on their behalf, which would support the hypothesis that the wampum belt from Lorette that was presented by a Huron chief to the king of England in 1825 was Kondiaronk's. They could also have been represented by other chiefs, such as those of the Iroquois of Sault St Louis, as part of the federation of the Seven Fires – if it existed at that time, which is doubtful – because the Iroquois of Sault St Louis were its honorary leaders.[45]

The case of the Dakota Sioux also merits discussion. The French wanted to include them in the general peace but the French allies refused. In the 1680s increasing numbers of coureurs de bois had gone into the upper Mississippi region in search of beaver and had initiated trading relations with the Dakota Sioux, who were enemies of the Great Lakes nations. In 1695 Le Sueur, a trader, had returned to Montreal with a Sioux chief, and Governor Frontenac had seen this as an opportunity to make an official alliance with that nation.[46] In 1701, once again, Governor Callière hoped to convince his allies to bury the hatchet with the Sioux. In July 1703 Vaudreuil, his successor, addressed Huron delegates: "With respect to the Sioux, you know that when your late father [Callière] made peace between all the nations, our allies, and the Iroquois, the hatchet of the Sioux was buried with all the others."[47] This speech was deceptive for in fact the Sioux were not included in the peace of 1701. This was because not only did the Sioux send no delegates to the general meeting,[48] but no one represented them as had been done for the Illinois, for whom the Potawatomi chief Onanguicé spoke. The allies, who were at war with the Sioux, refused to extend the roots of the Tree of Peace westward; unlike the French, they did not want to include the Sioux in the alliance.

Nicolas Vincent Isawanhonhi, chief of the Hurons of Lorette, holding the wampum belt he presented to King George IV of England in 1825. The origin of this belt is uncertain; it may have been presented by Kondiaronk at the negotiations for the Peace of Montreal, or it may symbolize the peace with the English that began in 1760. (National Archives of Canada, c-38948.)

A LAVISH CONFERENCE IN MONTREAL

From 21 July to 7 August, Montreal was a lively, colourful arena where cultures, languages, and customs mixed and mingled in a climate of reconciliation and peace – but also a place of sadness and mourning, since the conference was struck by an epidemic. Each day was filled with diplomatic rituals, official conference sessions, trade activities, festivities, speeches and more speeches. For nearly twenty days, Montreal, more than ever, moved to the rhythm of Native civilization.

The Arrival of the Ambassadors

When the flotillas of delegates from Iroquoia and the Great Lakes arrived in the colony, they did not go directly to Montreal but spent a day a few kilometres south, at the Iroquois mission village of Sault St Louis, respecting the protocol of conferences and marking the importance of this diplomatic site. The Onondaga, Cayuga, and Oneida ambassadors arrived there on 21 July, a day before the Senecas, who had been delayed by an accident.[49] "As soon as they were close enough to see the Fort," La Potherie wrote, "they saluted it with several gunshots," and their brothers at the mission, lined up on the bank, answered them in the same way.[50] A council was held shortly afterwards and a "little fire of dried brambles" was lighted in symbolic preparation for the great blazing fire in Montreal. The guests then smoked "with great composure for a good quarter of an hour,"[51] and their arrival was greeted with the customary metaphors. "My brothers," the chief of Sault St Louis said, "we are happy to see you here having escaped all the perils along the way. Indeed, how many accidents could have happened to you? How many rocks or rapids where you could have perished, if you did not have all the skill and persistence to Overcome them that you have always shown in perilous circumstances?"[52] Then this chief, carrying three strings of wampum, pronounced the "three rare words" of the ritual of condolence – wiping of tears, clearing of ears, and opening of the throat – in order to properly prepare them for the coming peace talks.[53]

The next day, just as the Iroquois were leaving Sault St Louis for Montreal, the delegation from the Great Lakes arrived. The new arrivals were greeted with respect. "From every direction in the Fort, people hurried to receive them, the grasses in the streets had been cut, and they had been swept to make them cleaner." "All the delegates and important persons" from the Great Lakes were ushered into the longhouse of an Iroquois chief, and there they performed their distinctive dance, the calumet dance, while the feast was being prepared in a neighbouring hut. An Odawa delegate entertained the crowd by skilfully manipulating a red stone pipe decorated with feathers, while twelve men in a circle sang to the beat of their rattles. "There was a Chief who stood up a quarter of an hour later," reported La Potherie, "and, taking a hatchet, struck a post with it. The Musicians immediately fell silent. 'I killed,' he said, 'four Iroquois five years ago' ... and, tearing off a piece of tobacco, 'I take this as a medicine to restore my spirit.' The Musicians applauded him with shouts and rapid movements of their gourds, the sound of two to three hundred Savages was heard from one end of the hut to the other."[54] The ritual of the calumet, incorporating dances, songs, and speeches, served to dissipate fears and rivalries between hosts and visitors, and foster feelings of friendship, understanding, and peace. It was the best way to prepare the participants for the diplomatic negotiations that were to follow, since the peace pipe was for Native people "a gift that the Sun sent to men to establish and confirm peace among them."[55]

The following day, after shooting the last rapids, the ambassadors from the west reached Montreal, where the "true fire" was.[56] When they came within "musket range of the town," the two hundred canoes "moved close to each other to form a single line," and the Amerindians, firing their guns or uttering "great cries," were greeted by the French cannon salute. The Senecas reached Montreal the same day, and Joncaire came to greet their "great chief" Tekanoet, eighty years old, who stood in his canoe and lamented the dead according to custom. The French diplomat, familiar with Native protocol, took the old sachem by the arm and, in accordance with the ritual of condolence, led him hand in hand with the other chiefs to the location for the grand council, where Onontio waited.[57]

Trade at the Peace Conference

The big summer meeting of 1701 was like a revival of the huge annual fairs that had earlier been held in Montreal, especially in the

1670s, when hundreds of traders from the Great Lakes came down-river to trade their furs on the French market. Some eight hundred visitors from the west attended the Montreal fair in 1674, and nearly five hundred in 1690.[58] In 1701 there were no less than thirteen hundred Native delegates present,[59] from the Great Lakes, Iroquoia, and the colony. This relatively high figure includes only part of the aboriginal population traditionally settled on the island of Montreal, which numbered approximately a thousand at the beginning of the eighteenth century.[60] Thirteen hundred Native people – the estimate is all the more impressive given that the French population of the island at the time was around twenty-six hundred, and that of the town of Montreal itself just twelve hundred.[61]

The arrival of the "far" delegates, from the Great Lakes, brought an Amerindian atmosphere to the town. They were distinguishable from the mission villagers, whose lifestyle, to judge from their clothing, was more influenced by French ways.[62] When the visitors from the west reached Montreal, they built their huts outside the town, between it and the river.[63] "Care was taken," noted La Potherie, "to have quantities of tree branches brought to them, to shelter them from the Sun."[64] Special attention was given to the Iroquois; some had the privilege of staying in the residence of Maricourt, who was accustomed to receiving Iroquois as guests, since he had been adopted by them. Predictably, the delegates from the west, especially the Hurons, complained about this preferential treatment.[65]

In parallel with the peace talks, trading officially began on 25 July at an assembly attended by Callière and the Odawas. During the assembly, the Native delegates gave their gifts to the French governor. The gates of the town were then opened, and the visiting Amerindians could enter the town freely throughout the day to trade their furs and visit the shops of the French merchants.[66] "They purchased powder, balls, hats, clothing in the French style trimmed with fake gold lace, which gave them a very grotesque appearance, vermilion, kettles, iron and copper pots, and all sorts of hardware," wrote La Potherie. "The town during that time resembled an inferno, because of the frightful appearance of all the Savages who strutted about prouder than ever, thinking they looked very fine ... The shouting, the din, the quarrels and discord, that occurred ... added to the horror of these spectacles." The Amerindians, he noted further, had "the freedom to come and go in the town, where all the shops were open to them." Lahontan had described the fairs of the 1680s with some poetic licence: "Tis a comical sight, to see 'em running from Shop to Shop, stark naked, with their Bow and Arrow." Interpreters offered their services to the shopkeepers, as La Potherie observed: "There was hardly a merchant in town without interpreters; they might receive a quarter of the profits, or half; anyway a goodly sum for their effort, because without interpreters, even if the shopkeepers had a thousand écus worth of merchandise, they could not sell so much as a pound of tobacco."[67]

Trading traditionally took place in an atmosphere of excitement conducive to disturbances,[68] and the unusual presence of thirteen hundred visitors, not to mention the political stakes of the conference, made the colonial authorities cautious. To prevent the outburst of violence, the governor and the intendant issued an order prohibiting the sale of alcohol during the conference. The troops stationed in the town by Callière were given the responsibility of enforcing this order.[69] All this was appreciated by many of the Native leaders, who were well aware of the dangers of spirits and were astonished that their "father" normally tolerated their being supplied with this "poison."[70] Hassaki, the representative of the Kiskakons, appealed to the French governor: "For pity's sake, do not give drink to [our] ... youth, [it would be their] ... ruin ... See to it ... that we can return safely to our country, so that our women and our children will be happy."[71] Similarly, another chief noted at the end of the conference, "There was during our assembly neither fighting, nor murder, nor any other disorder of the kind that usually happens when we are drunk."[72] And others "joked that they kept their ears and noses, which they would have ripped off each other with their teeth and eaten if the French had made them drunk." The bartering sessions were therefore not punctuated by the usual drinking bouts that could degenerate into brawls. "What made it so easy to execute this order," reported Intendant Beauharnois the following year,[73] "was that the public had an interest in complying, in order to contribute to the conclusion of a general peace treaty so necessary to the colony, which had been devastated by the long, cruel war."[74]

While the trading went on without violence, it did provoke lively discussions, which illustrate the problems inherent in the French-Amerindian economic alliance. Kondiaronk referred to these problems on 1 August, pointing out to Callière that trade had not been very active during the preceding days: "Consider a little, for your part, that we have not wanted to trade our Pelts yet. So establish some order, set the price of each thing yourself."[75] The furs brought by the Native people do not seem to have been of the best quality. Outoutagan, speaking for the four Odawa nations, told Callière at a special council meeting: "We bring only bad pelts, as the beaver is almost destroyed in our lands; we request your protection to make the merchants take pity on us and give us good prices."[76] This certainly shows that the beaver in the Great Lakes were in the process of being used up, but for this to be understood fully, it has to be interpreted in the context of Amerindian society. Let us examine the words of Potawatomi chief Onanguicé, who exhorted Callière "to have pity on them, and give them good prices on merchandise, because they had few beaver pelts."[77] The words of Outoutagan and Onanguicé are metaphorical and ritualistic in nature. The chiefs' purpose was to describe the destitution of their people symbolically in order to elicit compassion from the French and encourage them to be generous in trade. They were calling on Onontio to provide for the needs of his children.[78]

The rhetoric of pity and destitution was accompanied by more specific demands related to the terms of trade. These were expressed in the requests for "good prices" that were reiterated by all the orators from the Great Lakes to the governor. "Nothing should be hidden from us in the Merchants' shops," recommended Outoutagan.[79] Two views of trade were in conflict: the European conception of profit and the law of supply and demand, and the aboriginal one of gifts and reciprocity and general trade regardless of the amounts of goods available on the two sides. Thus, Amerindians with a poor supply of pelts asked their European partner to demonstrate their gift-giving spirit by providing the usual amount of trade goods.[80] The French merchants could not accept this logic of giving and reciprocity, as Outoutagan, who was well acquainted with them, was quite aware. "It is useless to ask you for low prices," he told Callière, "because we know very well that each one is master of his goods; at least ask them [the merchants] that they be at the same price as last year." For their part, the Amikwas pointed out "the consideration they had shown in not trading ... with the English, who sold to them at better prices."[81] This was an elegant way of warning the French, in the midst of the conference, that the nations of the west could be tempted at any time go trade in Albany rather than Montreal. New France's allies had been blackmailing the French this way for some years. Onontio was therefore obliged, for political reasons, to accept the role of provider. To satisfy the Natives traders and to compensate them for the low prices offered by the merchants, especially because of the scanty quantities of furs, Callière had gifts distributed to the delegates – food, blankets, powder, and so on – at each discussion[82] and promised to urge the merchants to make an effort to adjust their prices.[83]

A Deadly "Cold"

In a private session with Callière, the Miami chief Chichicatalo described the problems he had experienced during his voyage: "If we had the use of canoes, we would have come down in greater numbers ... I am saddened by the loss of two of our chiefs who died on the way."[84] The hazards of trade were not the only problem the French negotiators faced. A pall was cast over the Montreal conference by an epidemic that was probably of European origin, but that, according to Callière, had been brought from the Great Lakes by the Amerindians.[85] This explains why certain ambassadors turned back after setting out for the colony. Charlevoix reported, regarding the allies from the west: "Out of a fleet of a hundred and eighty canoes ... thirty were forced to put in to shore because of illness."[86] This was the case for the Illinois. In his first speech, on 23 July, the chief Kondiaronk, while following the standard Native imagery and rhetoric at the end of a long voyage, referred specifically to this problem:

Our Father, you see us near your mat; it is not without many dangers that we have endured on such a long voyage. The falls, the rapids, and a thousand other obstacles did not seem so difficult for us to surmount because of the desire we had to see you and to gather together here; we found many of our brothers dead along the river; our spirit was sorely tested by it; there had been much rumour that disease was great in Montreal. All those corpses eaten by birds that we constantly came upon were convincing proof of this. However, we made a Bridge of all those bodies, on which we walked with determination ... We are all sick with a cold that burdens us. You must judge from that how much we have been tested.[87]

This "cold" spread during the conference,[88] weakening or killing many Native delegates, particularly Huron-Petun and Miami chiefs. "It is unfortunate that, having come to hear your words ... we should fall sick," a Kiskakon chief observed to Callière.[89] This must have led Callière to rush the discussions, creating some tension between the French and their allies. Charlevoix reported: "The Hurons had been the most affected and they imagined that this was the result of a spell that had been cast to make them all perish. There were even some who went to find Father Anjelran [Enjalran] ['with a bundle of beaver pelts'[90]] to have him persuade the clergy of the Seminary to lift the so-called evil spell."[91] The Amerindians, the Hurons in particular, had long associated the epidemics that periodically struck their country with the presence of the Europeans, especially the missionaries, whom they saw as powerful sorcerers, given the shamans' inability to counter the new diseases.[92] La Potherie stated, "The majority refused to go to the Hôtel-Dieu [hospital], where they would have had all possible assistance, imagining that they would be poisoned there."[93] The tension was so great that a rumour – obviously false – spread that "the French were only assembling so many Peoples in their territory in order to destroy them."[94]

On 1 August during a council between the French and the Huron-Petuns, Kondiaronk fell sick with a violent fever. "He received care very promptly," wrote Charlevoix, "especially because the Governor General based on him his main hope for the success of his great work ... the general peace."[95] "He first sat down on a folding chair," La Potherie reported, "they had a large comfortable chair brought so that he could rest and speak at his ease, he was given wine to fortify him. He asked to drink herbs, and they realized that he wanted maidenhair," a Native remedy. Weakened, almost unconscious, Kondiaronk – a confirmed orator – "revived somewhat and spoke in a rather listless tone for two hours." He expressed his sorrow "at being made the dupe of the Iroquois, who had brought back no prisoners from his Nation," and then spoke at length about the diplomatic role he had played since the conference in September.[96] The Huron chief was listened to with "infinite attention,"[97] and "at each different matter of which he spoke," his compatriots "applauded him with voices that came from deep in the stomach." "We could not help but be touched by the eloquence with which he spoke, and admit at the same time that he was a man of merit," commented La Potherie.[98] His speech completed, Kondiaronk became so weak that he was unable to return to his hut. He was carried in a chair to the hospital, where his condition continued to deteriorate. He died the following day at two o'clock in the morning.[99]

This death caused widespread grief and probably contributed to reconciliation and mutual understanding.[100] Callière and Champigny, bowing to Native ritual, "covered the deceased," who was carried back to his hut and carefully prepared. "He was laid out on Beaver pelts [and] a hat trimmed with a new red plume was placed on his head. He was covered with a large scarlet cover," and close to him were laid a pot, a gun, and a sword. By their varied origins, the deathbed objects expressed the mixing of cultures that prevailed in the diplomatic meetings.[101] The visit by the French representatives was followed by that of some sixty Iroquois, mostly Senecas, who had asked Joncaire to walk at their head. They entered the hut of the Huron chief in a solemn procession. "When they came near the body, they formed a circle, and all sat down on the ground," except for the Seneca chief Tonatakout, who continued to walk back and forth for a quarter of an hour, lamenting the death of Kondiaronk with tragic dignity. He was then replaced by the Seneca orator Aouenano, who carried out the ritual of condolence, drying tears and opening throats to pour in "a sweet medicine" intended to restore the grieving Hurons. The orator, displaying a wampum belt, then declared to the Huron-Petun chiefs: "The Sun is eclipsed today, it is the death of our brother Le Rat [Kondiaronk] that is the cause. We ask you to have the same spirit, the same sentiments as he had to hereafter make only one body, one cauldron." They must continue to follow the path to peace that had been cleared by Kondiaronk.[102]

Pomp and Cross-Cultural Diplomacy

The conference of 1701 was in many respects exceptional, and the French authorities, for whom luxury and pageantry were the best symbols of political power,[103] organized it as befit the occasion with a display worthy of Louis XIV. The Native ambassadors were received with great pomp by the representatives of the Sun King, who as usual took care to respect to the letter the thousand and one details of Native diplomatic protocol. In its reception ceremonies,

Portrait of Louis XIV, c. 1701. Engraved by Pierre Drevet after Hyacinthe Rigaud. McCord Museum, M10018.

private sessions, and assemblies, the Montreal conference was thus marked by the forms and etiquette of the Native political world, which, even more than its European counterpart,[104] raised diplomacy to the level of spectacle. The European protocol was truly a blend of the two diplomatic traditions, giving rise to original, hybrid rituals.

Throughout the conference, at every political meeting, the Native orators accompanied their speeches with gifts; for the Huron-Petuns and other groups from the Great Lakes region, these were wampum belts or bundles of beaver pelts, and for the Iroquois, generally, wampum belts. Callière, in turn, had to follow a similar ritual, and with the help of his interpreters, he punctuated each meeting with various gifts, offering, among other things, "bread and wine" to each Native delegate in the European tradition.[105] Beyond these traditional elements of diplomatic protocol,[106] the Montreal conference was the setting for two imposing events, the funeral of Kondiaronk and the general assembly of 4 August.

The funeral of the great Huron chief took place on 3 August. The French wanted it to be magnificent to let everyone know how deeply they felt the loss of this chief "who had been so commendable."[107] Kondiaronk's challenge to Denonville's policy in 1688 seems to have been forgotten. The captain of the troops, Pierre de Saint-Ours, headed up the procession, leading an escort of sixty soldiers. After them came sixteen Huron-Petun warriors walking four by four, wearing long beaver pelts, their faces blackened as a sign of mourning and their guns pointed to the ground. Then came the members of the clergy, followed by six war chiefs who carried the flower-covered coffin, on which had been placed "a hat with a plume, a sword, and a gorget." Next came the family of the late chief – his brother and children – and many Huron and Odawa warriors. Madame de Champigny, Philippe de Rigaud de Vaudreuil, and all the officers brought up the rear of the funeral procession. Two volleys of musket fire followed the celebration of the Catholic service,[108] and then the body of Kondiaronk was buried in Notre Dame Church in Montreal. All the warriors and soldiers then fired a last round in turn, and on the grave they put the inscription "Here lies Le Rat, chief of the Hurons."[109] The military honours given Kondiaronk belong to the language of political spectacle of the period of Louis XIV. It was considered appropriate to display his power visually, to express it in concrete symbols. The French, by honouring deceased of recognized merit, sought above all to impress the Native people present and encourage them to behave in the same way as the departed chiefs.[110] One hour after the funeral, Joncaire, leading some fifty Iroquois from La Montagne, went to the Hurons and urged them, "with a porcelain Sun, supported by two Collars," not to leave the light of peace.[111]

The peace treaty was ratified the next day, 4 August, in a magnificent assembly organized by the French authorities. Callière, anxious that the ceremony have a resounding impact, particularly on the Native delegates, spared no expense. "Everything was displayed for two days," reported La Potherie, and "many women savages were summoned to prepare the Collars."[112] A huge rectangular arena, forty-three metres long and twenty-four wide, was created on a large plain south of what is now Pointe-à-Callière,[113] between the town and the river. It was bordered by a double enclosure of tree branches that formed an alley three metres wide where one could stroll. A hall ten metres long and almost square, and covered with leaves, was built at one end of the area. This summery, rustic setting, which had been prepared with a good deal of care, was then enlivened by the addition of a colourful crowd. Whether playing leading roles or bit parts, or attending as spectators, everyone was there to celebrate peace. The theatre was full: two to three thousand people, perhaps more, were assembled there. First there were the approximately thirteen hundred Native representatives. They arranged themselves by nation inside the enclosure, "in a very orderly fashion," most sitting on the ground quietly smoking the peace pipe. Facing them were the French plenipotentiaries – Callière, Champigny, Vaudreuil – and other officers, as well as scribes and interpreters. But there were also many other people, for all of Montreal society was represented at this majestic assembly. It had attracted the elite of the citizenry, the farmers, the tradesmen, and the various clergy, including Jesuits, Sulpicians, and Récollets. "People of quality" – ladies and gentlemen and prominent citizens – had the privilege of attending the ceremony in the covered hall, which was outfitted with tiers of seats. Dozens of French soldiers were placed around the palisade surrounding the area.[114]

This multicoloured, baroque grand council, where the multiplicity of languages was matched only by that of dress and adornment, where Native chiefs "wearing their long robes of pelts," with painted faces and feathered head-dresses, rubbed shoulders with stiff, bewigged officers in uniform and elegant ladies in their most beautiful finery, was a spectacular expression of Canadian multiculturalism in its "colonial" version.[115] In this context, the interpreters provided an indispensable service. There were five of them, of whom four were Jesuits. Father Garnier translated for Callière and the Hurons; Father Bigot, for the Algonquins and Abenakis; Father Enjalran, for the Odawas; Father Bruyas, for the Iroquois; and Nicolas Perrot, finally, for most of the Great Lakes nations.

Governor Callière, as host of the conference, gave the first speech, standing on a platform, paper in hand:

It is with extreme joy that I see all my children assembled here now, you Hurons, Sable Odawas, Kiskakons, Sinago Odawas, [Odawas] nation of the Fork, Saulteurs [Ojibwas], Potawatomis, Sauks, Puants [Winnebagos], Folles Avoines [Menominees], Foxes, Mascoutens, Miamis, Illinois, Amikwas, Nipissings, Algonquins, Timiskamings, Crees, Gens des terres, Kickapoos, people from the Sault, from La Montagne, Abenakis, and you the Iroquois nations; having one and all placed your interests in my hands that I can have you all live in tranquillity, I therefore today ratify the peace agreement that we have made ... as I am determined that there be no more talk of the attacks made during the war, and I gather up again all your hatchets, and all your other instruments of war, which I place with mine in a pit so deep that no one can take them back to disturb the tranquillity that I have re-established among my children, and I recommend to you when you meet to treat each other as brothers, and make arrangements for the hunt together so that there will be no quarrels among you ... I attach my words to the collars I will give to each one of your nations so that the elders may have them carried out by their young people, I invite you all to smoke this calumet which I will be the first to smoke, and to eat meat and broth that I have had prepared for you so that I have like a good father the satisfaction of seeing all my children united.[116]

When Callière's words were translated by the interpreters, who had a written copy of them, the Native delegates all cheered and shouted their approval. The French governor was clearly affirming his role as mediator and father ("you ... having one and all placed your interests in my hands"; "this calumet which I will be the first to smoke"). Similarly, when the chief of the Kiskakons offered a peace pipe to the Iroquois, it symbolically was first taken to Onontio, who then had it given to the old Seneca chief

Tekanoet.[117] But while affirming his pre-eminence – which was not only rhetorical – Callière was also acting according to Native political rules. His power of mediation was based on that of an Amerindian chief, and his speech was studded with Native references: the pit in which the hatchets were buried, the wampum belts, the peace pipe, the broth in the pot. In this way, Callière enhanced his ability to convince his partners. To authenticate what he had said, he then offered the delegates thirty-one wampum collars, which were hung on a large rod at the entry to the area.[118]

Then the Native orators, carrying wampum collars, took the floor one after the other. Each one was dressed in pelts and adorned with ceremonial care, and spoke with majestic dignity. Charlevoix reported with his usual ethnocentrism: "This ceremony, as serious as it was for the Savages, was for the French a kind of comedy, which they enjoyed very much. Most of the Delegates, especially those from the most distant Nations, were dressed and adorned in a completely grotesque manner, which made an extremely amusing contrast with the gravity and seriousness they affected."[119] The Natives' love of theatricality, which equalled that of the French, was expressed through the use of pantomime, dance, and song, but also in the great attention they paid to costumes, head-dresses, and ornamentation. "The savages in general," noted a Jesuit, "put their main glory in the adornment of their heads, especially their hair, whether long or short, according to the diversity of the nations."[120] This concern for appearance led to innovations in dress during cross-cultural conferences.

Hassaki, the Kiskakon chief, was the first Native orator to speak, thus indicating the pre-eminence of the Odawas within the French-Amerindian alliance. Dressed in a "robe of beaver that hung to the ground" and displaying a wampum string and collar, he walked "in a majestic manner, leading four very handsome Iroquois, who had their eyes lowered," whom he "had sit at his feet" before beginning his oration.[121] A little later, after the Hurons, the other Odawas, and the Miamis had spoken, it was the Potawatomi chief Onanguicé's turn to take the floor. According to Charlevoix, he wore a head-dress that was made from a bison head, "with the horns hanging over his ears," and which he removed when he started his speech.[122] The Ojibwa chief Ouabangué had also taken pains with his head-dress: "[H]e had a red plume around his head in the form of rays of light," noted La Potherie.[123] As for the Algonquin chief, a "tall, remarkably well-built young man," the very man who three years earlier had defeated La Chaudière Noire's Iroquois war party, he was dressed in the "Canadian" style and his hair, in the shape of a crest, was decorated with a red plume that fell to his shoulders.[124]

It was Miskouensa, however, the orator for the Foxes, who was undoubtedly the most ceremonious and theatrical. Accompanied by three Iroquois prisoners, he walked from "the far end of the enclosure" to the centre of the area. His face was painted red and he had covered his head with an old wig that was "heavily powdered and very badly combed." "He had made himself an ornament of it to follow the French manner ... and, wanting to show that he knew how to act, he saluted the Chevalier de Callière with it as if with a hat. In spite of the composure that one is obliged to maintain before people who are so solemn, especially in such serious circumstances, we could not help but burst out laughing; and asked him at the same time very seriously to put it back on."[125] Miskouensa, not at all bothered by this, launched into his speech with eloquence, even implying that he had already made peace with the Iroquois and telling Callière he did not plan to do so with the Sioux.[126] It was his "horrible and ridiculous appearance," noted Charlevoix, and his comical gestures, that caused the French diplomats to laugh. He seemed "horrible" to the French because he shocked their sense of good taste and offended their aesthetic sensibilities, "ridiculous" in that he was dressed in a style outside his condition, outside his "savagery." By borrowing in this way, the Fox delegate was not attempting to make his French counterparts laugh, but to distinguish himself. He was asserting himself politically by putting on a performance, making an exhibition of himself, presenting – without malice or sarcasm – a mirror-image of the world of the Other. He was therefore not at all taken aback by the laughter of the French, since, according to Charlevoix, he took it "for applause."[127]

This scene, like those in which the French diplomats bowed to Native rituals, illustrates the creative aspect of the encounter and highlights the intensity of the cultural exchange. Each side was attempting to adapt to the other by mirroring its culture. Miskouensa, by adopting for his own purposes the representative signs (the wig) and gestures (the salute) of the European aristocrat, created an original costume that through metonymy expressed the invention of a New World in the cosmopolitan Montreal of that summer. This borrowing shows the Amerindians' desire to appropriate otherness in order to eradicate it. Many authors have noted their propensity of to copy the Europeans in this way. The Amerindians were particularly fond of wearing hats, which, like wigs, were a key article of the European culture of appearances. This mimicry was in no way facetious. It was rather a ritualistic, superficial form of acculturation intended to "cannibalize" otherness. The European officers had quite different motives in imitating the gestures of the Native delegates; they were imitating the Other only for the purpose of manipulation. This does not mean that the Amerindians were more naive, but that their culture did not incline them to subjugate their alliance partners. In imitating their partners, they sought to integrate them by appropriating their difference, essentially adopting them as their own.[128]

By sending their best orators, all the nations were able to express their positions. Aouenano, speaking on behalf of the Iroquois, finished the round of speeches. The governor then had the peace treaty brought out, which the various chiefs signed by making their distinctive pictographs,[129] and the assembly, despite the deadly atmosphere resulting from the "cold" (epidemic), ended in a mood of festivity and rejoicing. To "confirm this great Alliance ... and to do it with all possible circumspection," the French and the Indians performed the ritual of the calumet. One by one, Callière, Champigny, Vaudreuil, and all the Native delegates spent a long time smoking the big peace pipe that Chichicatalo had given the French governor.[130] Then three Frenchmen distinguished themselves by "singing" the calumet, swinging around the Native ambassadors sitting on the grass. They "stepped in cadence, their faces animated, and the movement of their bodies expressing the vehemence of their words." After this the "Te Deum" was also sung, and then all the participants were welcomed to share in the feast that had been prepared: three oxen boiled in ten huge cauldrons. According to La Potherie, this was "rather frugal for so many people."[131] "Everyone was served without noise or confusion," wrote Charlevoix, "and all went well and happily."[132] In the evening, to the sound of musket and artillery fire, everyone gathered at a bonfire, the closing note of this memorable day's festivities.[133] The all-important distribution of gifts was organized in the following days. La Potherie noted that "the marks of esteem and friendship we had shown until then to all our allies would have made little impression on their minds if we had not at the same time done something more real and more effective, to acknowledge all the good services they had rendered to us. We therefore planned to give them the presents that had been prepared in the storehouses of the King."[134]

The Private Sessions

The events of 4 August must be seen within the framework of the conference, which involved constant diplomatic activity. From 23 July to 7 August, there was a succession of daily political councils between the French governor and various Native ambassadors.

On 25 July, after the visitors had rested and held discussions within their respective groups, the councils themselves began. Callière received the many Native representatives in succession in the courtyard of his residence. Some of them sat on chairs, others on the ground. The Native orators were almost always the first to speak, and then it was the governor's turn. These private sessions, which continued until 1 August, encouraged secret discussions, and each delegate took care to defend the particular interests of his nation above and beyond the more general problems related to trade and the exchange of prisoners.[135] Thus the Foxes, less concerned than the Huron-Petuns, for example, with the Iroquois war, took advantage of being in Montreal to present various requests to Callière, whom they saw as both a mediator and a provider. They tried to settle their dispute with the Ojibwas and requested that a Jesuit, a blacksmith, and the interpreter Nicolas Perrot be sent to their territory.[136] All the chiefs arranged to be received several times by the governor. "Some," commented Charlevoix, "never tired of bothering him; but when he found himself pressed, he extricated himself with promises, and with his pleasant, engaging manners ... Jean Le Blanc [Outoutagan] was the one who gave him the most trouble. This savage was very clever ... he saw more clearly than would have been desired in a matter of such consequence." Various problems arose in the course of the discussions, and tact and skilled diplomacy were constantly required of all the participants.[137]

The private sessions were replaced, on 2 and 3 August – which were marked by the death and funeral of Kondiaronk – by public meetings of either the nations of the west or the Iroquois of the League.[138] The impressive general assembly was held the following day, and 5 August was probably spent in intense debates within each delegation. On 6 and 7 August, finally, the two closing sessions were held. In the first one, Callière negotiated with all the allied delegations, dealing mostly with the questions of Detroit and the war in the west. The following day he met with the delegates of the four western Iroquois nations, with whom he discussed the issues of prisoners, Detroit, and their neutrality.[139]

8 The Tree of Peace

When the conference was over, the Amerindians from the west, still weakened by a "violent cold," headed back home, some taking the Ottawa River to Michilimackinac, others the St Lawrence and the southern lakes to Detroit. Before leaving Montreal, Outoutagan addressed Callière on behalf of the Great Lakes nations: "Pray to the Master of Life to preserve us on our voyage, to dispel our stomachaches and headaches, so that our relatives will see us all happy."[1] It was the task of Vaudreuil, as governor of the town, to accompany the ambassadors from the west "for more than eight leagues." The next day, the Iroquois also bid farewell. Montreal returned to normal, but the long visit by the plenipotentiaries from the Great Lakes and Iroquoia had left its imprint on the town's history. Without doubt, important agreements had been negotiated over the course of the conference.

PEACE: METAPHORS AND FOUNDATIONS

The provisional peace agreement of the previous September was now extended to all the Great Lakes nations. With the darkness dissipated[2] and the hatchet buried,[3] the western nations and the Iroquois would now be able to live as "brothers"[4] and travel without being disturbed. The peace, symbolized by the Tree of Peace, was based on shared access to hunting territories and the exchange of prisoners.

Philippe de Rigaud, Marquis de Vaudreuil (ca. 1643–1725). Copied from the original by Léopold Darangel. National Archives of Canada, C-100374.

Vaudreuil emigrated to New France in 1687 and led French campaigns against the Iroquois between 1690 and 1700. In 1698 he succeeded Callière as governor of Montreal, and five years later became governor general of Canada.

"The Tree of Peace is now planted
on the highest mountain"

In the language of the Native diplomats, the Iroquois in particular, the Tree of Peace was a metaphor for general peace. Symbolically, it was "planted" or "raised" on "the highest mountain of the Earth," and it was provided with "deep roots so that it could never be uprooted." Its branches and foliage, which rose "to the heavens," provided "dense shade," so that "those who [sat] under it [were] ... refreshed, ... sheltered from any storms that might threaten them," and, lastly, able to "do good business."[5] The protective aura of the tree was seen as creating a space of internal peace in which individuals were united in a common kinship.[6] The Native orators referred to it constantly during the conference. Let us look at some of their brilliant speeches addressed to Onontio, all intended to celebrate peace. L'Aigle, on 4 August, spoke on behalf of the Iroquois of Kahnawake (Sault St Louis):

Onontio, our father, you no doubt feel joy in seeing all your children gathered here on your mat today. You must believe that since we have the fortune to be here in such numbers, we share it with you. The swiftness with which so many different Nations have left from the far reaches of this vast country, the courage and perseverance that they have shown in overcoming distance, fatigue, and the dangers of travel in order to come hear your voice shows well their disposition to obey it faithfully. All your views are so just and so reasonable, that one would have to not be a man to refuse to submit to them. You must therefore believe that neither the diversity of the many languages they speak, nor their particular interests and resentments, will by any means be an obstacle to the proper understanding in which you order them to live together in the future. They will now pay attention only to the desire you have to make them happy, by stopping the disastrous pursuit of war, through the Peace that you have just established among them. For us who have the advantage of knowing more intimately and from a closer distance than they the true feelings of your heart, we readily throw down the hatchet on your word ... and give the Tree of Peace that you have erected such strong, deep roots, that neither winds nor storms, nor other misfortune will be able to uproot it.[7]

During the meeting of the allied nations on 6 August, their chiefs adopted a similar tone. The Huron Quarante Sols stated the following before the assembly: "The hatchet is stopped, we have buried it during these days here in the deepest place in the earth, so that it will not be taken up again by one side or the other."[8] And the chief of the Potawatomis, Onanguicé, said to Callière: "Be assured ... that my Nation and the one on the far side of Lake Huron will not forget what you have so happily completed; the earth is now made level. The Tree of Peace is now planted on the highest mountain; the Iroquois and all your Allies will have to look up to it often."[9] The Iroquois ambassadors also expressed satisfaction. Aouenano, their main orator, stated on 4 August: "Here we are assembled, our father, as you wished. You planted last year a tree of peace and you gave it roots and leaves so that we would be sheltered there. We now hope that everyone hears what you say, that no one will touch that tree, for we assure you, by these four collars, that we will comply with everything that you have arranged ... Now ... the doors are open for peace."[10]

The Common "Bowl"

The Great Peace of Montreal included a territorial agreement, but it is important not to misunderstand its significance. For some authors, such as W.A. Starna and J.A. Brandão, the territorial issue was at the heart of the 1701 agreements. War and peace for the Amerindians, these two scholars explain, were essentially related to the desire to protect or extend hunting territories.[11] I feel that this rationalist perspective needs to be qualified. Territory was of course no minor issue for the Native people in the context of colonial pressures and the fur trade, but the dynamics of war (and its structural corollary, peace) were of a different nature. Hunting, traditionally, was not really the major reason for conflicts. "[The Amerindians] do not make war to invade the lands of their neighbours nor to plunder them ... it is solely for the pleasure of killing men," observed Intendant Raudot at the beginning of the eighteenth century. Hunting, in this perspective, appears to have offered the most favourable *opportunity* to kill one's enemies, since it took place at the fringes of the territory. In June 1701, for example, Father Enjalran succeeded in taking "from the hands of the Kiskakons two [Iroquois] prisoners they had captured in the spring after their hunt."[12] Hunters who killed one another during their trapping activities, therefore, were not necessarily doing it for territory. Certainly the Iroquois' victories in the 1650s had given them a certain hegemony in Ontario that lasted until the 1680s, and it is therefore likely that they took a dim view of the return of the hunters from the western tribes to this region. It may be, then, that war was increasingly associated with territorial issues, but if the hunters attacked one another, it was basically more because they were warriors and it was the nature of a warrior to kill or capture his enemy.

Brandão and Starna's analysis of the sources merits critical discussion. First of all, a small point should be made concerning their reading of the Amerindians' speeches. They say that "many of the Western Indians had either depleted the local supply of beavers or were dangerously close to doing so."[13] Indeed, it seems clear that the beaver were in the process of being wiped out in the Great Lakes region – various documents attest to this – but we should not forget the ritualized nature of the Native petitions, which by definition exaggerated poverty and penury. This is not the most important point, however. According to Brandão and Starna, "The Western Indians had come to the Iroquois to request that they share hunting territories." In this view, the objective of the Amerindians from the Great Lakes in 1701 was to ask the Five Nations to authorize their settling "north of Lake Ontario."[14] Nothing in the French sources seems to justify these remarks. As W.J. Eccles points out, "By 1701, the Iroquois no longer had any hunting grounds north and west of the Great Lakes"; they "had been driven out of their few villages on the north shore of Lake Ontario by the Mississaugas, Ottawas, Tionontates [Huron-Petuns] and Ojibwas."[15]

Eccles, taking the opposite view to that of Brandão and Starna, goes so far as to state that there is no "mention of Callière having told the Iroquois that they could hunt peacefully with their old enemies." "Neither in the Montreal 1700 Treaty, or the 1701 ratification of that Treaty," he says further, "is there any mention of Iroquois hunting rights anywhere." To support his statements, Eccles expresses his mistrust of the writings of La Potherie, which he considers not very reliable.[16] This view is totally unfounded. La Potherie, who witnessed the ceremonies of the Great Peace of Montreal, was generally a sensible, meticulous chronicler, and his remarks regarding the hunting territories are confirmed by other sources.

Onontio and the Native diplomats used the image of the kettle or the dish during the 1701 negotiations. The hunters should no longer kill each other when they met – in other words, they should share the same "dish" as "brothers." The culinary imagery that was sometimes associated with war (e.g., the kettle was used to cook enemies) has here become symbolic of peace. "Let us now live in peace," proclaimed the chief Onanguicé. "Let us eat from the same kettle when we meet during the hunt." "So it is today that the Sun shines," continued the Miami chief Chichicatalo, "that the land will be united, and that we will no longer have any more quarrels. When we meet, we will look on each other as brothers, and we will eat the same meal together."[17] According to Gédéon de Catalogne, "the peace treaty was concluded on these terms, that their father [the French governor] give them a bowl in which he put a knife to cut the meat and a *micouanne* [large ladle] to eat the soup or sagamite; and to seal the agreement they all smoked the same pipe." The "bowl," he noted, "signified all the hunting and fishing territories." Vaudreuil, Callière's successor, anxious to maintain peace between the Iroquois and his allies in the west, reminded some Onondaga delegates in 1710 of what to him was "the main provision" of the Montreal treaty: "The Chevalier de Callière, at the general peace, presented you with a large dish, and gave you each a knife and a *miscouaine* to eat the meat and drink the broth all together. This big dish is the hunting territories where you all have permission to go, all being brothers through the peace."[18]

In a speech given in 1791 by an Iroquois chief from Kahnawake to the British authorities, there is a reference to a territorial agreement that, at first glance, appears to date from 1701:

[T]hen the king of France summoned to a council all the savages of the continent, Kanawageronons [Iroquois from Kahnawake], Hurons, Algonquins, Nipissings; he brought a big dish in which there was a piece of meat, broth, a *micouanne*, a knife, and he said to us: "My children! you are all brothers, all the same colour, and by the grace of god of the same religion; until this day you have been at war for your hunting territories. What I desire from you today is that you make a peace forever. Here is a dish of meat, of broth, a *micouanne* and a knife that you will take paying attention not to hurt yourselves; use all this without quarrelling over it. The one who has the greater appetite will eat more, without the other having anything to complain about." My Father! this parable signifies our hunting territories, that the king of France placed in common. And he then placed the great fire in the village known as gana8age [Kahnawake] where the big dish was placed and that we have kept until this day.

The memory of this great sharing has been to some degree distorted over time, but also by the context and the orator's interests. He speaks of "all the savages of the continent," but he is really talking about Onontio's allies settled in the colony, as indicated by several elements: the nations listed (no mention of the Amerindians of the Great Lakes); the reference to the "same religion" (Catholicism); and, finally, the fact that the dish "was placed" in the village of Kahnawake, which was the capital of the Seven Fires, that is, of the settled Natives of the St Lawrence Valley. There is no evidence that this Amerindian agreement does, in fact, date back to the Great Peace of Montreal. The French documents make no mention of the role played by Kahnawake in the sharing of the "big dish."[19]

In 1701 the hunting territories were open to all the allies. According to many historians, the shared zones were even specified. Starna, for example, writes that "the rights of the Five Nations to their hunting territories north and west of Lake Ontario and Lake Erie were recognized and guaranteed."[20] In fact, the sources never say this explicitly. There are, however, two specific geographic references, although they do not appear in the minutes of the Montreal treaty.

The first reference concerns the area around Fort Frontenac. In March 1701 some Onondagas had complained to Callière that his allies in the west were not respecting their hunting territories: "The tongue of land at Fort Frontenac belongs to us, it is the place where we have been hunting since the world is the world, and no other nation has ever hunted there. We were surprised to find both Algonquins and Nipissings there numbering two hundred, who have taken over those areas that belong to us."[21] In fact, the Iroquois had not always been the only ones to hunt in these areas. The argument of occupation from time immemorial ("since the world is the world"), which is very dubious from a scientific point of view, deserves further discussion. This kind of discourse was certainly used systematically in the colonial context because it was understood by the French and the Iroquois had to take advantage of their mediation. We can assume that the "tongue of land" that the Iroquois orator talked about was particularly rich in game at that time.[22]

The second mention concerns the Detroit region, which Teganissorens described to Callière in May 1701 as "a place that was the only one that we had for hunting." In fact, the Iroquois probably used other trapping territories as well. The Detroit region was part of the area where warriors/hunters from the two groups encountered each other. The Iroquois, who had often been beaten by their enemies from the west, had not been in control there for many years. Callière told Teganissorens that Cadillac was building his post "in order to maintain the peace we have made together [in September 1700] between the Great Lakes nations and you [the Iroquois], and, so that if there occur any disputes when you are both hunting in that region, the commander that I place there can resolve the matter to your mutual satisfaction, as the one at Fort Frontenac did last winter with the nations who were hunting in the area."[23]

In short, the common "bowl" was probably one of the objectives of the peace (in the case of the Iroquois), but it was also, especially, one of its foundations, as could be the exchange of gifts and prisoners. The purpose of the sharing of territories was to establish peace and avoid having hunters kill one another and set off a new round of wars. The territorial question should not distract us from the fact that it was the peace settlement, and not the sharing of hunting territories, that was the major issue at the 1701 conference.

The Exchange of Prisoners

While the general peace was finally approved by every ambassador, the problem of prisoners was the stumbling block that almost proved insurmountable. The exchange of prisoners had for many years been one of the thorny issues in the negotiations. It was a real issue, in particular for the nations of the west. Prisoners were pivotal to the Native culture of war and peace. War made possible the taking of prisoners, and peace their recovery. Peace was often seen as an interlude, and since it was based on exchange (of gifts, women, territory, etc.), it was also an opportunity (and even the pretext) to recover prisoners. There are many personal accounts that show the importance the Natives placed on recovering their compatriots. In 1701 Father Marest, a Jesuit missionary at Michilimackinac, observed that for the Odawas, the return of "slaves ... was the most essential article of the peace agreement."

And La Potherie considered that "the Iroquois have no goal" in the peace negotiations "other than recovering their prisoners without problems."[24]

Kondiaronk addressed Callière as follows early in the conference:

My Father, I come to say to you that I obey your voice; remember that you told us last fall that you wanted absolutely that we bring you all the Iroquois Slaves who are among us. We obeyed you and we are obeying since we bring them. Let us see at the same time if the Iroquois obey you, and how many they have brought back of our nephews who were taken since the beginning of the war ... If they have done so, it is a mark of their sincerity; if they have not done so, they are dishonest. I know, however, that they have not brought any. I told you last year that it was better if they brought us our Prisoners first, and now you see how it is, and how they have deceived us." "This chief's reasoning was correct," remarked La Potherie, "and we saw at once the predicament that confronted us."[25]

In all, the delegates of the nations of the west – in particular the Kiskakons, Sable Odawas, Huron-Petuns, Potawatomis, Mississaugas, and Miamis – returned more than thirty Iroquois prisoners. These were, of course, only a fraction of the adopted prisoners. Chichicatalo, the Miami chief, stated frankly to Callière on 2 August: "We are here like passengers who took advantage of our neighbour's canoes. We are not used to them, so we have brought you only eight slaves." According to Onanguicé, there was another reason for the absence of a large number of Iroquois prisoners: "We would have brought you many Prisoners, but we ate them all; they [the Iroquois] do the same with us, they put us in the kettle when they take us."[26]

"As our people had taken some Iroquois, I withdrew them before they were mistreated," stated Outoutagan on 4 August. As for the Miamis, according to La Potherie, they "had forced their Prisoners to follow them." At the general assembly, their chief Chichicatalo, "followed by two Iroquois men and three women, who looked very sad," told Onontio:

I come to present you today with Prisoners that I had intended for the fire, but the Frenchman [Courtemanche] who explained your thoughts to us, convinced us to give you absolute control of them. If I had had canoes, I would have brought a great number, as I have already told you. We have more, and I am prepared to open the doors for them. I confess to you that I feel bitter resentment against the Iroquois who burned my Son a few years ago; the fate of the war decided that he would be a prisoner; but the fact that they killed him because they knew he was my Son, I confess that I was deeply affected by that. However, I forget all that today.

The same eagerness for peace motivated the Hurons, who came with "eleven Iroquois," although six of them did not want to return to Iroquoia.[27]

The ambassadors of the Five Nations returned twelve French prisoners[28] and only two Native prisoners, a Mahican and an Algonquin.[29] During the Onondaga conference in June 1701, Onontio's delegates "had spoken little on the subject of the allies" and had been primarily concerned with prisoners of French origin. "It was deemed appropriate," reported La Potherie, "to blame this omission on Maricourt, captain of the troops, who was the head of that delegation, and Joncaire, on behalf of the Chevalier de Callière, accepted sole responsibility for this error. He did so, and told [the Iroquois] ... that being their adoptive Son, it seemed he should carry the burden of all this, beseeching them to give him the means to resolve such a predicament." The French had to clear the Iroquois in the eyes of the allied delegates in order to ensure peace.[30]

The Iroquois, who had suffered substantial losses during the previous decade, certainly wanted to give up as few prisoners as possible. It was difficult for the chiefs to force families to give up people they had adopted, and Tekanoet, speaking on behalf of the Five Nations, presented this argument to Callière. It is likely that this was also a pretext. The leaders of the Great Lakes nations, which, albeit reluctantly, had brought back a sizable proportion of their prisoners, did not possess greater authority in their societies than the chiefs of the Iroquois League in theirs.[31] The governor also expressed his displeasure: "I cannot accept your excuse ... since you should have used all sorts of means to take them from the hands of those who had adopted them, as they [Amerindians of the west] have done."[32] We may also hypothesize that the prisoners of the Iroquois had been adopted earlier than those returned by the western nations and that they therefore had a greater emotional value for their captors. This is suggested by the speech of an Iroquois chief to the governor: "Do not you see that for four years we have made no attacks against your allies in spite of those they have made against us?"[33] The prisoners returned by the Great Lakes nations may thus have been recently captured.

In any case, Onanguicé, who mistrusted the Iroquois, had been proven right during the negotiations the previous spring in Michili-mackinac, and like Kondiaronk, all the delegates from the Great Lakes complained to Callière about the behaviour of the Iroquois,[34] even threatening to take back their prisoners.[35] The peace treaty was suddenly in jeopardy. "We did not know what to think about all the incidents that could occur from all these complaints, because the Odawas [here meaning the allies in the west] had reason to complain bitterly about our bad faith in making all the promises to them to take back their slaves at the same time as ours," reported La Potherie.[36] The representatives of the Five Nations, he said, "consulted each other at length in private. It was noted that they were extremely troubled, as the matter was more important than they had thought." "They had something to meditate on for a few days concerning the uncertainty in which they found themselves about the Peace settlement." The problem seemed impossible to resolve, and it required the combined efforts of the governor and the Huron chiefs to untangle the knot. Callière noted in his report to Versailles: "I spoke sternly to the Iroquois ... who promised me they would correct their error, and once I had won over the Hurons, who brought me their prisoners and placed their interests in my hands, all the other savages of the Pays d'en Haut followed their example and did the same thing." Kondiaronk played a crucial role. Overcoming his own disappointment over the "duplicity" of the Iroquois, he managed, on the strength of a solemn promise by them that they would very soon return all the prisoners "detained" in the Five Nations' villages, to convince the ambassadors from the west to return their prisoners and sign the treaty. He was not the only one to demonstrate his talents as a conciliator. Shortly after Kondiaronk's death, Quarante Sols, another Huron leader, told Callière: "You had proposed to us that we leave here the Slaves that we brought to you until the Iroquois return our people to us, and I say to you on behalf of our Nation that we want you to return them to them, without waiting for the return of our people." The Amerindians of the west did not, however, intend to stop there. Quarante Sols explained to the governor that "the feeling of Le Rat [Kondiaronk], our chief, who has just died," was that the prisoners should be recovered directly, "without having them brought here [to Montreal]," but "by way of Niagara."[37]

On 6 August, two days after the return of the prisoners, Chief Outoutagan spoke in the same vein on behalf of the allied nations: "We are happy that the prisoners of the Iroquois whom we are giving back are returning with their people to their villages, but we ask that you be firm about having ours back. We ask these prisoners when they are home to remember the good treatment they received from us, and when we meet each other while hunting or elsewhere, to regard us as their brothers, we who adopted them."[38]

During the farewell session given for the Iroquois the next day, Callière told them that the

Savages of the Great Lakes Nations ... gave me your Prisoners ... Therefore I want to return them to you now, except for five who wanted to stay with the Hurons, so that you will all return home content with me, and I give you Sieur de Joncaire as you wished, to bring back their people to me; do not fail to redeem the error that you made by leaving them in your Villages, to overcome all the difficulties that you may encounter among the individuals who have them, in order that I also satisfy my Allies ... and convince them of your sincerity, so that starting this winter you can hunt together in peace, and without them mistrusting you. I ask you again, too, for the rest of my Frenchmen, so that these matters may be entirely concluded.[39]

A few days after the conference, Joncaire was therefore sent to Iroquoia. He brought only six prisoners back to Montreal a few weeks later, but the Iroquois had promised to return the others directly by way of Niagara or Detroit, according to the Hurons' wishes.[40] It was the latter post, which was built by Cadillac in July 1701 and had become the new centre of the Pax Gallica, that was the setting for the return of a few prisoners (including some Iroquois, it seems) in the following months. This attenuated the discontent of certain groups from the Great Lakes region. In December 1701, for example, the Seneca chief Aouenano arrived in Detroit accompanied by "three women of the Miami nation." "Onontio told me to bring them here," he said. "I would not be angry to go in person to change the minds of the Miamis." Cadillac gave him safe passage and Aouenano went to a Miami village on the St Joseph River early in 1702 to return the three prisoners and smoke the peace pipe.[41]

IROQUOIS NEUTRALITY

In addition to establishing peace between the Five Nations and the members of the French-Native alliance, the Treaty of Montreal provided for Iroquois neutrality in the event of a new war between the French and the English. This agreement was the result of French diplomacy. Callière developed the idea shortly after the treaty of September 1700, and in a dispatch to the minister of marine, he stated: "I hope that the peace [of 1700] with the Iroquois can be used to settle to the advantage of the King the boundaries between us and the English, and if we could not obtain ownership of the land of the former, we could ... render them neutral." The agreement on neutrality was prepared during the Montreal meeting in May 1701 with Teganissorens and, in particular, during the visit of Bruyas, Maricourt, and Joncaire to Iroquoia the following month. On 6 August 1701 the governor was able to write, "I do not doubt that, in the disposition in which I have put them, they will accept ... the neutrality I propose to them."[42]

The next day, Callière told the delegates from the Iroquois League: "I have informed you ... that if the war began again between us [the French] and the English ... you should not think of becoming involved. I repeat to you again ... by this Collar, that in the event that war comes, you should remain peacefully smoking on your mats, without taking any part in our troubles, because otherwise they will again involve you in war with me and with all my Allies, who will block the way from your lands to here, and in all your settlements, where you are now free to come and go to get your necessities."[43] The Iroquois delegates agreed to Callière's request: "We would be angry if you were at war with the English, because you are our friends and they are too. However, if that occurred, we would leave you, smoking peacefully on [our] mats, as you ask."[44]

In the opinion of D.K. Richter, who draws on the work of W.J. Eccles and F. Jennings, "neutrality was more imposed on the Five Nations by the victorious French than it was the original idea of shrewd Iroquois diplomats."[45] The Iroquois nevertheless accepted it readily, as it corresponded to one of their political options. Discussed as early as 1688 by the Onondaga leader Otreouti,[46] the idea of neutrality was taken up again by Teganissorens around 1700.[47] The role of the Iroquois ambassadors present in Montreal in 1701 was to implement the policy of balance initiated by Teganissorens. As neutrals, the Iroquois maintained full political independence from the two colonial empires, which they could now play against each other if necessary, and which, in addition, represented two separate potential sources of supply. Furthermore, they would not have to get involved in the new European war that seemed imminent, and this reduced the risk of renewed conflict with the French and, consequently, the nations of the west. Neutrality was thus also a diplomatic weapon in the eyes of the Iroquois. As Father Bruyas said to his hosts in June 1701 in Onondaga, "[It is by] smoking peacefully on your mats [that] ... you keep the path open to go to Orange [Albany] and to come to Montreal to get whatever you need with the freedom to hunt, without Onontio's savage allies bothering you."[48] The following year, an orator for the Five Nations described the relative success of the rapprochement of the Iroquois factions: "[Teganissorens] is pulled by one arm to Montreal by you Onnontio, and Corlard pulls him by the other to Orange, his body remains always in Onontagué [Onondaga]."[49]

Pax Gallica in the West

The 1701 conference was also an opportunity for Onontio to strengthen the Pax Gallica in the Great Lakes region, that is, to extend French influence and work for peace in spite of the abandoning of its posts. Along these lines, Callière reaffirmed a clause already included in the agreements of September 1700. "If it happened that one of my children struck another," proclaimed Callière on 4 August, "the one who was attacked should not take revenge, neither he nor any of his people, but he should come to find me so that I can have justice done for him ... [and] if the offending party refused to make reasonable satisfaction, I and my other allies will join with the offended party to Compel him, which I do not believe would happen, because of the obedience owed to me by my children, who will remember again what we are deciding now together."[50] Onontio was setting himself up as an arbitrator in international relations, and to a certain extent he was one, but there was nothing absolute about his power as such, since it was based on the Amerindian tradition of chiefs, and the alliance was an association of sovereign nations even though the French had a certain hegemony.[51]

The French also wanted to reduce tensions between themselves and some of the western peoples. Callière agreed to forgive the robbing of coureurs de bois, for example, declaring on 6 August to Chief Onanguicé, who represented the Illinois, "You will tell them that I am willing to forget ... their robbing of certain Frenchmen." The governor intended to maintain the alliance with the Illinois even though they had not been present in Montreal, and therefore he used the customary language of alliances: "I honour the Illinois who died coming here and I ask you to give them this present, and to tell them everything that has happened here."[52]

The Pax Gallica also depended on the circulation of information. Onanguicé, who also spoke on behalf of the Sauks, brought to Onontio's attention the case of a Frenchman killed by a warrior of that nation: "I come here in fear, through the apprehension I have that you will resent the death of a Frenchman that a reckless young man from our Nation killed in a battle with the Sioux. However, since you are a good Father I ventured to present myself before you."[53] Callière answered that he forgave the Sauks; Onanguicé, to mourn the death of the Frenchman, "presented a small slave along with the beavers and continued: 'Here is a little flesh that we offer you; we took it in a country where the People go on horse. We wipe the mat stained with the blood of this Frenchman by dedicating it to you.'"[54] By displaying moderation and accepting the Native custom of compensation, the governor consolidated the alliance in the Great Lakes region.

The French also wanted to calm the habitual tensions among their allies, for example between the Foxes and the Ojibwas. Noro, who represented the Foxes, asked Callière to mediate so that the Ojibwas, who had killed a man of his nation, would make reparation to him. Ouabangué, the chief of the Ojibwas, replied that the killing had been committed to avenge the murder of one of his people by the Foxes, but Noro rejected this accusation and stated that he and the members of his nation had been at war with the Sioux at the time of the killing. Ouabangué then yielded, acknowledging that the arrow that had killed the Ojibwa had not been made by the Foxes.[55] The two delegations were reconciled,[56] and Callière confirmed the peace between the two nations: "We mourned the death of the Outagamis [Foxes] whom ... [the Ojibwas] had killed, with a present to 'the Porcupine' [Noro]. He was presented with the calumet, which he smoked, in order, they say, to swallow the revenge he

Fox warrior, c. 1710–1730. Anonymous watercolour, Bibliothèque nationale de France, Paris.

Note the elaborate tattooes covering much of his body and the European linen shirt tied around his waist. Comments written below the image indicate that the French author admired the prowess of the Fox in warfare.

could have taken. Ouabangué, the chief of the Saulteurs [Ojibwas], did the same, and thus the alliance was solemnized. All the chiefs of the other Nations smoked as witnesses at this meeting."[57]

Callière knew that the Ojibwa ambassador only represented some of his people, probably a group settled at Sault Ste Marie. He intended to extend this peace to the Ojibwas of Chagouamigon, at the western end of Lake Superior. He therefore instructed Ouabangué to "tell your brothers from Chagouamigon Point as soon as you can that I intend that all these disputes with the Foxes end."[58]

As we have already noted, Callière tried in vain to put an end to the wars between his allies and the Sioux. He hinted at this impasse in a letter to the minister: "As for the conflicts between the Miamis, the Illinois, and the six nations of the bay [Potawatomis, Sauks, Winnebagos, Foxes, Mascoutens, and Kickapoos] and the Sioux, since there is no one in the latter nation to whom I could send my orders to stop their acts of hostility, all I could do was to have the former call a truce, which I do not believe can last a long time."[59] In Montreal the allies never referred in their speeches to a peace with the Sioux. The Fox delegate, at the 4 August assembly, even mentioned to Callière that he was "on bad terms with the Sioux." La Potherie noted that "no one wanted to address the latter issue," which was particularly sensitive and which came up just when peace was being negotiated with the Iroquois.[60] Callière told his allies that he would stop the supply of guns and ammunition to their Sioux enemies from the French coureurs de bois, but he was not able to convince them of this.[61] The allies, consequently, imposed limits on the westward extension of the roots of the Tree of Peace, refusing to broaden the network of alliances as the French desired.

The Montreal conference finally allowed Callière to bring up the question of Detroit. Cadillac, accompanied by about one hundred men, had gone there in June to establish a post. It was necessary to inform the various nations of this and convince them of the merits of the project.[62] The French governor repeated to the Iroquois sachems the arguments he had already presented to Teganissorens the previous May, namely that Detroit could be used as a supply station for their hunters and that it would help in maintaining peace between the Iroquois and the western nations.[63] The ambassadors from the League gave their approval to the project,[64] and the Senecas, who were particularly pleased, even promised to bring corn to Cadillac and his men.[65] Similarly, since Versailles had decided, despite the edict of 1696, to allow trading with the Iroquois at Fort Frontenac, the clause to this effect – which had already been included in the peace agreement of September 1700 – was renewed.[66] Not surprisingly, the Iroquois were completely satisfied with it, especially since it enabled them to trade anywhere in the colony on the St Lawrence.[67]

Cadillac planned to establish the Hurons and Odawas of Michilimackinac and the Hurons of St Joseph River at Detroit.[68] Such a move seems to have corresponded to the wishes of these nations prior to Cadillac's plan.[69] In Montreal, the delegates from the west agreed, without any particular enthusiasm,[70] to comply with the French plans.[71] The Huron-Petuns and Odawas who moved to Detroit were attracted by the presence of a French commander, the fertility of the land, the abundance of game, and the possibility of trading more easily with the British. However, in the following months many Odawas expressed the desire to remain in Michilimackinac.[72]

9 1701: A New Situation

The Treaty of Montreal of 1701 involved the French, their Amerindian allies, and the Five Nations directly, and the English in New York indirectly. The Montreal agreements, along with those negotiated in Albany at the same time among the members of the Covenant Chain (the English and the Iroquois), are sometimes referred to as "the Grand Settlement of 1701."[1] It is important to analyse the balance of power in the diplomatic arena of northeastern North America at this time, and to determine how the Treaty of Montreal and the Albany Agreements affected it. We need to assess the situation of the various actors, taking care to consider the limits of the peace, since the Montreal treaty, as important as it is, certainly did not end the Amerindian wars in New France.

THE ALBANY AGREEMENTS OF JULY 1701: A CONTROVERSIAL DEED

Thirty-three sachems from the Five Nations (nine Mohawks, five Oneidas, twelve Onondagas, four Cayugas, and three Senecas) went to Albany to meet with John Nanfan, the new governor of New York, from 12 to 21 July 1701. These were the pro-English leaders, but like those who went to Montreal, they were motivated by the neutralist principles of Teganissorens. Their goal was to clarify the terms of the Covenant Chain in light of the treaty being signed that same summer in Montreal. The Iroquois thus had to strike a deli-

cate balance, confirming the alliance with the English in spite of
their peace treaty with the French. Nanfan, who was backed by
Robert Livingston, the secretary for Indian affairs, intended to obtain an explanation concerning the French-Iroquois negotiations in
June in Onondaga, to settle the missionary issue in his favour, and
to counter French plans to establish a post at Detroit.[2]

When the English governor complained that the Iroquois were
negotiating separately with the French and were about to sign a
peace treaty in Montreal, as Teganissorens had stated in Onondaga
the previous month, the Mohawk orator Onucheranorum replied
in a manner that was both defiant and evasive: "We have made
strict enquiry among all our people and can learn nothing but what
the people you sent thither are privy to, and what the[y] entred
down in writing, if you know of anything else then what they have
given you an account of, pray tell us, wee shall be glad to be informed."[3] The Iroquois managed to preserve the principle of their
neutrality while notifying the English repeatedly that they were
counting on their protection in the event of war with the French:
"if a warr should break out between us and the French, wee desire
you to come and stay here in this place [Albany], that you may be
ready to assist and defend us."[4] Similarly, the delegates from the
League clearly intended to use the British to counter French activities in the west. They asked that Livingston be sent "to Corakhoo
the great King of England to acquaint how that the French of
Canada encroach upon our territories by building a Forte att
Tjughsaghrondie [Detroit] and to pray that our great King will use
all means to prevent itt."[5] Cadillac's post could represent a threat
to the Iroquois, but even more so to the English. Onucheranorum
is said to have then made the offer to Nanfan and Livingston to
"give and render up all that land where the Beaver hunting is
which wee won with the sword eighty years ago to Coraghkoo our
great King and pray that he may be our protector and defender
there." Thus, on 19 July 1701, the well-known "Deed from the
Five Nations to the King of their Beaver Hunting Ground" was
signed (by Nanfan and twenty Iroquois headmen). Through this
deed, the Iroquois placed under the protection of the English a
huge territory situated approximately, from east to west, from
Lake Ontario to Lake Michigan and, from north to south, from
Lake Erie to Lake Superior (Detroit and Michilimackinac, for
example, were within this territory).[6]

The interpretation of this deed is controversial. According to many authors, it was a challenge issued by the Five Nations to their English allies, forcing them to respect the military dimension of the Covenant Chain and protect the Iroquois' activities in the Great Lakes region. Brandão and Starna, for example, write: "This was a bold move made to draw out and compel the English to protect them against the French and their Indian allies, thus guaranteeing the Iroquois continued and unimpeded access to their vital hunting territories." For D.K. Richter, similarly, the deed "seems to have been the Five Nations' idea."[7] F. Jennings, following A. Trelease, has particularly emphasized the symbolic and even fictitious nature of this agreement. The territory in question, far from being under Iroquois sovereignty, was in fact under the control of the Amerindians of the Great Lakes and their French allies. "This 'deed' was a worthless piece of paper," writes Jennings. "It purported to set forth the rights of the Iroquois to vast hunting territories in the west by rights of conquest over the Hurons and other Indians during the beaver wars, and it conveyed those asserted rights to the English Crown. But the conveyance was made precisely because the Iroquois had been driven out of those supposedly conquered lands." For the English, Jennings explains further, this deed was a document for the future: "The Iroquois gave a 'deed' ... absurd on its face but taken seriously because it was later to be advanced in diplomacy to justify England's claims against France."[8]

The Canadian historian W.J. Eccles goes further. He suspects the New York authorities of fabricating this deed behind the backs of the Iroquois chiefs: "The 'Deed' is a spurious document contrived by Lieutenant Governor Nanfan and his Albany Officials without the participation or sanction of the Five Nations." And he continues: "The totems marks of the Iroquois sachems ... bear no resemblance to those of the sachems on the Montreal Treaty, which I incline to think are authentic. I suspect that the Iroquois totems on the 'deed,' like the burden of the text, were contrived by an Albany official." The document, according to Eccles, is so contaminated with English legal language (for example, "To all Christian and Indian People in this part of the World and in Europe ..."; "wee ... have freely and voluntary surrended delivered up and for ever quit claim, and by these presents doe for us our heires and successors absolutly surrender, deliver up and for ever quit claime unto our great Lord and Master the King of England ...") that it loses all credibility. He also points out several examples of geographical errors, observes that the Amerindians did not measure distances in miles but in time, and, like Jennings, mentions the fact that the Iroquois no longer had control over their so-called Beaver Hunting Ground.[9]

Whether or not this deed was understood by the Iroquois, it was deceptive in that it was based on an extremely distorted representation of the balance of power in the Great Lakes region. How could the English guarantee to the Iroquois the possession of territories that no longer belonged to them? However, the idea of the Five Nations placing themselves under the protective wing of the English is not entirely lacking in credibility,[10] since the League had been weakened and such an agreement was in keeping with the logic of European-Native relations in colonial North America. It is not impossible that the original document recording the Iroquois orations had been rewritten by the New York authorities in "British" language before being sent to London.[11] It could also be that the Iroquois had adopted into their own discourse the rules of colonial politics, in particular the European rhetoric on the right of conquest. They would then have used the English imperial desire for expansion to win back a little of what they had lost.

During the Albany conference, the Iroquois sachems also renewed the economic alliance and took a conciliatory stance on the missionaries. In fact, Onucheranorum stated that the Iroquois had decided not to allow any Jesuits among them.[12] He did not, however, make any commitment to accept Protestant ministers.[13]

A DIPLOMATIC FAILURE FOR NEW YORK

"Only New York was a loser by the treaty [of Montreal]," states F. Jennings. Governor Bellomont and his successor, Nanfan, were not able to prevent the Iroquois from making peace under the aegis of the French and they were forced to accept the principle of Iroquois neutrality between the empires. On the eve of a new war with New France, the treaty of 1701 thus deprived New York of an ally that had been very valuable to it in the previous war, the Iroquois having essentially fought on its behalf. In addition, by getting the Five Nations to accept the French fort at Detroit, the treaty in the short term destroyed English hopes of expansion towards the Great Lakes.[14] While New York seemed highly satisfied with the Albany Deed of July 1701,[15] it actually had little reason to be. The territorial cession they claimed to have won in the west was fictitious and at the very most could only be used as a diplomatic argument in negotiations with the French.[16]

There were, however, positive aspects for the British. As Starna writes, "the peace with the western Indians could only increase the flow of furs to Albany."[17] Moreover, the neutrality of the Five Nations prevented the French from making expeditions through Iroquoia. A buffer had been created between New France and New York, and when war again broke out between the two empires, New York was able to escape the horrors of guerrilla warfare from Canada. New England was not so lucky; starting in 1702, it suffered a great deal from border raids by the French and Abenakis.[18] Finally, in spite of the Montreal treaty, Nanfan was able to reconfirm the Covenant Chain with the Iroquois.

WERE THE IROQUOIS THE WINNERS OR THE LOSERS?

Scholars have always agreed that the Grand Settlement of 1701 was a turning point in the history of the Five Nations. However, when it comes to analysing this turning point and assessing the diplomatic and military situation of the League at this time, their interpretations are widely divergent. There are two opposing positions. W.J. Eccles takes the view that the Iroquois were forced to capitulate in 1701 in Montreal, and that this admission of failure was the prelude to their irreversible decline. In this view, they were so weakened over the course of the eighteenth century that they were unable to pursue any ambitious objectives.[19] Brandão and Starna have a completely different analysis. According to them, the agreements of 1701 represent not a military defeat for the Five Nations but "the triumph of Iroquois diplomacy."[20]

Both positions have their flaws – but especially the latter. Let us start with that of Eccles, however. He fails to take into account the positive aspects of the Great Peace for the Iroquois, aspects that have been brought out by the historian Wallace and then by other scholars following him, such as Haan and Richter – in addition to Brandão and Starna.[21] The Iroquois' prospects for the future were in fact quite favourable, and they were not limited to the advantages of neutrality. Trade links with Albany were maintained, and now the Iroquois also had access to French sources of supplies –

Fort Frontenac, Detroit, and also Montreal.[22] The peace of 1701 also led to the success of the Iroquois' diplomatic and commercial overtures in the west.[23] Finally – something that has barely been mentioned by historians – the Iroquois recovered some thirty prisoners, which was one of their objectives. As well, according to D.K. Richter, the most important result obtained by the Five Nations in the negotiations of 1700–1701 was a partial solution to the internal quarrels that had divided the League for a decade and threatened to destroy it. In spite of enormous internal tensions, the Iroquois had reached a new consensus based on a kind of compromise, and they owed this in large part to the political genius of the Onondaga chief Teganissorens, who had been able to make the French strategy of neutralization of the Five Nations part of his program in order to resolve the internal struggles of the confederacy.[24] By thus preserving the League's unity and its autonomy vis-à-vis the colonial powers, he established the conditions for a new Iroquois offensive, this time a diplomatic one.

It is Starna and Brandão who are the most emphatic about the "singularly positive" results achieved by the Five Nations in 1701.[25] In their view, the League had sufficient manoeuvring room to negotiate a favourable agreement with the two European colonies. This view is shared by O.P. Dickason, who sees the Iroquois as deceiving both the English and the French. She says, for example, that in Albany they hid from the English their neutrality and the fact that they no longer controlled the territories covered in the deed. They "were playing both ends against the middle with great skill," she writes, in my view overestimating their ability to escape colonial pressures.[26] According to Starna and Brandão as well, the Iroquois did not have their backs against the wall in 1701: "They had not been defeated. And they did not come on their knees."[27] However, the French and New York sources, as we have seen, taken together with several Amerindian oral accounts, show that the Iroquois had suffered many defeats in the 1690s. Starna, contradicting himself somewhat, actually acknowledges this fact: "Several Onondaga and Oneida headmen brought their complaints of continued raids and the killing of their people to Governor Callière."[28] Of course, F. Jennings may have overstated the case in his harsh verdict that "the Iroquois sued for peace because they had no alternative but complete collapse and disintegration."[29] The Five Nations had not lost all military capacity, and although they were in a position of weakness, they negotiated as equals with the French and their allies, obtaining the best terms possible. One fact clearly shows that the Iroquois were not totally defeated: they managed to obtain a peace agreement and, without returning their captives from the nations of the west, recovered their own prisoners, even though reciprocal exchange had been a central issue in the negotiations. However, as already stated, neutrality was more a French idea than an Iroquois one, and it was imposed on them. Had the Iroquois wanted to oppose it, would they have had the means to do so? What is certain is that the peace of 1701 consolidated the military victory of the French-Amerindian alliance – it was the military raids of the western nations that induced the Five Nations to accept peace – just as the dispersion of the Hurons and their neighbours in the years 1640 to 1660 had represented a victory for the Iroquois.

I therefore do not share the conclusion of O.P. Dickason, who writes: "What had been achieved by the century of war? It had shifted the balance of Amerindian regional power from Huronia to Iroquoia." This historian seems to be confusing the 1660s with the 1690s. She continues: "The Five Nations emerged with expanded territory, although not so much as they claimed." In the same vein, Starna, who is clearly obsessed with the issue of territory, goes so far as to assert: "Therefore, practically speaking, it was the Five Nations who were in the best overall position to exercise control over the lands described in the 1701 [Albany] deed."[30] This is completely false. How could the Iroquois control territories dominated by the allies of the French-Amerindian diplomatic network? The Iroquois, of course, were in a much more favourable situation in 1701 than they had been between 1697 and 1700 – the Grand Settlement of 1701, as we have seen, was advantageous to them in many ways – but it would be an exaggeration to speak of a triumph. If there was a triumph for anyone, it was for the French. The Tree of Peace had been planted in Montreal, not in Onondaga.

NEW FRANCE: A CORNERSTONE
IN THE CONSTRUCTION OF THE EMPIRE

Shortly after the signing of the Montreal treaty, Callière explained to Minister of Marine Pontchartrain that "the separate peace made with the Iroquois in 1700, and which was made common in 1701 to all the known savage Nations, achieved for the King a certain, indisputable superiority in Canada over all New England."[31] While attributing the glory of this treaty to the king, the governor was obviously eager to take credit for its success, which was all the greater given that a new war was brewing across the Atlantic. Callière's judgment was too optimistic, however, because, in spite of the diplomatic defeat suffered by New York, the English colonies still had the advantage of their enormous demographic superiority. But the French governor was not wrong about the importance of the peace settlement with the Iroquois or about the vitality of all the alliances with the Amerindians, which provided support to New France. While the treaty of 1701 did not deal with the structural weaknesses of the colony or resolve the question of withdrawal from the Great Lakes region, it was nevertheless an undeniable political success for the French in that it furthered their hegemonic ambitions in North America.

The primary achievement, peace, was the result of a long diplomatic process initiated by Frontenac in the final years of his administration and completed brilliantly by Callière. The Iroquois war, long a scourge of the colony on the St Lawrence, seemed to have been eliminated forever. This was an enormous relief for all the colonists, especially those in Montreal, who had been living under constant threat of attack by the Iroquois since the Lachine raid in 1689. Iroquois neutrality provided an additional guarantee in this regard. Callière knew that the British would still urge the Five Nations to fight on their side in the event of war; if the Iroquois maintained their neutrality, New York would be deprived of its first line of attack and the Iroquois would serve as a valuable buffer against the British. Moreover, the imperial rivalry with New York over the status of Iroquoia had turned in favour of the French, since the Treaty of Montreal denied any English sovereignty over the Five Nations.[32] It was the governor's hope that Jesuit missionaries might help to preserve the peace and even separate the Iroquois from the British alliance: "I hope ... that through the familiarity that peace will bring about between us [French and Iroquois] more and more, the time will become favourable so that they will propose to me themselves that I send them Jesuits because in that case they will be obliged to defend them against the insults that the English could make to them through drunkards and other people connected to them." Callière was right: at the instigation of the pro-French factions, Jesuit missionaries began to settle in Iroquoia the following year.[33]

During the War of the Spanish Succession (1702–13), the priority for Governor Vaudreuil, Callière's successor (Callière died in 1703), was to preserve the peace with the Iroquois that had been won at such great cost, even if this meant to some extent neglecting the allies of the Great Lakes region. Vaudreuil went so far as to give the new alliance with the Iroquois precedence over the one with the Odawas (the main partner of the French in the west); in the event of "war between [these] two nations ... we would be obliged to take the side of the Iroquois," he stated in 1706.[34] The fear felt by the Native people of the Pays d'en Haut, in particular Kondiaronk during the 1680s, of a French-Iroquois alliance at their expense was not unfounded. Vaudreuil gave clear expression to the temptation to make a shift of alliances, a temptation that had been a constant in French policy since the defeat of the Hurons in 1650. In 1656, for example, dozens of Huron refugees had been captured on Île d'Orléans by the Mohawks with the apparent blessing of the French authorities, who were more concerned about their relations with the Five Nations than about the fate of their defeated allies.[35] The governor's statement also confirmed that the Iroquois, although defeated, were still feared and respected by the French at the beginning of the eighteenth century.

It was not in the interest of New France to weaken the Five Nations too much, although not everyone accepted this view. Father Carheil in 1702 wrote from Michilimackinac with respect to the Iroquois nations: "It is the only enemy that we have to fear and that fights with us over trade with our savages whom they want to attach to the English; what reason did we have not to want to destroy them in the war that we had undertaken against them, why did we want to preserve them? What would we lose in destroying them as few as they are now? Their destruction and the possession of their lands would assure us of the trade with all the savage nations up here."[36] While these remarks revealed the weakening of the Iroquois and the existence of trade between the nations of the west and Albany, they were still faulty in terms of strategy. The French, with the assistance of their Native allies, were probably in a position to further weaken the Iroquois (Onontio had demonstrated that he was capable of invading Iroquoia, and he had taken the hatchet away from many of his allies in 1700), but as noted above, it was not in their interest to do so. As Lahontan wrote:

Those who alledge that the destruction of the *Iroquese*, would promote the interest of the Colonies of *New-France*, are strangers to the true interest of that Country; for if that were once accomplish'd, the Savages who are now the *French* Allies, would turn their greatest Enemies, as being then rid of their other fears. They would not fail to call in the *English*, by reason that their Commodities are at once cheaper, and more esteem'd then ours; and by that means the whole Commerce of that wide Country would be wrested out of our hands.

I conclude therefore, that 'tis the interest of the *French* to weaken the *Iroquese*, but not to see 'em intirely defeated.[37]

Since the time of Champlain, the Iroquois had served for New France as a barrier between its Native allies and the English or Dutch merchants,[38] and there was no question of the French renouncing this time-honoured principle.[39] Maintaining the Iroquois as a secondary force allowed the French to preserve a geostrategic buffer separating its English enemies from its allies in the west; the loss of that buffer could lead to the commercial and political ruin of New France. In short, as B.G. Trigger writes, "if the hostile Iroquois had not existed, the French would have had to invent them."[40] Contrary to Jennings's view, however, it was not solely for this reason that "the French refrained from demanding Iroquois subjection in the great treaty settlement";[41] it was also because, despite a certain superiority,[42] the French were not really in a position to do so, and they may have feared the effects of a resurgence of Iroquois guerrilla warfare, which would have hindered the development of the colony.[43]

"This Peace [of 1701] engages all the savages in the interests of France," wrote Callière in his report to the minister.[44] These "savages" of course included the Iroquois – who seemed at the very least to have been neutralized – but he was referring above all to the nations of the Pays d'en Haut and of the St Lawrence and Acadia,[45] "peoples who are the support of Canada" according to La Potherie.[46] Onontio thus had good reason to be satisfied; the multilateral alliance with his "children," which had been shaky in the west in the previous decade, was consecrated

by the treaty of 1701, in accordance with the very wishes of its
members.[47] As host for the peace negotiations and intermediary
between the allies of the west and the Iroquois, the governor
made official the strategy of arbitration and mediation that he
had applied in the Pays d'en Haut. The 1701 conference demonstrated in a most impressive way the central, influential place of
Onontio in the alliance. The chief Chichicatalo acknowledged
Callière's right to act in Native affairs when he asked him to
speak to the other Miamis in support of his decision to migrate
to the St Joseph River.[48] Similarly, if the allies in the west agreed
to make peace with the Iroquois, it was in part because of
Callière's entreaties, with gifts to back them up, during Courtemanche and Father Enjalran's diplomatic mission in the winter of
1700–1701.[49] In 1701 Onontio wanted to appear as the master
of war and peace, and in this case he managed to do so quite
well.

Certainly the Pax Gallica had its limits; the impossibility of ending the conflict between the nations of the west and the Sioux at-
tests to this. In addition, in spite of the establishment of Detroit,
the Treaty of Montreal had not provided any solution to the interruption in trade resulting from the edict of 1696, which in the
long term could result in the peoples of the Great Lakes trading
their pelts in the English markets, thus weakening the alliance. But
the Great Peace nonetheless constituted a success for New France.
Versailles was particularly pleased, for the treaty was signed at a
time when Louis xiv was giving new impetus to French imperial
policy in North America with the decision (demonstrated in the
founding of Detroit and, especially, Louisiana) to consolidate his
control of the area west of the Appalachians from the Great Lakes
to the Gulf of Mexico in order to prevent English expansion beyond the Appalachians.[50] Thus, 1701 must be seen as a pivotal
time in the building of the French empire in America. According
to W.A. Starna, "None of the parties to the 1701 treaties, whether
France, England or the Five Nations, could reasonably exercise
control over all or part of the territory described in the 1701 deed
and treaties." Eccles, disagreeing with Starna, replies, "The
French did." And they did, by means of their posts on both sides
of Iroquoia (Fort Frontenac and Detroit) and the indispensable
support of their allies.[51]

THE ALLIED NATIONS IN A POSITION
OF STRENGTH

The delegations from the Great Lakes did not go to Montreal only because Onontio had asked them to. They came to defend their own interests, as demonstrated by their determination to make the voyage in spite of the rumours – which were well founded – of an epidemic. Each group had its own motives, which depended on their relations with the Iroquois and the Sioux and on their place in the network of French-Amerindian alliances (the Odawas, Huron-Petuns, and Potawatomis, as we have seen, occupied a more central position than for example, the Foxes, the Mascoutens, or the Gens des Terres). Certain nations – and sometimes mere bands or factions – were already negotiating peace with the Iroquois independently of Onontio. But the majority accepted his request to bury the hatchet in 1700–1701.

The Huron-Petun chief Kondiaronk is the best illustration of the key role played by the Great Lakes nations in building the Great Peace of Montreal. He contributed through his raids (the battle on Lake Erie in 1697, for example) to the weakening of the Iroquois, and he was, with Onontio, one of the leaders of the faction in favour of a general peace in 1700–1701. On many occasions, Kondiaronk showed himself to be a man of compromise and conciliation, able to overcome the various obstacles on the path to peace. At least twice he played a decisive role in winning over the Amerindians of the west: first, at the Michilimackinac conference in May 1701, (where all the nations of the alliance were represented), when he managed to achieve a precarious but functional consensus; then, in Montreal in August of that same year, when, to the great relief of Callière, he settled the question of prisoners. It must also be noted that, in Montreal in September 1700 and August 1701, and also in separate meetings in the west in the absence of the French, Kondiaronk had the opportunity to talk directly with delegates from the Five Nations to persuade them to accept the terms of the general peace.[52] Thus, Kondiaronk was, with Onontio, one of the main artisans of the peace of 1701. He was probably also one of its initiators, but on this point the sources focus almost exclusively on the role of New France.

On the whole, we see in the year 1701 a reinforcement of the position of the nations of the Great Lakes. In fact, the peace settlement seems to have given them increased room to manoeuvre. The priority for most of the delegations, in addition to the recovery of prisoners, was to maintain the alliance with the French. As the governor and the intendant wrote, "permanent posts would do a great deal to satisfy our allied savages, who urgently asked Sieur Chevalier de Callières, when they were in Montreal for the peace negotiations, to be given Frenchmen among them."[53] The minutes of the treaty confirm that the allied chiefs asked repeatedly that officers, blacksmiths, and missionaries be sent to the Great Lakes region. In the following years, the Odawas would ask again and again for the reestablishment of a garrisoned post at Michilimackinac. Wanting to consolidate the alliance, these nations thus played on French imperial ambitions. Offering the French hospitality in the west, they intended to take advantage of their merchandise (in particular their weapons) and their power to mediate.[54]

The allies were in a favourable position in 1701 because through the peace settlement they had been reconciled with the Iroquois, and if the Five Nations gave them free passage through their territory, they might also have closer relations with Albany. The French strategy of maintaining the Iroquois as a buffer between the Native peoples of the west and the English was therefore not without its weak points. The general peace did in fact create the conditions for an alliance between the Great Lakes nations and the Iroquois.[55] It even opened the door to a shift of alliances in favour of the Covenant Chain, which was the policy favoured by the Huron chief Le Baron in the 1690s. In 1703 an administrator expressed his concern over this possibility: "It is not appropriate to bring together so closely the Iroquois with the Outaouais [Odawas], the Hurons and the other savages, we must use our skill to try to see that they are never too friendly."[56] Alliance with the English, which was likely to weaken their links with Onontio, was certainly not the plan of all the Amerindians of the Great Lakes region. As we have already seen, it is hardly possible, given the factional manoeuvring, to speak of common strategies, and the Amerindians' propensity for war could hinder plans of alliance. But it was an option that several groups would take advantage of in the ensuing years. As shown by the words of the Amikwa delegate at the Montreal conference, the intention of the nations of the west was not to leave the comfortable bosom of the French alliance, but rather to put pressure on Onontio to be more generous in trade, and to take advantage on occasion of the attractive New York market. In this sense, the nations of Great Lakes came out of the 1701 peace settlement more powerful, as they had become potentially less dependent on the French.

Onontio's influence on the Christian Iroquois was also declining somewhat at the turn of the eighteenth century. After 1701, Delâge notes, the settled Iroquois "were distancing themselves from the French. They shared the geopolitical analysis of the leaders of the League, that of Teganissorens in particular, who recognized the threat that the colonial societies represented to their security and who favoured a strategy aimed at intensifying competition between the colonial powers in order to neutralize their negative impact as much as possible. Breaking with the rules of the French-Amerindian alliance, according to which the enemies of one were the enemies of all, they refused to regard the British as enemies simply because they were the enemies of Onontio."[57] The peace settlement of 1701, to which the agreement concluded in 1696 between the Iroquois of the League and the Iroquois in the réductions contributed, did even more to bring these two Amerindian groups together. Thanks to the Five Nations, in fact, the settled Iroquois obtained the freedom to trade with New York, which, unbeknownst to the French, consolidated their union with the Iroquois of the League.[58] The Iroquois settled in Montreal would thus act as middlemen in the "contraband" trading that was beginning and would soon flourish between Albany and Montreal.[59] The "great alliance,"[60] born of the Treaty of Montreal, that brought together the French, their allies, and the Five Nations was indeed a double-edged political weapon for New France.

THE LIMITS OF THE PEACE

"From then [1701] on," writes W.J. Eccles, "peace reigned in the west, until the resumption of Anglo-French hostilities in 1754."[61] This judgment needs to be qualified. Let us begin by looking at what La Potherie wrote shortly after the treaty of 1701: "So here is the peace made with the Iroquois, but I can assure you, Monseigneur, that our allies who have their people [prisoners] among the Iroquois will not fail to take revenge on the former if they meet them in their hunting parties."[62] La Potherie, who was not on good terms with Governor Callière, wanted to play down the diplomatic success of the treaty. But he was right about the importance of the problem of prisoners and the danger of a resumption of war. It should be pointed out that while the Great Peace of Montreal put an end to the open warfare of the preceding decades, it was not scrupulously respected in the Great Lakes region. The skirmishing of previous years between the Iroquois and the nations of the west continued sporadically at the instigation of certain groups or individuals. "[They] have uprooted the tree of peace," some Senecas complained to Vaudreuil in 1704. Attacked by Miami, Ouiatenon, Illinois, and Mascouten warriors in spite of the peace treaty of 1701 and the diplomatic voyage of Chief Aouenano to the Miamis at the beginning of 1702, these Iroquois appealed for the protection and arbitration of the French.[63] The Odawas of Michilimackinac – those, that is, who had not migrated to Detroit – also continued to make war with the Iroquois regardless of the general peace. In 1704 they attacked some Iroquois living "on the doorstep of Fort Frontenac" and captured forty of them. According to D.K. Richter, "the majority of the victims were dedicated francophiles who had placed their trust in French promises to keep the peace."[64]

These clashes did not prevent other western bands from forming trading relationships with the Iroquois and the English,[65] but they indicate how difficult it was to establish a lasting general peace. "My Father, all the men disobey you, they are all making war with each other and killing each other," exclaimed a Menominee chief in 1708.[66] For many Native people in the west, the peace of Montreal was a mere truce. In 1709 Governor Vaudreuil reminded the allies in the Pays d'en Haut of the agreements of 1701: "You have all forgotten the promise you made at the general peace; you all promised not to take revenge if someone attacked, but to rely on me to get satisfaction for it. You have not, however, done this and that is what today is causing your misfortunes."[67] The following year, some Onondaga and Seneca delegates complained to Vaudreuil under the terms of this arbitration clause: "Until now we have done as you wished. The Outaouais [Odawas] have not done the same, they have attacked us many times since the general peace. We have been struck almost everywhere on our bodies, we are now completely fed up, but we have not taken revenge because you have until now always prevented it. Without that, our father, the Odawas would be no more, they must be persuaded that we do not fear them. They know like many others that when we go to war, it is not to kill two or three men, but to take an entire village."[68] The orator was

anxious to affirm the power of his people, and his words to this effect were not without foundation. The Iroquois had since 1701 captured many enemies in attacks on southern tribes. This was not just
a *petite guerre* but open warfare involving the capture of villages,
like that waged against the western nations from 1640 to 1670,
though certainly on a smaller scale.[69] The ambassador's main objective was to take advantage of French mediation to solve the
League's problems with the Great Lakes nations. This remedy, inci-
dentally, would have been unthinkable in 1690, evidence that the
Iroquois had truly been defeated by the end of the century.[70]

Throughout the eighteenth century, then, when it was in their interest, the Iroquois reaffirmed the general peace agreement concluded in 1701. In 1757, for example, at a conference held in
Montreal, the orator for the Five Nations reminded the French,
"We can't write but know all that has past between us having good
memories." He continued: "After the Warrs and troubles we together met you at this place [Montreal] where every trouble was
buried and a fire kindled here. Where was to meet and Treat peace-
bly; you are daily now working disturbances and Seem to forget the
old agreement ... The Tree Seems to be falling, let it be now put up
the Roots spread and the leaves flowrish as before."[71]

In addition to the tensions between the Great Lakes nations and
the Iroquois, there were also occasional conflicts among the nations of the French-Amerindian alliance. For example, the peace
negotiated between the Foxes and Ojibwas under Callière's auspices did not last. The Ojibwas were related both to the Sioux and
to other Algonquian groups (Odawas, etc.), which created conflicts within the league of the Pays d'en Haut. There were recurring tensions between the Ojibwas, on one side, and the Foxes,
Menominees, Potawatomis, and Sauks, on the other.[72] There were
also tensions between the Odawas and the Hurons and Miamis,
which degenerated into open warfare at Detroit in 1706.[73] It was
also at Detroit, in 1712, that the French became involved in a terrible battle between the Foxes and several allied groups, including
the Odawas and Potawatomis. This battle was the prelude to a
long war that pitted the French and their allies against the Foxes,
Mascoutens, and Kickapoos, a war that continued until 1738.[74]
Callière had hoped to arrange a truce with the Sioux, but this had
proved impossible because the Sioux had not been present in
Montreal in 1701.[75]

While it essentially ended the Iroquois Wars, the treaty of 1701 did not stop the "Indian wars" in Canada. This was, first of all, because the French did not have the means to impose peace on all the groups as they would have liked to and, secondly – and especially – because of the inherently military nature of the aboriginal societies.[76] It is important to understand the significance of the Amerindians' concepts of war and peace. "Wars are eternal among the savages," stated Charlevoix. War was a permanent condition, and peace, tactical and temporary, was often intended only to recover prisoners. Nicolas Perrot expressed the view that "there is no savage nation that does not have a grudge against another. The Miamis and the Illinois hate each other, the Iroquois detest the Outaouais [Odawas] and Saulteurs [Ojibwas], and so forth. There is none of these nations that does not say it is justified in making war with others." Perrot was describing the prevalence of war and the unstable nature of alliances, which constantly had to be reactivated if they were to last. Alliances were not by nature inviolable contracts, and intertribal relations were thus marked by a structural alternation between phases of war and phases of peace. From one period to another, the cycle went from the violence of war to the exchange of gifts or women (or prisoners). Peace was even more fragile because war making was often an individual undertaking, carried out by reckless young men in defiance of the wisdom of the elders. Even the Iroquois, who in 1701 longed for peace with the nations of the west, were subject to this structural aspect of war, which hampered their strategy of rapprochement with the nations in the Great Lakes. As Richter explains, "When women mourned their dead kin and called on young men to bring them captives or scalps to ease their grief, and especially when warriors with no other foes at hand were in their cups, western Indians on their way to Albany made tempting targets."[77]

If the Amerindians of the west and the Iroquois were at war less after 1701 than during the seventeenth century, it is because they had opportunities to express their warrior ethos in other places and against other enemies. The concept of "universal peace" was unknown to the Natives, who, while they valued the military support or neutrality of allies, always had an adversary to fight and prisoners to be adopted or tortured. La Potherie observed that the Iroquois "never made Peace with any Nation without planning to make War elsewhere." And Intendant Raudot, speaking of Amerindians in general, said, "When they are not at war against any of

their neighbours, they usually go to the lands of very distant nations."[78] This is exactly what the Iroquois did after 1701. Once
the peace agreement was concluded with the allies of the French,
they resumed and intensified their raids against the "Flatheads"
(Catawbas, Choctaws, and various other southern peoples) in the
Carolinas and Virginia, ending a truce that had lasted from 1692
to 1701,[79] the period when they had been on the defensive vis-à-
vis the Great Lakes nations. These raids do not seem to have had
an economic basis. They were part of the tradition of wars of capture, as an Iroquois orator stated in 1719: "It seems that God in a
particular manner is pleasd to Strengthen us by Severall prisoners
which we do take from those people."[80] As for the western allies,
they had no intention of making peace with both the Iroquois and
the Sioux. As some Hurons told Vaudreuil in 1703, "You make
war against the English, so let us go against the Sioux."[81] They
continued to fight the Sioux and increased their raids against various groups in the Mississippi Valley, such as the Akansas, as well
as the Flatheads, which brought them closer to Iroquoia.[82]

The French-Iroquois peace depended on the Five Nations' maintaining their neutrality, in particular in the event of a war between
the French and the English, and on New France's attitude to the
trading relationships its allies in the west and the Five Nations
might form. Vaudreuil endeavoured to discourage the development
of trade cooperation between the two groups, even arranging the
murder, in 1709, of the Métis Alexander Montour – the son of a
French officer and a Mohawk woman – who was acting as a guide
in Iroquoia for Mississaugas, Ojibwas, Odawas, Huron-Petuns, and
Miamis on their way to Albany. This did not help maintain the
peace of 1701. It also explains in part why the Iroquois broke their
promise of neutrality in 1709 and 1711.[83]

Because of factional manoeuvring, it was difficult for the Iroquois
League to maintain neutrality when the French and the British were
at war, as between 1702 and 1713. An Onondaga orator in 1710
expressed the reservations of the League to Vaudreuil: "Today I am
on my mat and it is with sorrow that I see that you are fighting with
the English. Are you both drunk …?"[84] As R. Haan has shown, the
policy of balance between the empires was not always as successful
during the eighteenth century as Wallace has asserted. Richter, in
the same vein, writes, "[T]he diplomatic balancing act never seems
to have worked very well in periods when the imperial powers

pressed the Five Nations to choose sides." At least until 1720, Richter goes on, "anglophile, francophile, and neutralist factions continued to disagree." Neutrality, in 1701, was one option for the Iroquois; it did not necessarily have their unanimous support.[85]

During two attempts by the British to invade Canada – both unsuccessful – the Iroquois departed from the principle of neutrality, joining the English camp. In 1709 only the Senecas remained neutral. In 1711 warriors from all of the Five Nations (a total of 656 men) went to Albany to join an expedition that was planned against New France. But in subsequent years the League returned to a strict policy of neutrality. The policy would again be put to the test, however, during the War of the Austrian Succession (1744–48) and after 1754, during the Seven Years' War.[86]

10 Conclusion

The year 1701 is a date that has traditionally been ignored in the imperial – and therefore Eurocentric – account of North American history. While 1713, the year that saw the end of the War of the Spanish Succession with the signature of the Treaty of Utrecht (which took Acadia, Newfoundland, and Hudson Bay away from New France), is certainly essential to an understanding of the fate of Canada, for the colonists of the St Lawrence, as for the Native people in the colony and the Great Lakes region, the events of 1701 are indisputably more significant. That year Louis XIV inaugurated a new imperial policy in North America by notifying the Canadian administrators that New France, including the new colony of Louisiana, now had to serve as a barrier to English expansion into the interior of the continent.[1] In June the officer Lamothe Cadillac founded the colony of Detroit, thus reshaping the geopolitics of the Great Lakes region, and later in the summer the Montreal treaty was signed between the French authorities and some forty Amerindian nations.[2] The importance of the peace agreement of 1701 should not be exaggerated: it did not completely end the fighting, nor did it transform the nature of European-Native relations. The epithet *great* or *grand* that has usually been attached to it is not, however, inappropriate, for two reasons: first, because of the importance of the agreements concluded, and second, because the treaty is a manifestation of an original and relatively successful form of colonization.

The treaty of 1701 in part determined the diplomatic and military history of Canada until the end of the French régime in 1760. Unlike many of the treaties signed in the previous century, the peace with the Five Nations was lasting. New France, and the Montreal region in particular, no longer had to live, as it once had, under the permanent threat of Iroquois raids. While the Five Nations, under the influence of the British, attacked the French again during the imperial wars of the eighteenth century, their hostility towards Canada was largely a thing of the past. The negotiations of 1700–1701 established the principle of Iroquois neutrality, which was advantageous for the Five Nations and, as R. Aquila writes, was respected most of time: "With the brief exceptions of the aberrations during Queen Anne's War [the War of the Spanish Succession] and King George's War [the War of the Austrian Succession], the Iroquois Confederacy maintained a policy of neutrality from 1701 until 1754." The League was always divided into factions but from about 1715 on, according to D.K. Richter, "the vast majority of the Iroquois now agreed with the neutralists."[3]

The treaty of 1701 reflected not the triumph but the reorientation of Five Nations diplomacy. For example, the League undertook a policy of alliance with the nations of the west, and this policy, paradoxically, was encouraged by the French, who had orchestrated the Treaty of Montreal. Of course, the Tree of Peace was sometimes uprooted in the Great Lakes region, but the confrontations of the eighteenth century were limited to a few skirmishes. Finally, the peace of 1701 put an end to French-Amerindian military expeditions into Iroquois territory, which had particularly affected the Senecas. The Iroquois Wars in Canada were thus over.

The reading of the Treaty of Montreal should not be limited to an analysis of what was agreed; the treaty is also interesting in that it provides a striking and evocative image of French colonization in North America. The gathering of thirteen hundred Amerindians from as far away as the Mississippi Valley and Acadia – which justifies the use of the expression *Great Peace* – is a reflection of the relative success of the French colonial enterprise at the dawn of the eighteenth century. In spite of their small population, the French had managed to extend their influence over a large part of the continent. The Great Peace of Montreal is a powerful illustration of the success of the French-Amerindian alliance. "New England ... has twice the population of New France," wrote Callière in 1701, "but the people there are surprisingly cowardly, absolutely unprepared to fight, and lacking any experience of war; the smallest savage war party has always made them run away."[4] The French governor was, however, greatly minimizing the demographic handicap; since the ratio was not 1 to 2, but close to 1 to 20; at the beginning of the eighteenth century, New France had 16,000 inhabitants of European origin, as opposed to 300,000 in all the English colonies.[5] But his remark is still an accurate reflection of the strength of the French colony, which was drawn largely from its alliance with the Native nations, expressed in Callière's remarks in terms of the "indianization" of the war. The Great Peace of Montreal, in this sense, was the crowning achievement of a certain form of colonialism based not on agricultural expansion and settlement, but on alliance with the indigenous peoples and adaptation (in large part tactical and manipulative) to their political customs. The Montreal ceremonies of 1701 were a spectacular expression of this spirit of adaptation and of the intensity of cultural exchange in the diplomatic sphere.

While it marked a political success for New France, the year 1701 was not at all a break with history. From 1600 to 1760, the existence of New France was dependent on a policy of alliance with the aboriginal peoples. Governor Vaudreuil and Intendant Raudot in 1708 reminded the court of the importance of "maintaining a good union with all the savages ... it is only this union that makes the happiness and safety of this colony." Vaudreuil further stated, "The policy of a governor of Canada does not consist so much in taking care of the French who are within the scope of his government as in maintaining a close union with the savage Nations that are his Allies."[6] This strategy had an economic basis – the fur trade – and a political-military dimension, since the Amerindians of the colony on the St Lawrence, the Atlantic region, and the Great Lakes region constituted an essential auxiliary force in the wars against the Iroquois and then, in the eighteenth century, in the conflict with Great Britain. The British were perfectly aware of this. Cadwallader Colden, in a report on the fur trade in 1724, attested to the success of the French-Amerindian alliance, although he predicted its downfall in favour of the British colonial power.[7] This alliance was clearly the key to the survival of New France. Bougainville, a French officer in the Seven Years' War, in 1757 expressed the view that the colony would be "lost" without the alliance with the Amerindians: "[W]e sustain ourselves only through the good will of the savages; that is the counterweight that tips the scales to our side."

And he stated further that "it is the affection they have for us that has preserved Canada until now."[8] Thus, the Great Peace of Montreal seemingly marked the success of French colonization in North America – only seemingly, however, because although the network of the French-Amerindian alliance would be maintained until 1760, the demographic imbalance between New France and the British colonies was already making itself felt in 1701.

The French-Amerindian alliance was able to endure in the eighteenth century for two principal reasons. The existence of French forts in the west made it possible for the Amerindians to reduce the cost of transporting and repairing their goods, an advantage the English lacked. As well, fear of the expansionism of the British colonists was, in the words of Governor Vaudreuil, giving rise to a "natural antipathy" on the part of the Amerindians,[9] who considered the military support of the French essential to counter this threat. Some settled Iroquois expressed their fear of English expansion in 1754 in a speech intended for their brothers in the League: "Do not you know, our brothers, what a difference there is between our father [Onontio] and the English? See the forts that our father has established and you will see that the lands beneath their walls are still hunting grounds, [the forts] being placed in our hunting grounds only to facilitate our needs; when the English on the contrary take possession of land, the game is forced to desert it, the woods fall before them, the land is laid bare."[10] In 1701 the issue was not ceding territory, but peace and alliance. Onontio was certainly motivated by a desire for conquest, and the seeds of subjugation were already apparent in the time of Louis XIV, but the French were too dependent on the Amerindians to opt for any strategy other than that of alliance.

The Montreal conference thus gave rise to a historical reality of which the celebration of the tricentennial in 2001 should be a powerful reminder. Forty sovereign nations signed the Treaty of Montreal: this was de facto recognition by the French of the independence of the Native nations. Amerindians were key actors in the history of North America, as is clearly demonstrated by the events of 1701. Many Native chiefs shared with the French leaders in building the peace, and the conference was a triumph for Amerindian diplomatic customs. The Native people as well as the Europeans were indeed the founders of Quebec and Canada. There is also, perhaps, a lesson to be learned from the peace of 1701, although the current context bears little resemblance to colonial times. It was a tremendous achievement to bring together in Montreal the delegates of some forty nations, from the Missouri to north of Lake Superior and from Iroquoia to Acadia – some of whom were nomadic and others sedentary, some of whom were accustomed to using canoes and others for whom it was unusual – and to overcome the intertribal hatreds and the passion for war of so many and induce them to sign a peace treaty. If they were capable of doing that three hundred years ago – regardless of the limitations of the peace treaty of 1701, and regardless of the French desire for conquest – then perhaps today's problems between Native peoples and Euro-Americans are not as insurmountable as they sometimes seem.

The Nature of the Treaty
and the Amerindian Pictographs

The Montreal treaty of 4 August 1701 (shown on pages 112–18 and, translated into English, in Appendix 3) begins with a preamble by Governor Callière and then is divided into three parts: first, the speech the governor delivered to the Native delegates; second, the words of the various Native speakers, obviously summarized; and finally, the signatures of the chiefs and the colonial administrators.[1]

The treaty is a written document characteristic of European diplomatic culture. It made official, through pen and ink, the proposals put forth in the speeches, "transforming into law what until then was only words."[2] The French diplomats were therefore concerned to have the Amerindian chiefs with whom they had negotiated the agreement ratify the treaty by putting their "marks" on it. It is probable that the written document was not initially considered official in nature by the Native participants, most of whom, contrary to European custom, did not keep a written copy of the treaty. Moreover, diplomatic agreements were not set down on paper in the indigenous languages. In August 1701 the chiefs from the Great Lakes returned to their villages with no written copies of the treaty. In 1716, however, Louvigny, who made peace with the Fox nation, reported, "I left them a copy on a sheet of paper as authentic testimony of our agreements."[3] Did these particular Amerindians, then, attribute a political value to the French written document even though they would not have been able to read it? Or should we regard these French-Amerindian treaties as being just for show? It is clear that they were diplomatic instruments for internal use by the French. The written treaty was an object recognizable both to the king, whom the governor had to reassure about the proper management of Native affairs, and to the rival imperialist powers in the event of a diplomatic dispute over some colonial claim by France. But these treaties also involved the Native peoples, who used wampum belts to validate the negotiations and the oral tradition to remember them. A French-Amerindian treaty was therefore just as valid as a French-English or French-Spanish treaty, even if the Amerindians did not have proper written copies.[4]

It should be noted that the Amerindians never signed such documents to validate the words written in them; rather they were validating the words that had been delivered in their language by an interpreter. This could lead to misunderstandings,[5] but that was not the case for the 1701 conference. First of all, there were many participants, and the scope of the negotiations precluded the possibility of specific agreements at the expense of the greater number; secondly, the treaty did not include any transfers of territory, which usually involved deception; and finally, the dependence of the French on Amerindian alliances and their interest in this peace led them to make sure that everyone, and not just some factions, took part.[6]

While the treaty – as a document – was intended for the French authorities and not the Indian chiefs, its form is a syncretic product of French-Native diplomacy. The Native oral tradition is in fact part of it. In Europe, diplomatic documents were written in a standard form, with numbered clauses listing the points agreed to by the parties. While the text of the French-Iroquois treaty of 1665, for example, follows this model quite faithfully, that is not the case for the treaties of 1700–1701, which owe a great deal to the Native tradition of "words." The signatures do not follow a series of clauses, but rather a series of orations delivered during the conferences by the plenipotentiaries from each nation and written down by a French scribe. The form of the treaty of 1701 thus combines both European and Native elements.[7]

The document that has come down to us is not the original. We may conclude from the relative uniformity of the pictographs that it is a copy made by a scribe of the governor. Callière is quite clear on this point when he wrote to the minister of marine: "I attach the *copy* of what occurred in this assembly [of August 4] at the bottom of which I have had their signatures very well imitated" (emphasis

added). The terse phrase at the end of the list of Amerindian signatures confirms this: "Signed: Le chevalier de Callière, Bochart
Champigny, and others." The expression "and others" is additional
evidence of copying done by the scribe. On the original document,
which has disappeared, it was the Native delegates who signed, as
La Potherie and Charlevoix reported. The former wrote, "All the
delegates ratified the Peace by each putting their arms," and the latter reported, "The Savages signed ... by each one putting the mark
of his Nation at the bottom of the Treaty."[8]

There are thirty-eight or thirty-nine Amerindian pictographs on
the treaty of 1701 (compared to thirteen on the treaty of 1700).
What do they correspond to? According to Charlevoix, "Each tribe
bears the name of an animal, and the whole Nation also has its
own, from which it takes its name and of which its mark is the symbol or, if you wish, its coat of arms. These treaties are not signed
otherwise than by drawing these figures, unless there are particular
reasons for substituting others."[9] In the iconographic corpus, the
animal world, including both actual species and mythological crea-
tures (such as the thunderbird), is predominant, but there are also
human figures, plants, and various objects, such as the arrow, the
peace pipe, or the scalp pole.[10] There could also be totemic em-
blems,[11] but there was not actually anything systematic about their
use to formalize agreements, since signing treaties was new for the
Native people.

The nature of the pictographs depended in part on the position
of the signatory, who could be a peace chief (in keeping with his
role), a war chief (who for ending the war was entitled to sign the
peace treaty), or just an ambassador. Certain figures that are
difficult to interpret identify a chief ("chief's mark": should we
speak here of "individual" totemism?) or a village ("village
mark").[12] Others, no doubt, are sociological symbols corresponding to a nation, clan, phratry, or moiety. The glyph is sometimes a tribal symbol; this may perhaps be the case for the fork
drawn in the name of the Nassauaketons – the Odawa nation "of
the Fork" – or the pipe drawn by the ambassador of the Cayugas,
who were called the "People of the Great Pipe." The tribal value
of the symbol may also come from a clan motif. It is not surprising, for example, that the Sauk ambassador used a sturgeon on
the treaty; as the main tribal chief, who was a peace chief, belonged to the clan symbolized by this fish. The Seneca signatory

drew a tortoise, perhaps because he belonged to that clan or because that was the clan entrusted with diplomatic responsibilities. Ouabangué, the Ojibwa delegate, drew a crane; according to Ojibwa oral tradition in the nineteenth century, the crane was the emblem of the most prestigious clan and thus the one overseeing relations with the Europeans.[13]

My final example is that of two thunderbirds with their backs to each other, drawn by the Winnebago and Menominee representatives. It is possible that the mirror image is intentional, and that the pictographs reflect the dualistic organization of these nations. Among the Winnebagos, there is a sky moiety, which is the peace moiety, and an earth moiety, which is associated with war. The clan of the thunderbird belongs to the peace moiety, which is also, in the residential structure of the village, the western moiety. The signatory, a representative of the thunder clan, is therefore the peace chief, and the bird is also looking towards the west, in the direction of peace. Among the Menominees, the thunder clan is the main clan of the sky moiety, but in this case it is the war chiefs who come from this clan. The signatory of the treaty of 1701 is thus a war chief. However, the figure is facing east, towards peace, since the Menominee peace chiefs were on the eastern side at tribal councils.[14]

Whether he signed with a personal symbol (individual totemism) or with a symbol of a sociological nature (nation, clan, moiety, etc.), the Native delegate committed himself on behalf of the nation of whom he was the agent.[15] Under almost every emblem the French scribes put the names of the chief and his community, in order to clarify the document for themselves. With respect to the delegates who agreed to the peace of September 1700, the signatures were usually the same from one treaty to the next. The Seneca ambassador, Toarenguenion, twice used a tortoise, and the Onondaga ambassador, Ohonsiowanne, twice used a wading bird. But there is a surprising counter-example: the barely identifiable signature of Garonhiaron, a Cayuga delegate, on the treaty of 1700 does not look at all like the pipe he drew at the general meeting on 4 August 1701. Was the first instance the totem symbolizing his clan, and the second the symbol of his nation?[16]

The Native delegates signed in accordance with the European convention of written documents, but this was not a major concession; this practice was formally in keeping with the pre-European pictorial tradition. While the Amerindians were amazed by writing, which they saw as truly magical, they were not unfamiliar with graphic communication. They were accustomed to the use of pictographic symbols, which had a spiritual value, a sociological meaning, or a mnemonic and narrative function.[17] The symbols drawn on the treaties were related to the traditional representational art created by the peoples in the Great Lakes region on various surfaces: human or animal hide, bark, and rock. J. Bernard Bossu, an eighteenth-century French officer, observed that the Amerindians of the Mississippi made tattoos representing animals or objects as a sign of recognition of the military merit of individuals. "It is a sort of order of knights," noted Bossu, "to which one is admitted only for outstanding deeds."[18] As Lahontan explained, the bark was also used for pictographs extolling war: "When a Party of Savages have routed their Enemies in any Place whatsoever, the Conquerours take care to pull the Bark off the Trees ... to give all Passangers to understand what Exploits they have done. The Arms of the Nation, and sometimes a particular Mark of the Leader of the Party, are painted in colours upon these strip'd Trees."[19]

Finally, there is a continuity between the pictographs on the peace treaties and the old tradition of shapes painted or engraved on rock; the style and even the iconographic lexicon are the same. The petroglyphs, according to anthropologist Emmanuel Désveaux, are associated with the Native vision quest, which some groups depicted by creating representations on rock of the entities encountered in the visions.[20] These representations were also created on other surfaces, such as skin. The adolescent, after the vision, made a kind of contract with his guardian spirit by having "the figure of his Okki or his Manitou," as Charlevoix wrote, "pricked on the body."[21] If there were cultural concessions on the part of the Native peoples, then, it was not because they drew glyphs but rather because they adapted to a new medium, paper.

The Cast of Characters in the Great Peace of Montreal

The purpose of this section is to provide further information on the lives of those people who played direct and indirect roles in the Great Peace of Montreal. It includes both French personalities – officers, diplomats, missionaries, interpreters – and Native leaders, most of whom took part in the conference. It was necessary to be selective, and I have left out those persons for whom the only information available is that they were present in Montreal in August 1701. Data on the Native participants is, of course, sketchy. *The Dictionary of Canadian Biography* is the source of a good deal of the information provided in this appendix, especially for the Europeans. Other sources used will be mentioned in this section's endnotes.

AOUENANO Civil chief and orator of the Senecas, Aouenano suffered great personal losses in war. In the summer of 1699, his entire family was killed in an attack by the Amerindians of the west. This perhaps induced him to pursue peace with the French even more actively. Considered one of the leaders of the pro-French faction of the Iroquois League, Aouenano went to Montreal in July 1700 with three other Seneca chiefs and two Onondaga sachems to ask Callière to stop the raids by the groups from the west, and to notify him of the four western Iroquois nations' acceptance of the peace terms dictated by the French. During the general conference the following year, he and Tekanoet were the main orators of the Iroquois delegation and he led the condolence ritual for Kondiaronk's mourners.[1]

ARADGI It appears that Aradgi, Arratio, and Haratsion were one and the same person. A pro-French sachem of the Onondaga nation, Aradgi led an Iroquois delegation to Quebec in November 1697 and remained there as Frontenac's hostage in order to guarantee peace. He was apparently freed in March 1699, when he returned to Onondaga. It was there, in April 1700, that in his capacity as League orator he presided over a meeting with an English delegate, Peter Schuyler. In July he travelled to Montreal with five other Iroquois delegates and gave a decisive impetus to the peace process.[2] Aradgi, however, did not attend the Montreal conference in 1701.[3]

VINCENT BIGOT (1649–1720) Born in Bourges and a member of the Society of Jesus since 1664, Vincent Bigot arrived in Canada in 1680 and worked as a missionary until his return to France thirty-three years later. Founder in 1694 of the mission at Pentagouet, in Acadia, he also was responsible for maintaining the alliance with the Abenakis. He knew their language well, which earned him the position of official interpreter at the Montreal conference of 1701. From 1704 to 1710, Father Bigot held the office of superior general of the Jesuit missions in Canada. He died in France in 1720.[4]

JACQUES BRUYAS (1635–1712) Born in Lyon in 1635, Jacques Bruyas became a Jesuit novice in 1651 and arrived in New France in 1666. A missionary among the Oneidas from 1667 to 1670 and among the Mohawks until 1679, he then took charge of the mission at Sault St Louis (Kahnawake), where he died in 1712. Callière gave him, with Joncaire and Maricourt, effective responsibility for Iroquois affairs, and he was such a capable diplomat that he represented the governor in Boston in 1699. Familiar with Iroquois protocol and an interpreter as well, he was a delegate to Iroquoia in August 1700, where he took part in the League Council. Then in June 1701, he was sent to convince the Five Nations to send representatives to Montreal the following month. At the peace conferences of 1700 and 1701, Bruyas translated Callière's speeches into Iroquois and the Iroquois speeches into French.[5]

CADILLAC [ANTOINE LAUMET, KNOWN AS DE LAMOTHE CADILLAC] (1658–1730) Antoine Laumet was born into a provincial bourgeois family from Gascony and took a noble title under the name de Lamothe Cadillac. He emigrated to Canada in about 1683. Thanks to Governor Frontenac, who had taken him under his protection in 1691, he was first made a lieutenant and then a captain in the marine, and then, in 1694, he was promoted to commander of Michilimackinac, the most important post in the Pays d'en Haut. He made large profits in the fur trade, with the collusion of the governor. Three years after his arrival at the post, when his captain's pay was 1,080 *livres* per year, he sent 27,596 *livres* to France in letters of exchange. To build his fortune, he permitted the sale of alcohol to the Native people, in defiance of regulations and to the indignation of the Jesuit fathers (of whom he became a sworn enemy), and made the coureurs de bois give him a share of their furs. Cadillac was a brilliant figure (intelligent, charming, a talented writer), but he was concerned above all about his purse and his power, and was ambitious, quarrelsome, and manipulative.

Following Louis XIV's edict ordering the closing of the posts in the west, Cadillac returned to the colony and sailed for France in 1698. His goal was to obtain the support of Versailles for a plan to establish a colony on the shores of the strait between lakes Erie and St Clair. It took a second voyage to France, in 1699, for him to finally win the minister of marine, Pontchartrain, over to his cause and thus overcome the objections of Callière and Champigny. In the summer of 1701, with some fifty soldiers and as many colonists, Cadillac went to lay the foundations of his little colony, Detroit, which soon became an intertribal meeting point. He reigned there for nine years, becoming increasingly despotic, extorting money through the sale of alcohol, various taxes, and bribes, earning the enmity of colonists and Amerindians alike, and jeopardizing the French network of alliances. In 1710 Minister Pontchartrain, who had rashly supported him, finally became aware of his excesses – and sent him to Louisiana as governor. Cadillac went there only in 1713 and, in association with financier Antoine Crozat, took part in an unsuccessful colonization program. Four years later, he was once again removed from his position, and he even spent a few months in the Bastille for contradicting official propaganda that portrayed Louisiana as the new El Dorado. He spent his final years in France, near Montauban, in Castelsarrasin, where he had purchased the office of governor.[6]

LOUIS   HECTOR   DE   CALLIÈRE(S)   (1648–1703)
Louis Hector de Callière (usually spelled Callières, but he signed
without the *s*) was born in Thorigny-sur-Vire, in Normandy, to a
noble family originally from the province of Angoumois. His father,
Jacques de Callières, a brigadier-general in the royal army and
sometime writer, served as governor of the town of Cherbourg, in
Normandy. Louis Hector's older brother, François, also had a literary and political career. Elected to the French Academy in 1689,
François became a distinguished diplomat at the end of the century,
playing a major role as Louis XIV's representative in the negotiation
of the Treaty of Ryswick, and was the author of a famous book on
ambassadors (*De la manière de négocier avec les souverains*).[7] He
even rose to the powerful position of secretary of the king's cabinet
and took advantage of it on occasion to further Louis Hector's
career in New France.

Louis Hector, who joined the army in about 1664, had already
taken part in several of Louis XIV's campaigns when he was appointed governor of Montreal in 1684. Sometimes disliked because
of his taste for authority and his severity, Callière was nevertheless
for the twenty years of his stay in Canada a devoted, competent officer, at ease in both military and diplomatic matters. Quickly gaining expertise in guerrilla warfare, he fortified Montreal and its
surroundings to ward off enemy attack and organized many raids
against the Five Nations. He also took part in expeditions into the
heart of Iroquoia, assisting Denonville in 1687 and then Frontenac
in 1696. Callière also proved himself a shrewd diplomat in his
many meetings with Iroquois ambassadors[8] and a clear-sighted
strategist with respect to the geopolitical situation in New France.
He criticized Frontenac's policy of *petite guerre*, which was very
costly in men and matériel, and though he supported the expeditions of 1693 and 1696 into Iroquoia, he thought that it would be
disastrous to destroy the Five Nations completely, since their presence in moderate strength was essential to the economic and political security of the colony. In 1694 he explained to the minister of
marine that if the Iroquois were to be weakened, they must still be
left strong enough to act as an effective barrier between the western
nations and Albany.[9]

Frontenac died in November 1698, and Callière replaced him as
governor general of the colony. He was officially appointed to the

position in the spring of 1699, following a request by his brother
François to the king. While Frontenac would undoubtedly have
concluded the peace agreement of 1701 as Callière did, the latter
was perhaps better prepared for this task. On many occasions, the
new governor questioned the policies of Versailles. He felt that the
edict of 1696 decreeing French withdrawal from the posts in the
west threatened to destroy New France's system of Native alliances.
He was also critical of the plans for Detroit and, especially, Louisiana, an independent colony outside his jurisdiction. Pontchartrain,
however, paid little attention to his advice, although he was grateful
to him for his skill in concluding the Great Peace of Montreal.

In 1702 Callière decisively oriented the policy of New France in the
War of the Spanish Succession. Pontchartrain had wanted to form an
offensive alliance with the Iroquois to fight New York, but Callière
did not agree, arguing that they had to respect the Treaty of Montreal
and therefore leave New York and the Iroquois in peace – which did
not preclude border raids against New England. Callière, wrote
Charlevoix, "died in Quebec on 26 May 1703, much regretted, as the
most accomplished General this colony has ever had."[10]

JEAN BOCHART DE CHAMPIGNY (C. 1645–1720)
Born to an illustrious family of the *noblesse de robe*, Bochart de
Champigny landed at Quebec in 1686 and subsequently served as
intendant of New France for sixteen years, responsible for justice,
administration, and finances. He had not had the opportunity to
serve the king in France, but he did so with skill in Canada. Like
Colbert, he was hesitant about expansion into the west, but he was
conscious that maintaining the network of alliances in the Great
Lakes region was vital to the colony.[11] In 1687 he assisted the Marquis de Denonville in the campaign against the Senecas, using
shrewd tactics to capture dozens of Iroquois living near Fort
Frontenac; these captives were afterwards sent to France as galley
slaves. He later served under Frontenac and then Callière, and in
1701 played an active role in the organization of the peace conference.[12] Appointed intendant at Le Havre by the king, Champigny
left the colony the next year and was succeeded by Beauharnois.[13]

CHICHICATALO (?–1701) Chief of the Miamis of the
St Joseph River, Chichicatalo was one of the leading figures of the

Great Peace of Montreal. Described by La Potherie as "a personage of singular merit, whose bearing much resembled that of the Roman Emperors,"[14] he was one of his nation's most enthusiastic supporters of the French alliance. In 1701 he presented himself to Callière as an ambassador of all the Miamis and asked him to support their gathering "in a single place, near the St Joseph River."[15] While speaking of the military superiority of his people over the Iroquois, he said he was completely satisfied with the peace settlement and offered the governor a peace pipe, which the plenipotentiaries smoked at the meeting of 4 August. Before leaving Montreal on 6 August, he made an important speech: "My Father," he said, "I am delighted to see the Iroquois together with our people. My Father, I fear one thing, that he is deceiving you; for often he has spoken to me with his mouth, but his heart did not correspond to his words. I feel joy in no longer hearing the sound of weapons clashing together to avenge the insult he made to us. So today the Sun shines, the land will be united, and we will have no more quarrels. When we meet, we will look on each other as brothers, we will eat the same meal together ... So, my Father, I bid you adieu, perhaps I will never return, for I am very weary."[16] According to La Potherie, "it was not without reason that Chichicatalo made this adieu, which became eternal."[17] He died a few days later, probably as a result of the epidemic in Montreal, which had already taken several Miami chiefs.[18]

CHINGOUESSI (?–1701) A Sinago Odawa chief, Chingouessi is mentioned twice in the sources prior to his participation in the 1701 conference. In 1695 he took part in an important conference in Michilimackinac in the presence of Cadillac and several chiefs from the region.[19] Three years later, he led an Odawa delegation to Quebec and told Frontenac privately that the Sable Odawas and the Kiskakons were planning "to leave their fire at Michilimackinac to go make a fire elsewhere." Opposed to this plan, Chingouessi managed to counter it by using the influence of the French governor.[20] At the end of the century, he seems to have been involved in the war waged by the Great Lakes nations against the Iroquois, as shown by the colourful speech he made to Callière on 2 August 1701: "I bring you no Iroquois because I have eaten all the ones I captured."[21] Chingouessi died on the way back to Detroit, where he had perhaps planned to settle.[22]

AUGUSTIN LE GARDEUR DE COURTEMANCHE
(1663–1717) Born in Quebec in 1663, Courtemanche spent
the first half of his career as a soldier and diplomat in the service of
the colonial authorities. In 1689 he participated in an expedition to
New England and the following year took part in the defence of
Quebec against the English. Courtemanche was seen by Frontenac,
and then Callière, as an expert in Native relations, and he was given
various missions in the west. An ambassador to the Odawas in
1691,[23] he was in 1693 appointed commander of the post on the
St Joseph River, in Miami country, where he directed the war effort
against the Iroquois.[24] In the autumn of 1700, he was again sent to
the Great Lakes region to persuade all the allies to take part in the
general conference. He went to Michilimackinac, to the St Joseph
River, in Illinois country, to Chicago, and to Green Bay, meeting
with many groups. In July 1701 he was back in Michilimackinac
"after a journey of more than four hundred leagues, then set off
with a fleet of one hundred and eighty canoes."[25] From 1702 to
1717, Courtemanche spent most of his time on the Labrador coast,
trying to advance France's ambitions for that region.[26]

JEAN ENJALRAN (1639–1718) A member of the Society
of Jesus from the age of fifteen, Jean Enjalran came to Canada in
1676, where he carried out his apostolic work among the Odawas.
He lived at St Ignace (Michilimackinac) and like all the missionaries
played both a political and religious role among the Amerindians.
In 1684 he tried to persuade the Odawas and Huron-Petuns to join
La Barre's expedition. He played a similar role in 1687 during Denonville's campaign, in which he took part as chaplain of the forces
in the west. A proponent, unlike other Jesuits, of Cadillac's plan to
convince the Native people of St Ignace to go to Detroit, he was
asked in 1700 to give up his missionary work in Canada. At that
time he played a prominent diplomatic role, going to Michilimackinac on Callière's behalf to invite the nations of the west to take part
in the peace conference. In Montreal, in August 1701, Father Enjalran translated the speeches of the governor for the Odawas and Algonquins. He left New France the following year and died in his
native town of Rodez in 1718.[27]

FRONTENAC [LOUIS DE BUADE DE FRONTENAC
ET DE PALLUAU] (1622–1698) Born into an old family

of the *noblesse d'épée* from Périgord, Frontenac divided the first half of his career between the court of the king and the battlefields of the Thirty Years' War. Appointed governor general of New France in 1672, he quickly became involved in the fur trade for his own benefit, promoting expansion into the west. In 1682 his constant quarrels with the intendant, the Sovereign Council, and the clergy led to his recall to France. La Barre and then Denonville succeeded him, but he was restored to his position as governor in 1689. The defender of Quebec against the English in 1690, Frontenac organized military campaigns against the Iroquois in 1693 and then in 1696. During this period, he promoted the creation of new trading posts in the Great Lakes region, in defiance of directives from Versailles.[28] He repeatedly – in 1690, in 1693–94, and then in 1697–98 – attempted to negotiate a lasting peace with the Iroquois, and thus, in a sense, planted the seeds for the Great Peace of Montreal. His efforts came to fruition thanks to the skills of Callière, his successor as governor.

During his long career in New France – nineteen years – Frontenac consistently demonstrated his abilities as a diplomat at conferences with the Native peoples, both the Iroquois and the allies in the west.[29] For both the French and the Amerindians in the early eighteenth century, Frontenac remained the "father" par excellence, the embodiment of the perfect Onontio.[30] From 1673 on, he insisted that the Iroquois use the term *father* "in all the conferences when they came to ask him for peace."[31] Around 1680 he affirmed his double role as protector and provider to the allies in the west, whom he received in Montreal and called his "children."[32] Frontenac was an exceptional diplomat, frequently inviting Native ambassadors to share his table and putting them at ease with his charming manner. He was capable of joining them, tomahawk in hand, in their war dances.[33] He was considered to have a real capacity to influence the Natives, and Charlevoix even remarked that he knew how to "manipulate ... [their] minds."[34] The Huron chief Kondiaronk considered him one of the rare "men of ability" in the colony.[35]

JULIEN GARNIER (1643–1730)   Born in Brittany in the diocese of Saint-Brieuc, Julien Garnier entered the Society of Jesus in 1660 and went to New France two years later. He taught at the Jesuit college in Quebec and studied Native languages in preparation for missionary work. Father Garnier served in Iroquoia from

1668 to 1685, promoting peace between the French and the Five Nations, and later worked at the Sault St Louis (Kahnawake) mission. Lafitau, who was introduced by Garnier to the world of the Amerindians, said of him: "He knew the Algonkian language fairly well, but he was master particularly of the Huron language and the five Iroquois dialects." This knowledge of Native languages prepared him well to take part in the diplomatic talks, and he served as an interpreter at the Montreal conference. In 1702 he continued his conversion work in Iroquoia, among the Senecas, and in 1716 he became the superior of all the missions in New France. He died in Quebec in 1730.[36]

LOUIS THOMAS CHABERT DE JONCAIRE (1670–1739) Born in France around 1670, Chabert de Joncaire went to Canada a little before 1690 and served in Governor Frontenac's guard. Captured by the Senecas shortly after his arrival, he was saved from the torture post at the last minute by the intervention of a clan mother, who may have belonged to the family of Tonatakout[37] and who decided to adopt him. Mutual friendship and trust then developed between Joncaire and his Iroquois hosts, a relationship that would on several occasions assist diplomatic negotiations between the French and the Five Nations.[38] In 1700–1701 Joncaire, along with Maricourt and Father Bruyas, directed the comings and goings of delegations between Montreal and Onondaga, and managed to convince the Iroquois to go to New France to negotiate a general peace. His familiarity with the Iroquois permitted him to play a predominant role in the conference. In subsequent years, he worked under Governor Vaudreuil to preserve the achievements of 1701 among the Iroquois, and in 1720 used his influence with the Senecas to obtain their permission to build a fort at Niagara. The commander of the post until 1726, Joncaire died in 1739.[39]

KINONGÉ Kinongé, or Le Brochet ("The Pike"), was a chief of the Sable Odawas of Michilimackinac. Historian D. Chaput traced his activities over a very long period, from 1660 to 1713, but it is possible that Chaput confused two individuals, since the names of chiefs were transferred ritually from generation to generation. The first mention of him dates from 1660, when he had a disagreement with a Jesuit father who criticized him for having several wives. The Kinongé of 1683 (perhaps the same one) was an influential chief. In fact, it was in his house that Duluth, La Barre's agent, organized the trial of some Amerindians who had murdered two French coureurs de bois. During the 1690s, Kinongé seems to have belonged to the pro-French faction of Michilimackinac. He was a signatory of the two Montreal treaties of 1700 and 1701, but it was Outoutagan, as an orator, who apparently had the greatest influence among the Sable Odawas. Kinongé did not subsequently go to Detroit as most of his people did, but he nonetheless played an important role in the "Le Pesant affair" in 1706–7.[40]

KONDIARONK (C. 1649–1701) Born, according to W.N. Fenton, around 1649, at the time of the fall of Huronia, Kondiaronk died on 2 August 1701 in Montreal, during the peace conference with the Iroquois, as a result of a "violent fever." Kondiaronk (or Gaspar Soiaga, Souoias, or Sastaretsi) was better known to the French under the name of "Le Rat" ("The Muskrat").[41] For some twenty years, from the beginning of the 1680s until his death in 1701, he was one of the main chiefs – if not the main chief – of the Huron-Petuns of Michilimackinac and a charismatic figure in the French-Amerindian alliance. According to Father Charlevoix, he was a "Man of talent, extremely brave, and the Savage of the greatest merit the French have ever known."[42] In a classical panegyric with an added touch of ethnocentrism, La Potherie wrote of him:

I cannot express to you ... the grief there was in his Nation at the loss of a man so full of good qualities. It was difficult to have a more penetrating mind than his, and if he had been born French he would have had the character to govern the thorniest affairs of a prosperous state. He was the soul and prime mover of the Outaouakse Nation, which is the most powerful of our allies. His words were like oracles, and when the Iroquois knew that he was moving to make a strike against them, they avoided fighting with him. He had the sentiments of a beautiful soul, and was a savage only in name.[43]

Kondiaronk bore the "dynastic" title of "Sastaretsi," which belonged to a member of the bear lineage, itself part of the prestigious deer phratry.[44] He was therefore a hereditary chief, but his influence as a leader owed much more to his qualities as a warrior,[45] mediator,[46] and orator. His speaking skills were much admired by the French. "He was naturally eloquent ... Nobody could ever have more wit than he," wrote Charlevoix. "He shone ... in private conversations, people often took pleasure in teasing him just to hear his repartee, which was always lively, colourful, and usually impossible to answer. He was in that the only Man in Canada who could stand up to Count Frontenac, who often invited him to his table for the pleasure of his Officers."[47] This chief may even have been the inspiration for a character created by one of Frontenac's protégés, the iconoclastic Baron de Lahontan, whose *Dialogues* feature a Huron philosopher named Adario (a partial anagram of Kondiaronk) who is harshly critical of European society, condemning private property, corruption, venality, social injustices, and religious dogmatism. A fictional character in the spirit of the Enlightenment, Adario is the perfect "Noble Savage," and he seems to owe little to the real Kondiaronk.[48]

Although Kondiaronk had rivals within his nation and among the Great Lakes nations allied with the League, his influence was unequalled around 1700. According to La Potherie, he was "the most able and most important person in the upper [Great Lakes] nations."[49] He had a special relationship with Frontenac and then with Callière, especially during the years 1695–1701. The first recorded meeting between Frontenac and Kondiaronk took place in Montreal in 1682, when the nations of Michilimackinac were seeking the protection of the French governor to counter the Iroquois threat. The Huron-Petun chief had declared: "Saretsi [Kondiaronk] your son, Onontio, formerly called himself your brother, but he stopped being your brother because he is now your son, and you sired him by the protection that you gave him against his enemies. You are his Father and he knows you as such, he obeys you as a child obeys his father."[50] In saying that the term *father* better described Kondiaronk's relationship to Onontio than *brother,* the term that prevailed in the time of Huronia, the chief was recognizing Onontio's central role in the alliance but there was no question of submission, and in subsequent years Kondiaronk did not hesitate to defy the French alliance. He feared more than anything a separate peace between the French and the Iroquois, and in the summer of 1688, he used trickery to break up negotiations then taking place between Denonville and Teganissorens, the great Onondaga leader. Kondiaronk also occasionally attempted rapprochement with the Iroquois. In 1689, according to Nicolas Perrot, "Le Rat ... went to find the Iroquois and propose to them the destruction of the Outa-ouais [Odawa] nations." He added, "We know very well that the Hurons have always wanted to destroy the nations of the Pays d'en Haut, and that they have never been strongly attached to the French."[51]

Around 1694–95, however, Kondiaronk joined the pro-French factions of the Great Lakes villages, and he played a central role in establishing the Great Peace, relaying Onontio's words to the west.[52] In 1697, "at the head of one hundred and fifty warriors," he defeated a party of sixty Iroquois in a fierce canoe battle "of more than two hours" on Lake Erie. "Le Rat was then," observed Charlevoix, "sincerely attached to the interests of the French; it was he alone who had prevented all the Hurons of Michilimackinac from following Le Baron, to New York. He also did a great service to the Miamis, by warning them to beware of Le Baron; for he had realized that this Traitor, on the pretext of forming an alliance with these savages, was thinking only of betraying them."[53]

Kondiaronk remained in the area of Michilimackinac for the following three years, but he returned to Montreal in September 1700 to sign the peace treaty with the Iroquois. On this occasion, he made a long speech in which he reminded the Iroquois delegates

that the Tsonnontouans [Senecas] had formerly violated the general peace ... [and] were bent only on the complete destruction of the French, planning not even to spare their Father, whom they intended to be the first to be put into the Kettle, for an Iroquois threatened Monsieur de Frontenac that he would drink his blood from his skull ...; that their brother Corlard treated them so harshly, they who had always been so loyal, that they had lost most of their warriors by supporting his side in that war, that he had not protected them from the burning of their villages and their forts ... that their hands were bloody with the blood of our allies, that their flesh was even still between their teeth, and that their lips were all gory with it, that secret hearts were known ... that they preferred to walk in the darkness of war ... [but] today ... the Sun dissipated all these clouds to reveal that beautiful Tree of Peace which was already planted on the highest mountain of the earth.[54]

Shortly after this peace treaty was signed, Kondiaronk returned to Michilimackinac and during the winter and spring endeavoured to convince all his allies to attend the great fire in Montreal in July. His diplomatic activity met with complete success. Kondiaronk was indeed the principal Native architect of the Great Peace of Montreal, as Charlevoix stated unequivocally: "The Governor General placed in him his main hope for the success of his great enterprise. *He was almost totally obliged to him for this marvellous agreement, and this unprecedented meeting of so many Nations for the General Peace*" (emphasis added).[55]

KOUTAOILIBOE   This Odawa Kiskakon chief took part in the Montreal peace conference in September 1700, representing four Odawa nations. He then went west to support the diplomatic mission of Enjalran and Courtemanche. From 1701 to 1712, he remained in Michilimackinac. He was one of the intermediaries who helped Governor Vaudreuil establish his Pax Gallica. He played a particularly important role in resolving the crisis that arose in Detroit in 1706–7.[56]

LA POTHERIE (CLAUDE-CHARLES LE ROY, *DIT* BACQUEVILLE DE LA POTHERIE) (1663–1736) Born in Paris in 1663, La Potherie began his career in Brest, in 1691, as chief writer in the Marine, a position he held until 1697. He was then appointed commissary of the Marine and took part in d'Iberville's expedition against the English in Hudson Bay. In 1698 he became comptroller of the marine and of the fortifications in New France, where he stayed for only three years. During this time, La Potherie took an intense interest in the negotiations for the Great Peace of Montreal, although to his great dismay he did not take part. He harboured resentment against Governor Callière for this and perhaps found consolation in his writing. His *Histoire de l'Amérique Septentrionale*, which was not published until 1722 and of which three volumes out of four are devoted entirely to the Native peoples, is an invaluable work on the history of New France. For events prior to 1698, he gathered information from officers and voyageurs such as Nicolas Perrot. An attentive witness and meticulous observer, La Potherie chronicled the ceremonies of the Great Peace of Montreal. He witnessed the councils held in Kahnawake on 21 and 22 July 1701, and then went to Montreal. A rigorous historian – although he neglected to date the events he was describing – he also consulted the correspondence of the governor and the intendant and even copied long passages verbatim. In 1701, shortly after the general peace treaty was signed, La Potherie left Canada for Guadeloupe, where he had been appointed adjutant of a company. He died there in 1736.[57]

LE BARON   This Huron-Petun chief was given the name "Le Baron" by the French, but his real name is not known.[58] There were, in fact, two Le Barons in the 1690s. The first, who presented himself to Governor Frontenac as an ardent defender of the French alliance died, at an extremely old age, during a general conference held in Quebec with the Iroquois in 1694.[59] The second Le Baron – the successor of the first – was the leader of the Huron anti-French faction around 1695–97. He was, in the eyes of the French, "a dangerous person,"[60] because he carried on negotiations with both the Iroquois and the English. He managed to convince certain Odawa groups to negotiate with the Iroquois and thus weakened New France's system of alliances organized around Michilimackinac. His plans were foiled by the pro-French factions (Kondiaronk among the Huron-Petuns, Onaské among the Odawas), and in 1697 he went to live near Albany "with thirty families from his Nation."[61] This "famous chief"[62] embodied a policy that proved unsuccessful, at least in 1701. Le Baron apparently wanted the Huron-Petuns and the Odawas to make peace with the Iroquois independently of the French and to join the diplomatic and trade network of the Covenant Chain. The sources make no mention of Le Baron beyond 1697.[63]

PAUL LE MOYNE DE MARICOURT (1663–1704) The fourth of twelve sons of Charles Le Moyne de Longueuil and brother of Pierre Le Moyne d'Iberville, Maricourt was born in Montreal in 1663. A talented canoeist and a soldier by vocation, he played an active role in the years 1686–96 in the fight against the English and the Iroquois. He participated in military expeditions to Hudson Bay against the English in 1686, 1688, and 1696, as well as in the defence of Quebec in 1690, and commanded the Abenakis and the Sault St Louis Amerindians in Frontenac's campaign against the Onondagas in 1696. On several occasions, he traded his soldier's uniform for the garb of a diplomat, proving an invaluable assistant to Frontenac and then Callière in negotiations with the Five Nations. Maricourt was given this role because of his knowledge of the Iroquois language and his influence among the Onondagas, who had adopted him. That did not prevent Teganissorens, in 1701, from remarking shrewdly: "You come and speak of peace and have scarcely sat down to smoke a pipe, but talk of coming and knocking us on the head, and therefore I say nobody knows your heart."[64] In 1700–1701 Maricourt twice went to Iroquoia with other French emissaries to ensure the success of the peace talks. For the negotiations in Montreal in the summer of 1701, he acted as host to the Iroquois and probably played an important role in the discussions and festivities. Maricourt undertook a further mission to Onondaga in 1702.[65]

ONANGUICÉ (?–1701 OR 1702) This Potawatomi, who may have been of Sauk origin, was one of the most influential chiefs in the league of the Great Lakes around 1700.[66] "A man of intelligent mind, and who spoke well," according to Charlevoix,[67] he, like Kondiaronk, had a considerable reputation in the west. La Potherie wrote: "There would have been many negative effects for Canada if this chief had abandoned our interests. He would have taken with him other allies, the complete loss of trade would not have been the only ill we would have had to fear ... The garrisons we might have left in the various posts of these nations would have run the risk every day of having their throats cut."[68] The French, who knew his influence, tried to make him an intermediary for the Pax Gallica, but he always showed a strong spirit of independence. Onanguicé was first received by Frontenac in Montreal in 1679.[69] In 1695 Frontenac criticized him at a conference in Quebec: "I am very happy to see you. I thought that a son I loved had disappeared forever from my presence, and far from following the wishes of his Father, tried to oppose them. This is what I have been told about you but I would like to forget it ... I cleanse you of everything you have done if you do well in the future."[70] Two years later, when the French were abandoning their post in the west, Onanguicé threatened the governor with leaving the alliance. "Onanguicé ... spoke on behalf of all, and said ... that they had often been assured that they would not be left lacking for ammunition, and that was more than a year ago, and they had not been supplied any; that the English did not treat the Iroquois this way and that if they continued to abandon them in this way, they would no longer come to Montreal."[71]

In 1700 he hesitated to come to Montreal to make peace with the Iroquois because he feared that they would not bring their prisoners. In 1701 Callière did not criticize him for his hesitancy. "It was even appropriate," noted La Potherie, "to stifle the resentment that we may have had against him. Onanguicé ... is a true friend of the French. He has given us in these recent wars clear evidence of his loyalty."[72] Onanguicé did not play as important a role as Kondiaronk in the establishment of the Great Peace of Montreal. He was, however, the orator for the Potawatomis, Sauks, and Illinois, and in a special session he declared to Governor Callière, "I am the reason that all the nations of Lake Huron have come [to participate in the conference]."[73] On 6 August he even spoke on behalf of most of the nations of the west. He had come to Montreal in 1701 above all to preserve Onontio's alliance and the special position of his nation within that alliance. He thus expressed his attachment to the role of mediator that the French governor now officially played.[74] Onanguicé died in the months following the peace conference.[75]

OUENEMEK (OUILAMEK)   Ouenemek is – I believe, mistakenly – presented by J. Clifton as being the same person as Ouilamette (or Ouiouilamette), a Loup (Mahican) who had accompanied La Salle on the voyages the explorer undertook around 1680, and who acted as intermediary with the nations of Michigan.[76] Born of a Sauk father and a Fox mother,[77] Ouenemek was a chief of the Potawatomis of the St Joseph River in the seventeenth century. With Onaské, an Odawa chief, he was the leader of a victorious raid against the Iroquois in 1696, and thus contributed to the success of the pro-French factions in the west.[78] He took part in the Montreal peace conference of 1701 but did not have the influence of Onanguicé. In subsequent years, he was an invaluable alliance chief for Onontio in the Great Lakes, although he tried to change the anti-Fox policy of the French after 1712.[79]

OUTOUTAGAN   The son of Le Talon – an important Sable Odawa chief – and brother of Miscouaky, Outoutagan was better known to the French under the name of Jean Le Blanc, a name given to him, reported La Potherie, "because his mother had very white skin."[80] The first mention of Outoutagan seems to date from September 1695, when he represented the Sable Odawas at a conference of the French and the Great Lakes nations. On that occasion, Frontenac said to him:

Your father was always loyal to my voice, and until his death he maintained his youth in the obedience they owe to Onontio ... It is up to you who now occupy his place to imitate him, and you cannot do this better than by vigorously making war with the Iroquois ... I am satisfied that you have come here on purpose, as you assure me, to warn me of the Peace that the Hurons want to make with the Iroquois, and of the collars that they send to them in which it is said you took part ... Otonthagan, my son, perhaps you have been led by surprise into this nasty business, because you are still young, but ... I wish nevertheless to forget it.[81]

A participant in the separate negotiations between the Iroquois and the Odawas around 1694–95, Outoutagan made an about-face in the following years, as shown by his presence in Montreal in 1701. He enjoyed a great deal of prestige in the French-Amerindian alliance at this conference, and on 25 July he was given the privilege of being the first Native delegate to be received by the governor. On 2 and 6 August he spoke on behalf of many Great Lakes nations. "This savage," noted Charlevoix, "possessed much talent, and though strongly attached to the French nation, he saw more clearly than we would have hoped in a matter of such importance."[82] Concerned to defend his people's interests, he discussed at length with Callière problems related to the fur trade and expressed a desire "to prevent the sale of alcohol to anyone among his allies."[83] The following year he went to Detroit and in all likelihood lived out his life there. In the dispute between the Odawas and the Miamis in 1706–7, he tried to exercise a moderating influence and once again represented his people before the French governor.[84]

NICOLAS PERROT (1644–1717) Born in Burgundy around 1644, the son of a justice official, Nicolas Perrot emigrated to Canada in 1660 as a Jesuit lay brother. Initially with the missionaries and then, starting in 1665, on his own, he visited many Native nations, learning their languages and cultures, and in the years 1670–1701 he was New France's most valuable agent in the Great Lakes region. Up to 1698, he made many voyages as an explorer, interpreter, or diplomat while also being involved in the fur trade. Entrusted with maintaining the colony's Amerindian alliances, he took part, in 1684 and then in 1687, in French expeditions against the Senecas, with the mission of convincing the Great Lakes nations to participate. In the 1690s his role on behalf of Frontenac was to constantly push the Odawas, Huron-Petuns, and other allies to make war against the Five Nations. On several occasions he acted as official interpreter in meetings with the Amerindians. For example, in 1670–71 he accompanied Daumont de Saint-Lusson, Louis XIV's delegate, who was charged with taking "possession" of the territories in the west, to Sault Ste Marie; in June 1688, in Montreal, he assisted Denonville in his discussions with the Onondaga chief Otreouti; and finally, in August 1701, he translated Callière's orations for most of the delegates from the west. By that time, he had permanently settled on his land grant at Bécancour, on the St Michel River, which he had obtained in 1677. A captain in the militia from 1708 until his death, which occurred in 1717, he left to posterity a memoir that shows his extensive knowledge of the Great Lakes country.[85]

QUARANTE SOLS (MICHIPICHY) A chief of the St Joseph River Hurons, Michipichy, who was called "Quarante Sols" by the French,[86] played an important part in the negotiation of the Great Peace of Montreal. Charlevoix spoke of him as a "treacherous, dangerous person" who was quick to disavow the French alliance.[87] If this was the case, it must be said that he hid his game admirably in 1701. He was apparently a former Iroquois. In 1695 Kondiaronk said, "I believe the word of Quarante Sols our ally, who, although a prisoner, has urged us not to trust the Iroquois."[88] Kondiaronk's statement is ambiguous. Quarante Sols could have been an Iroquois adopted by the Hurons (a prisoner) and eventually made a chief, but he could also have been a Huron who was temporarily a prisoner of the Iroquois. In 1697 Frontenac said to his allies, "Le Baron and Quarante Sols ... [have] urged the Iroquois to go eat the Miamis."[89] At the conference of 1701, however, Quarante Sols told Callière on behalf of the St Joseph River Hurons that he "made only one body" with the Miamis and Kondiaronk.[90] He even stated on several occasions that he had made a great deal of effort so that Chichicatalo and his people could go to Montreal, building them canoes and giving them many gifts.[91] Quarante Sols spoke in favour of the peace, like all the chiefs present, but stood out at the meeting of 6 August when he castigated Outoutagan, who wanted to stop the sale of alcohol in Michilimackinac.[92] Shortly after the negotiation of the Great Peace of Montreal, Quarante Sols went to Detroit, where he engaged in trade with the Iroquois and the English. He was also the instigator of an intertribal crisis at that post in 1706.[93]

TEGANISSORENS A chief of the Onondaga nation, Teganissorens played a decisive diplomatic role in Iroquoia between 1680 and 1720. In 1682 he went to Montreal and assured Governor Frontenac that the war the Iroquois were then waging in the west against the Illinois and Miamis was in no way directed against the French. He thus managed, until 1684, to prevent any counterattacks by Onontio. In 1688, when he was on his way to Montreal to negotiate a truce with Denonville, Teganissorens and his men were attacked and captured by a war party led by the Huron chief Kondiaronk, who, before releasing the Iroquois, convinced them that the attack had been carried out on behalf of the French. This seemed to put an end to the peace plans, and Teganissorens, very annoyed, had to return to Onondaga. Six years later, the Iroquois leader went to Quebec on behalf of the Five Nations. Frontenac welcomed him with great pomp, but no agreement was concluded. In 1700–1701 he was the strategist for the Five Nations' diplomatic efforts. Devastated by wars, epidemics, and emigration, and weakened by factional manoeuvring, the Iroquois at this time no longer had the means to carry out an aggressive policy. Teganissorens therefore opted for a neutral position between the two European empires and peace with all the members of the French-Amerindian alliance. Until about 1720 he spoke on behalf of the Iroquois on many occasions and endeavoured to maintain the policy established in 1701. Teganissorens appears to have died around 1725, in Sault St Louis, according to Father Charlevoix.[94]

TEKANOET According to La Potherie, at the time of the Great Peace of Montreal, Tekanoet was the "grand chief" of the Senecas.[95]

The first known mention of him is in September 1680, when he participated in a raid against the Illinois. Four years later he was taken hostage by La Barre at Fort Frontenac, and only obtained his release during the negotiations at La Famine, which were led by the Onondaga chief Otreouti. In August 1700 Tekanoet was host to Joncaire, who had just recovered the French prisoners of the Senecas. He went to Montreal the following year for the general peace negotiations. Already very old, he probably died shortly thereafter.[96]

TONATAKOUT   A Seneca chief, Tonatakout belonged to the pro-French faction of the Iroquois Confederacy in the early eighteenth century. In 1700 his people chose him to be "Joncaire's father," succeeding the previous "father," who had recently died and of whom he was the closest relative. As a member of the delegation that went to Montreal in July of that year, he spoke on behalf of the four western nations of the League. A participant in the 1701 conference, he, with Joncaire, presided over the condolence ritual that the Iroquois held for the family of Kondiaronk.[97]

PHILIPPE DE RIGAUD DE VAUDREUIL (c. 1643–1725)   Born into an old noble family in the province of Languedoc, Philippe de Rigaud de Vaudreuil began his military career in 1672 as a musketeer of the king. When he decided to emigrate to Canada in 1687, he was already a veteran of European wars and had distinguished himself in the Dutch war. He became commander of the troops in New France, and as a professional soldier played a very active role in the guerrilla war against the Iroquois in the 1690s. Highly regarded both in the colony and at the court, Vaudreuil in 1699 obtained the post of governor of Montreal, and in 1703, with the death of Callière, that of governor general. With the military and diplomatic experience he had acquired since his arrival in Canada, he governed the colony skilfully until his death in 1725. In particular he succeeded in maintaining peace with the Iroquois, preserving the alliance with the nations in the west, and, despite the Treaty of Utrecht, giving a new impetus to the empire in the Great Lakes region.[98]

APPENDIX 3

English Translation of the Montreal Treaty of 1701

[Beginning of the margin note illegible ...] From the Chevalier Callières Collection of peace treaties

Ratification of the Peace concluded in the month of September last, between the Colony of Canada, its Indian allies, and the Iroquois in a general assembly of the chiefs of each of those nations convened by the Chevalier de Callières, governor and Lieutenant-General of the King in New France.

AT MONTREAL THE FOURTH OF AUGUST 1701

As there were only delegates of the Hurons and the Odawa here last year when I concluded peace with the Iroquois for myself and all my allies, I considered it necessary to send the Sieur de Courtemanche, and the Reverend Father Anjalran [Enjalran] to visit all the other nations that are my allies who were absent to tell them about what had occurred, and to invite chiefs from each nation to come [to Montreal] with the Iroquois prisoners they had in order that they might all, together, hear my words.

It is with extreme joy that I see all my children assembled here now, you Hurons, Sable Odawas, Kiskakons, Sinago Odawas, [Odawas] nation of the Fork, Saulteurs [Ojibwas], Potawatomis, Sauks, Puants [Winnebagos], Folles Avoines [Menominees], Foxes, Mascoutens, Miamis, Illinois, Amikwas, Nipissings, Algonquins, Timiskamings, Crees, Gens des terres, Kickapoos, people from the

Sault, from La Montagne, Abenakis, and you the Iroquois nations, having one and all placed your interests in my hands that I can have you all live in tranquillity; I therefore today ratify the peace agreement that we have made in the month of August last, as I am determined that there be no more talk of the attacks made during the war, and I gather up again all your hatchets, and all your other instruments of war, which I place with mine in a pit so deep that no one can take them back to disturb the tranquillity that I have re-established among my children, and I recommend to you when you meet to treat each other as brothers, and make arrangements for the hunt together so that there will be no quarrels among you, and, so that this peace will not be disrupted, I repeat what I have already said in the treaty we have concluded, that if it happened that one of my children struck another, the one who was attacked should not take revenge, neither he nor any of his people, but he should come to find me so that I can have justice done for him, declaring to you that if the offending party refused to make reasonable satisfaction, I and my other allies will join with the offended party to compel him, which I do not believe would happen, because of the obedience owed to me by my children, who will remember again what we are deciding now together, and so that they will not be able to forget it, I attach my words to the collars I will give to each one of your nations so that the elders may have them carried out by their young people, I invite you all to smoke this calumet which I will be the first to smoke, and to eat meat and broth that I have had prepared for you so that I have like a good father the satisfaction of seeing all my children united.

I shall keep this calumet that was presented to me by the Miamis so that I can have you smoke it when you come to see me.

After all the above-mentioned nations had heard what the Chevalier de Callières said to them, they answered as follows:

THE CHIEF OF THE KISKAKONS I did not want to fail, my father, having learned that you were asking me for Iroquois prisoners, to bring them to you. Here are four that I present to you to do with as you please. It is with this wampum that I have released them and here is a calumet that I give the Iroquois to smoke together when we meet. I rejoice that you have united the land, which was in turmoil, and I willingly subscribe to everything you have done.

THE IROQUOIS   Here we are assembled, our father, as you wished; you planted last year a tree of peace and you gave it roots and leaves so that we would be sheltered there, we now hope that everyone hears what you say, that no one will touch that tree, for we assure you, by these four collars, that we will comply with everything that you have arranged; we are presenting you with two prisoners here with us, and we shall return the others that we have. We hope too, now that the doors are open for peace, that our people will be sent back to us.

THE HURONS   Here we are as you have asked. We present you with twelve prisoners, five of whom want to return with us. As for the seven others you will do with them as you please. We thank you for the peace that you have obtained for us and we ratify it with joy.

JEAN LE BLANC [OUTOUTAGAN], SABLE ODAWA   I obeyed you, my father, as soon as you asked me by bringing you two prisoners of whom you are master. When you commanded me to go to war I did it, and now when you forbid me I obey. I ask you my father with this collar that the Iroquois release to me my flesh that is in their country, and that they send it back to me (that is, the people of his nation).

SANGOUESSY [CHINGOUESSI], SINAGO ODAWA   I did not want to fail to obey your orders, my father, though I have no prisoners, However here are a woman and a child that I have ransomed with whom you will do as you please; and here is a calumet that I give to the Iroquois to smoke as brothers when we meet.

CHICHICATALO, CHIEF OF THE MIAMIS   I have obeyed you, my father, by bringing you eight Iroquois prisoners to do with as you please. If I had had canoes, I would have brought you a greater number, although I do not see here my people who are among the Iroquois. I will bring you those I still have, if you wish, or open the doors for them so that they may return.

ONANGUISSET [ONANGUICÉ] FOR THE SAUKS   I am of one body with you my Father, here is an Iroquois prisoner whom I took in war, in presenting him to you, permit me to give him a calumet to take back to his people to smoke when we meet, I thank you for lighting the sun which has been dark since the war.

ONANGUISSET [ONANGUICÉ], CHIEF OF THE POTAWATOMIS: I will not make you a long speech my father, I have only two prisoners left whom I place beside you to do with as you please. Here is a calumet that I present to you for you to keep, or for you to give to those two prisoners so that they will smoke it in their country. I am always ready to obey even to the death,

MIS8ENSA, CHIEF OF THE OUTAGAMIS [FOXES]: I have no prisoners to return to you, my father, but I thank you for the clear sky you give to the whole world through the peace. For myself I will never lose that light,

THE MASCOUTENS I do not bring you any Iroquois slaves because I have not been at war with them for some time, having amused myself in with making war with other nations, but I have come to obey you and thank you for the peace that you have obtained.

THE FOLLES AVOINES [MENOMINEES] I have only come, my father, to obey you and embrace the peace that you have made between the Iroquois and us.

THE SAULTEURS [OJIBWAS] AND THE PUANTS [WINNEBAGOS] I would have brought you, my father, Iroquois slaves if I had had any, wanting to obey you in whatever you command. I thank you for the light you have given us and I hope that it will be lasting.

THE NIPISSINGS I did not want to fail to come here like the others to listen to your voice. I had an Iroquois prisoner last year whom I returned to you. Here is a calumet that I present to you to give to the Iroquois if you please, so we can smoke together when we meet.

THE ALGONQUINS I have no prisoners to bring to you, my father. The Algonquin is one of your children who has always been yours, and who will be as long as he lives. I pray to the master of life that what you have done today will endure.

THE MIKOIS [AMIKWAS] Having no other desire than yours, I agree to what you have just done,

THE ABENAKIS: Although I am one of the last to speak, I am no less yours, my father. You know that I have always been attached to you, I have no more hatchets. You put them in a pit last year and I will take them up again only when you order me to.

THE PEOPLE FROM THE SAULT You know, you Iroquois, that we are attached to our father, we who dwell with him and live in his bosom. You sent us a collar three years ago to invite us to make peace for you. We sent you one in return. We also give you this one to tell you that we have laboured for that goal. We ask no more than that it be lasting. Do also for you part what needs to be done for peace.

THE PEOPLE FROM LA MONTAGNE You have assembled here, our father, all the nations to make a pile of hatchets and bury them in the ground with your own. As for me who had no other, I rejoice in what you are doing today, and I invite the Iroquois to look on us as brothers.

[Notes by the scribe under the signatures or marks of the chiefs in order]
8entsi8an [Ohonsiowanne], Onondaga; Toarenguenion, Seneca; Soue8on [Soueouon], for the Oneida; Garonhiaron, Cayuga; mark of "Le Rat" [Kondiaronk] chief of the Hurons; Le Brochet [Kinongé] for the Sable Odawas; Mesc8adoue [Meskouadoue], Abenakis of Acadia;8ta8libris [Outaliboi] for the Sinago Odawas; Haronhiateka, chief from the Sault; Mechayon, chief from La Montagne; Kile8iskingie [Kileouiskingié] for the Kiskakons; Ela8esse [Elaouesse] for the Odawas of the Fork; mark of the Missisaugas; mark of the Amikwas chief Mahingan; mark of the Saulteur chief 8abangué [Ouabangué]; mark of the Algonkins; mark of the village the Pangicheas [Piankashaws]; mark of Chichicatallos [Chichicatalo] chief of the village [Miamis]; [under the same pictograph or the same signature as the one before] mark of the village built on the

St Joseph River; mark of 8tilirine? 8tiliriue? [Outilirine], chief; mark of the village of the Kouera Kouitano [Coiracoentanons]; mark of the village of the Peauria [Peorias]; mark of the village of the Tapoueraüa [Tapouaroas]; mark of the village of the Monisgouena [Moingwenas]; mark of the village of the Maroua [Maroas]; [above the following pictograph] a stump and three roots, mark of the village of the Pout8atays [Potawatomis]; mark of the village of Kaskatia [Kaskakias]; [above the following pictogram] a quarry; mark of the village of the Oiatanon [Ouiatenons]; mark of the village; mark of the chief; mark of the Sakis [Sauks]; mark of the village; mark of Kinetouan, chief; mark of the Atagamis [Outagamis]; mark of the village of the Puants [Winnegabos] 8abarich [Ouabarich], chief; mark of the Malouminis (Menominees], chef Paitchico [Paintage] dessant; mark of village Nypynar, Couscain chief dessant; Milchicana dessant

Signed: Le Chevalier de Callière, Bochard de Champigny and others.

Note: "Collier," the term used in the original French treaty and other documents of the period, is straightforwardly translated as "collar" or "necklace" but the term invariably used in English-language documents in the archives of Albany, New York, referring to such exchanges is "belts." However, early accounts refer to Native people wearing and giving "disks" of wampum attached on "colliers" or to "colliers" worn about the neck or body. These seventeenth- and early eighteenth-century forms of wampum can also be seen in early drawings and engravings, although few have survived in museum collections. Thus in certain instances the English term "collar" may be accurate.

The symbol "8" that appears in the names of the Native signatories is derived from a phonetic symbol first used by the Jesuits and the French to approximate a Native consonant sound close to the "W" in Wendat, Wentsiwan, etc. The actual manuscript symbol consists of a Greek epsilon combined with a Greek omega, thus the 'open' appearance of the "8" in the facsimile of the signatures. As typographers of the time had no way of reproducing this symbol, they replaced it with the number 8, which, in turn, eventually made its way into manuscript usage.

The origin and meaning of the word "dessant," which appears after certain names of Native signatories of the treaty, are unknown.

Abbreviations

Notes

Note: Works in the Bibliography are cited in short form in the Notes.

INTRODUCTION

1 La Potherie, *Histoire*, 4:173. (Translators' note [hereafter TN]: our translation.)

2 W.N. Fenton, "Kondiaronk," in *Dictionnary of Canadian Biography* (hereafter *DCB*), 2:323. For more on Kondiaronk's funeral, see chap. 7.

3 Lahontan, *New Voyages*, 2:517–618; Lahontan, *Voyages to North America*, 517–618. T.C. McLuhan, in his well-known book *Touch the Earth* (New York: Outerbridge and Lazard, 1971), does not distinguish between Adario and Kondiaronk; G.E. Sioui (*For an Amerindian Auto-history*, 61–81) also considers them to be one person and sees the *Dialogues* by Lahontan as "an invaluable Amerindian source." Lahontan certainly had occasion to talk with Kondiaronk, in particular at the table of Governor Frontenac (see Lahontan, *Oeuvres*, 29–31; Charlevoix, *Histoire et description*, 2:277). But Adario is only a literary character based on Kondiaronk, and it would be a mistake to put all his words in Kondiaronk's mouth.

4 La Potherie, *Histoire*, 3:101–3. (TN: our translation.)

5 The term "la Grande Paix de Montréal" was coined by the historian Léo-Paul Desrosiers some fifty years ago, although his book had not yet been published (*Iroquoisie*, 4:336).

6 This is an established term designating the five Iroquois nations: the Mohawks, Oneidas, Onondagas, Cayugas, and Senecas (in French, the Agniers, Onneiouts, Onontagués, Goyogouins, and Tsonnontouans). The Five Nations, like the Hurons, belonged to the Iroquoian language family. The other main language family in this part of America was the Algonquian (which included the Algonquins).

7 The word *nation* should be understood in the seventeenth-century sense: in the *ancien régime* of France, it designated a "province" (for example, the Bretons, the Normans) or any group with representatives and specific jurisdictions. The term applies to any unified socio-political entity, any independent collectivity sharing the same culture and able to act collectively in the activities of daily life (hunting, war, trade, etc.): a tribe, but also a confederation, a village, or a single band. In North America, to use European terms, rather loose confederations were divided into several "nations" (this was the case for the Iroquois, but also for the Illinois and the Odawas). See Havard, "Empire et métissages," 136–44, 480–1.

8 This was the main provision of the Montreal agreement.

9 Tanner, ed., *Atlas of Great Lakes Indian History*, 34.

10 Archives nationales de France (hereafter ANF), Col., C11A, vol. 22, f. 102rv, mémoire de Raudot (TN: our translation). See Havard, "Empire et métissages," 221–25, 265.

11 On the problems of ethnohistory and Amerindian history, see Lurie, "Ethnohistory," 78–92; Fenton, "Ethnohistory and Its Problems"; Sturtevant, "Anthropology, History, and Ethnohistory," 1–51; Berkhofer, "New Indian History," 357–82; Carmack, "Ethnohistory," 227–46; Trigger, *The Children of Aataentsic;* 1:1–26; Trigger, "Indian and White History: Two Worlds or One?" in Foster, Campisi, and Mithun, eds., *Extending the Rafters*, 17–33; Trigger, *Natives and Newcomers*, 3–48, 164–72; Axtell, "Ethnohistory of Early America;" Axtell "Ethnohistory: An Historian's Viewpoint"; Jennings, "A Growing Partnership"; Marienstras, "Problèmes d'historiographie américaine"; Martin, ed., *The American Indian and the Problem of History*; Merrell, "Some Thoughts." For a critical discussion of the concept of ethnohistory (one might, for instance, prefer to use the term *history*), see Havard, "Empire et métissages," 16–20.

12 White, *The Middle Ground, xi.*

13 Delâge, "Les principaux paradigmes," 51–67; see also Havard, "Empire et métissages," 17–18.

14 For example, Garneau, *Histoire du Canada*; Lanctôt, *Histoire du Canada*. For a more recent overview, see Mathieu, *La Nouvelle-France*.

15 For example, Peckham, *The Colonial Wars*.

16 The other three volumes were not published until 1998. When *Iroquoisie* came out in 1947, First Nations culture drew little attention. In postwar Quebec there was no interest at all in their history. Historiography concerning New France was then dominated by authors such as F.X. Garneau, G. Lanctôt, and L. Groulx, all of whom focused on describing the heroic aspect of Canadian history and colonization, relegating the "savages" to the background. However, under the pen of Desrosiers, the Amerindians were present on every page; they were actors in history. Only A.G. Bailey, ten years earlier, with *The Conflict of European and Eastern Algonkian Cultures, 1504–1700*, had taken an interest in European-Native relations in Canada. Desrosiers's book, in the wake not only of Bailey's book but also of G.T. Hunt's *The Wars of the Iroquois*, was thus a ground-breaking work. Ahead of its time in many respects, it was met with indifference.

17 Wallace "Origins of Iroquois Neutrality."

18 Aquila, *The Iroquois Restoration*; Jennings, "The Constitutional Evolution"; Jennings, *Ambiguous Iroquois Empire*; Richter, "War and Culture"; Richter, "The Ordeal of the Longhouse"; Richter, *The Ordeal of the Longhouse*; Kent, *The Iroquois Indians*; Haan, "The Covenant Chain"; Haan, "The Problem of Iroquois Neutrality"; Fenton, *The Great Law and the Longhouse*. See also the pioneering work of Allen W. Trelease, *Indian Affairs in Colonial New York*. In these works, the Treaty of Montreal is examined in parallel with the Anglo-Iroquois agreements concluded the same year in Albany.

19 Goldstein, *French-Iroquois Relations*; Eccles, *Frontenac*; Zoltvany, "New France and the West"; Zoltvany, *Vaudreuil*. Works on the policies of various governors of New France provide quite good analysis of French strategies in North America, but pay little attention to the motivations of the Amerindians.

20 Delâge, "L'alliance franco-amérindienne"; Delâge, "Les Iroquois chrétiens, I"; Delâge, "Les Iroquois chrétiens, II"; Delâge, "War and the French-Indian Alliance"; Beaulieu, *Convertir les fils de Caïn*; Beaulieu, *Les autochtones du Québec*; Jetten, *Enclaves amérindiennes*; Grabowski, "The Common Ground"; Grabowski, "Les Amérindiens domiciliés"; Grabowski, "Le petit commerce"; Sawaya, *La fédération des Sept feux*; Vaugeois, ed., *Les Hurons de Lorette*.

21 For example, Clifton, *The Prairie People*; Edmunds, *The Potawatomis*.

22 White, *The Middle Ground*, x, 50, 143–5. White's book lays itself open to certain criticisms, but here is not the place to go into them (see, for example, Havard, "Empire et métissages").

23 Starna, "Concerning the Extent of 'Free Hunting' Territory"; Brandão and Starna, "The Treaties of 1701"; Brandão, *The Fyre shall burn no more.* See also Lytwyn, "Historical Research Report."

24 Alain Beaulieu and Michel Lavoie, "La Grande Paix de Montréal (1701) et l'Arbre de Paix iroquois," paper presented at the 53rd conference of the Institut d'histoire de l'Amérique française, Montreal, 19–21 October 2000.

25 Jennings, *Ambiguous Iroquois Empire.*

26 Havard, *La Grande Paix de Montréal de 1701.*

27 See Havard, "Empire et métissages," 20–7.

28 Eccles, "Report for the Ontario Ministry," 30–1.

29 See Trigger, *Natives and Newcomers*, chap. 3; Trigger, "Pour une histoire plus objective," 202; Trigger, "Ethnohistory," 10. It is also important to pay a great deal of attention to the slightest references to relations among the First Nations and to be sensitive to conflicts among Amerindians, in order to identify their motivations.

30 See Dickinson, "Annaotaha et Dollard"; Trigger, "Pour une histoire plus objective."

31 La Potherie, *Histoire*, 4 vol. This work is an invaluable source on the history of New France. After a detailed account of the expedition of Le Moyne d'Iberville to Hudson Bay in 1697 and a description of the colony on the St Lawrence, the author devotes most of his work to the Iroquois Wars and French-Native diplomacy in the Great Lakes in the late seventeenth century. During his stay in Canada as comptroller of the Marine and of the fortifications, from 1698 to 1701, La Potherie was a well-placed and attentive witness of the delicate negotiations that led to the Great Peace of Montreal. He gathered information on the Amerindians from officers, merchants, and coureurs de bois (Nicolas Perrot was his main informant), and copied down whole sections of the colonial correspondence word for word.

32 Le Blant, *Histoire de la Nouvelle-France*; 1:81. (TN: our translation.)

33 See Jennings, ed., *Iroquois Diplomacy.*

34 Day, "Oral Tradition as Complement."

CHAPTER ONE

1 Jennings, ed., *Iroquois Diplomacy*, 6–7.

2 See Chaunu, *Les Amériques*, 166–7.

3 Jennings, *Ambiguous Iroquois Empire*, 6.

4 English-Dutch and French-English conflicts, for example.

5 Jennings, ed., *Iroquois Diplomacy*, 38.

6 Quoted in Richter, "Iroquois versus Iroquois," 4.

7 See also Delâge, *Bitter Feast*, 110.

8 Jennings, ed., *Iroquois Diplomacy*, 38; Delâge, "L'alliance franco-amérindienne."

9 ANF, Col., CIIA, vol. 17, f. 204, Mémoire touchant le commerce des castors du Canada, 1699.

10 ANF, Col., CIIA, vol. 16, f. 233, Mémoire sur l'état présent de la ferme des castors, Canada, 6 octobre 1698 (TN: our translation). On the price differences between the English and French markets, see ANF, Col., CIIA, vol. 17, f. 48, Callière au ministre, Québec, 7 novembre 1700; ANF, Col., CIIA, vol. 17, f. 59, Champigny au ministre, Québec, 21 septembre 1699; ANF, Col., CIIA, vol. 17, f. 64, Champigny au ministre, Québec, 20 octobre 1699; ANF, Col., CIIA, vol. 17, f. 356, Mémoire sur l'état présent de la ferme des castors, 1699.

11 ANF, Col., CIIA, vol. 12, f. 24, Frontenac au Ministre, Québec, 15 septembre 1692 (TN: our translation). One should not, however, make the mistake of seeing the Amerindians as mere mercenaries; they were acting (or believed they were acting) first and foremost according to their own political interests. See also *The Jesuit Relations* (hereafter JR), 65:204. Similarly, without gifts the Amerindian leaders could not completely control "their" warriors (Haan, "Covenant Chain," 25).

12 Delâge, *Bitter Feast*, 97; Hurley, "Children or Brethren," 65.

13 La Potherie, *Histoire*, 4:131; Charlevoix, *Histoire*, 1:246.

14 The same conclusion was reached by an English officer in New York. See *Documents Relative to the Colonial History of the State of New-York* (hereafter NYCD) 4:977, Lord Cornbury to the Lords of Trade, Orange County, 29 September 1702. See also La Potherie, *Histoire*, 3:195.

15 ANF, Col., B, vol. 22.4, 63, mémoire du Roy à Callière et Champigny, Versailles, 31 may 1701.

16 The French governor called the Amerindians his "children," and he was called "father" by his allies and by the Iroquois at the end of the seventeenth century. See chapter 2. On the systematization of gift giving in European terms, see JR, 15:204–6; ANF, Col., CIIA, vol. 17, f. 103, mémoire du Sieur La Motte Cadillac, 20 octobre 1699.

17 Delâge, "L'alliance franco-amérindienne," 7.

18 See ANF, Col., B, vol. 20.1, 44, présents des sauvages de l'Acadie; ANF, Col., CIIA, vol. 14, f. 305–6, mémoire sur les affaires du Canada, 1696.

19 Jennings, ed., *Iroquois Diplomacy*, 22.

20 Goldstein, *French-Iroquois Relations*, 97.

21 William J. Eccles, "Bochart de Champigny," DCB, 2:73.

22 Lahontan, *New Voyages*, 2:517–618.

23 Charlevoix, *Histoire*, 2:200–1; ANF, Col., CIIA, vol. 15, f. 5, Relation de ce qui s'est passé de plus remarquable en Canada depuis le départ des vaisseaux 1696 jusqu'à ceux de l'automne de l'année suivante 1697. (TN: our translation.)

24 These could be Iroquois with the French or the nations of the west, or the latter with the Iroquois or the English.

25 La Potherie, *Histoire*, 4:84. (TN: our translation.)

26 Ibid., 124. (TN: our translation.)

27 H.C. Burleigh, "Oureouhare," DCB, 1:528.

28 See Charlevoix, *Histoire*, 2:66, 95.

29 Delâge, "Les Iroquois chrétiens, 11," 40. And see, for example, Charlevoix, *Histoire*, 2:170–1, in which he says that the Onondagas had been informed of the French attack of 1696.

30 Hurley, "Children or Brethren," 60–1; Trelease, *Indian Affairs*, 329, 354.

31 La Potherie, *Histoire*, 4:38–9.

32 Another form of democracy.

33 La Potherie, *Histoire*, 3:214 (TN: our translation); see ANF, Col., CIIA, vol. 13, f. 145, Députations et Colliers des Iroquois pour la paix.

34 La Potherie, *Histoire*, 4:84–8.

35 ANF, Col., CIIA, vol. 18, f. 83; La Potherie, *Histoire*, 4:146.

36 It should be noted that the speeches of the Euro-Americans were never made in the name of the colonies, but in the name of their respective kings.

37 See Jennings, ed., *Iroquois Diplomacy*, 3–36, 85–98, 99–114, 115–24; Snyderman, "The Functions of Wampum"; Richter and Merrell, *Beyond the Covenant Chain*, 29–39; Vachon, "Colliers et ceintures de porcelaine chez les Indiens de la Nouvelle-France"; Vachon, "Colliers et ceintures de porcelaine"; Vachon, *Éloquence indienne*, 5–11; Therrien, *Parole et pouvoir*, 126–48; Jennings, *The Invasion of America*, 118–24.

38 On the conclusion of a peace treaty including the French, Iroquois, Odawas and Michilimackinac Hurons, among others.

39 ANF, Col., CIIA, vol. 18, f. 85; ANF, Col., CIIA, vol. 18, f. 64, Callière au ministre, Québec, 16 octobre 1700.

40 Charlevoix, *Histoire*, 2:135.

41 La Potherie, *Histoire*, 3:175.

42 Quoted in La Potherie, *Histoire*, 3:211, 20 (TN: our translation). Other places in the west besides Michilimakinac were used for meetings between the Hurons and Iroquois (La Potherie, *Histoire*, 3:63–4, 260–1; ANF, Col., CIIA, vol. 13, f. 385, Callière au ministre, Montréal, 27 octobre 1695, which speaks of a "meeting in the Niagara area" [TN: our translation] between the Hurons-Odawas and the Senecas).

43 La Potherie, *Histoire*, 3:211. (TN: our translation.)

44 See ANF, Col., F3, vol. 8, f. 260, Instruction pour le Père Bruyas [...], 15 juin 1701.

45 L.M. Stone and D. Chaput, "History of the Upper Great Lakes Area," *Handbook of North American Indians* (hereafter *HNAI*), 15:617.

46 An example is the influence of Onanguicé in the network of French-Amerindian alliances (La Potherie, *Histoire*, 3:302–3).

47 Clastres, *Society against the State*, 153–5.

48 La Potherie, *Histoire*, 4:186; see *ibid.*, 148–9, and *NYCD*, 4:891, Journal of Messrs Bleeker and Schuyler's visit to Onondaga.

49 Iroquois in this case.

50 Charlevoix, *Histoire*, 2:245.

51 Ibid., 250.

52 For example, the Iroquois delegation that came to Quebec in May 1694 (ANF, Col., CIIA, vol. 13, f. 142, Députations et colliers des Iroquois pour la paix).

53 La Potherie, *Histoire*, 3:211.

54 Charlevoix, *Histoire*, 2:237.

55 Ibid., 246.

56 La Potherie, *Histoire*, 3:204; Charlevoix, *Histoire*, 3:212.

57 ANF, Col., CIIA, vol. 11, f. 8, Relation de ce qui s'est passé de plus remarquable [...] novembre 1689 [...] novembre 1690. (TN: our translation.)

58 Lahontan, *New Voyages*, 1:76.

59 The French documents use the term *porcelaine* (cowrie shell).

60 These bands are called collars, probably because the Amerindian ambassadors wore them around their necks.

61 Single strands of wampum might be called strings.

62 ANF, Col., CIIA, vol. 16, f. 168, Callière au ministre, Québec, 15 octobre 1698; other examples: La Potherie, *Histoire*, 3:106, 4:8, 100.

63 Lahontan, *New Voyages*, 2:431.

64 Vachon, *Éloquence indienne*, 5. (TN: our translation.)

65 ANF, Col., CIIA, vol. 11, f. 6, Relation de ce qui s'est passé de plus remarquable [...] novembre 1689 [...] novembre 1690.

66 For Amerindian metaphors, see La Potherie, *Histoire*, 3:101–3.

67 Charlevoix, *Histoire*, 1:264. (TN: our translation.)

68 Quoted in Lahontan, *New Voyages*, 1:84.

69 The forms of diplomatic protocol in northeastern North America gradually became fixed through cultural interaction among the different nations, which was encouraged as a result of contact. For example, the peace pipe appears to be an invention of the nations of the plains (La Potherie, *Histoire*, 2:14; Charlevoix, *Histoire*, 1:264 and 3:212–13).

70 ANF, Col., CIIA, vol. 11, f. 25, Relation [...] novembre 1689 [...] novembre 1690; La Potherie, *Histoire*, 3:97–8. (TN: our translation.)

71 ANF, Col., CIIA, vol. 18, f. 84. (TN: our translation.)

72 See the speech by Cadillac to Amerindian representatives from the west in Michilimakinac in 1695 in La Potherie, *Histoire*, 3:16–18; or the case of Joncaire speaking as if he were an Iroquois delegate, ibid., 3:249.

CHAPTER TWO

1 Delâge, "War and the French-Indian Alliance," 15.

2 Jennings, *Ambiguous Iroquois Empire*, 10–11.

3 Jennings, ed., *Iroquois Diplomacy*, xiv.

4 Jennings, *Invasion of America*, 118. On the Amerindians of the Great Lakes region, cf. Havard, "Empire et métissages," 479–85.

5 Havard, "Empire et métissages," 481–3.

6 Quoted in Charlevoix, *Histoire*, 1:431 (TN: our translation). The name Onontio ("big mountain") is the literal translation into Huron-Iroquois of Montmagny (or Mons Magnus), the name of the first governor of New France (1638–48). It was used as the name of all governors of New France from 1640 on by the Hurons and a little later by the Iroquois, probably at the initiative of the Jesuits (Charlevoix, *Histoire*, 1:226).

7 Eccles, *Essays on New France*, 98–9.

8 Jennings, ed., *Iroquois Diplomacy*, 119; Jennings, *Ambiguous Iroquois Empire*, 44–6.

9 The king of France in the traditional imagery was the father of the people, and Christians, at least at the end of the Middle Ages, were seen as one big diplomatic family whose father was the pope. See Havard, "Empire et métissages," 344–5.

10 See Jennings, "Evolution of the Covenant Chain," 89–90; Jennings, ed., *Iroquois Diplomacy*, 11; Jennings, *Ambiguous Iroquois Empire*, 45;

Nancy Shoemaker, "An Alliance between Men: Gender Metaphors in Eighteenth Century American Indian Diplomacy East of the Mississippi," *Ethnohistory* 46, no. 2 (1999): 253.

11 See La Potherie, *Histoire*, 4:7. In 1695 an Iroquois orator said of Frontenac, "We beseech Onontio to stay the hatchet of his nephews, the people of Lorette [Hurons of Lorette] and the Abenakis" (TN: our translation). Ibid., 7. Sometimes the Iroquois also used the term *children* to symbolize the relationship between Onontio and his settled allies; thus, nothing can be concluded with certainty.

12 See White, *The Middle Ground*, 84–5; Delâge, "Les Hurons de Lorette," 110–14; Havard, "Empire et métissages," 344–60.

13 The metaphor of brothers, which had been prevalent in the time of Huronia (before 1650), was officially supplanted by that of father and children in the 1670s; See ANF, Col., CIIA, vol. 6, f. 7, Montréal, le 13ᵉ août 1682. On the Iroquois, see Charlevoix, *Histoire*, 1:491; Havard, "Empire et métissages," 209.

14 La Potherie, *Histoire*, 1:245; Jennings, ed., *Iroquois Diplomacy*, 119–20.

15 It is possible (but this remains to be proved) that the kinship system of the Iroquois and the Hurons (Iroquoian groups) was the basis of the other Native groups' diplomacy. Cf. Delâge, "Les Hurons de Lorette," 111; Jennings, ed., *Iroquois Diplomacy*, 11.

16 Perrot, *Mémoire*, 72, 78. (TN: our translation.)

17 White, *The Middle Ground*, 143.

18 Delâge, "Les Hurons de Lorette," 112. White, in *The Middle Ground*, tends to underestimate the imperial paradigm.

19 B.G. Trigger, "Early Iroquoian Contacts with Europeans," HNAI, 15:347–51; Delâge, *Bitter Feast*, 95–7; Delâge, "Les Hurons de Lorette," 99–101.

20 E. Tooker, "Wyandot," HNAI, 15:398–9; L.M. Stone and D. Chaput, "History of the Upper Great Lakes Area," HNAI, 15:603; Perrot, *Mémoire*, 93; Goldstein, *French-Iroquois Relations*, 83; Havard, "Empire et métissages," 196.

21 See Charlevoix, *Histoire*, 1:437–9; or La Potherie, *Histoire*, 2:128–30.

22 Eccles, *Canadian Frontier*, 106–10. The main posts were Michilimackinac, on the straits between lakes Huron and Michigan, Fort St Joseph (Niles, Michigan), and Fort St Louis (Starved Rock and then Peoria), on the Illinois River.

23 See La Potherie, *Histoire*, 2:88–90.

24 See ANF, Col., CIIA, vol. 6, f. 11, Montréal, le 13ᵉ août 1682.

25 In the French-Amerindian political conferences held in Montreal in the 1680s, the Odawa delegates usually began the discussions: see, for example, La Potherie, *Histoire*, 3:299–300. On the Potawatomis, see La Potherie, *Histoire*, 2:77–8; 3:302; 4:52; and Charlevoix, *Histoire*, 1:438. On the influence of the Hurons of the Great Lakes in the grand councils of the alliance, see La Potherie, *Histoire*, 2:66; Charlevoix, *Histoire*, 3:199, 258. See also Delâge, "Les Hurons de Lorette," 103; Havard, "Empire et métissages," 214–18.

26 La Potherie, *Histoire*, 4:32–4; DCB, 2:xxxix.

27 ANF, Col., CIIA, vol. 17, f. 64, Champigny au ministre, Québec, 20 octobre 1699. (TN: our translation.) This was a recurring theme in the colonial correspondence.

28 ANF, Col., CIIA, vol. 17, f. 204, mémoire touchant le commerce des castors du Canada, 1699; ANF, Col., CIIA, vol. 13, f. 292, Frontenac au Ministre, Québec, 4 novembre 1695; Lahontan, *New Voyages*, 1:99. It should be noted that at that time there was a great demand in Europe for felt hats, in particular those made of beaver felt.

29 Dechêne, *Habitants and Merchants*, 91.

30 Jacquin, *Les Indiens blancs*, 119; Eccles, *Canadian Frontier*, 125. "Ottawa" (Odawa) is often used in the sources as a generic term for all the groups in the Great Lakes region that were allied with the French (see Smith, "Who Are the Mississauga?"). I am using it in its narrower sense as a "tribal" group. The Odawas were divided into four subgroups: the Sinagos, the Kiskakons, the Sable Odawas, and the Nation of the Fork (La Fourche).

31 ANF, Col., CIIA, vol. 12, f. 125, les P. Jésuites au Ministre, février 1692. (TN: our translation.)

32 ANF, Col., CIIA, vol. 16, f. 6, Frontenac et Champigny au ministre, Québec, 15 octobre 1698; Lahontan, *New Voyages*, 1:271.

33 Charlevoix, *Histoire*, 1:487.

34 Goldstein, *French-Iroquois Relations*, 152.

35 ANF, Col., CIIA, vol. 19, f. 232, Callière, projets sur la Nouvelle Angleterre, 1701.

36 This was true at least initially, since the *Canadiens* had at the very end of the seventeenth century adopted Native military techniques. See the description of the expedition of 1687 in Lahontan, *New Voyages*, 1:121ff.; see also Charlevoix, *Histoire*, 2:196. On the military role of the allies, see Havard, "Empire et métissages," 420–9.

37 Delâge, *Bitter Feast*, 132–3; Dechêne, *Habitants and Merchants*, 81; White, *The Middle Ground*, 128–41; Havard, "Empire et métissages," chap. 9.

38 La Potherie, *Histoire*, 3:94, 2:194–6.

39 Dechêne, *Habitants and Merchants*, 81.

40 La Potherie, *Histoire*, 3:147.

41 Charlevoix, *Histoire*, 1:438.

42 Dechêne, *Habitants and Merchants*, 81.

43 ANF, Col., F3, vol. 8, f. 263, pourparlez entre [...] Callière [...] et les sauvages descendus à Montréal pour la ratification de la paix, 29 juillet 1701. (TN: our translation.)

44 Dechêne, *Habitants and Merchants*, 81.

45 Jennings, *Ambiguous Iroquois Empire*, 81; Delâge, *Bitter Feast*, 136.

46 See, for example, ANF, Col., CIIA, vol. 19, f. 119, Callière au ministre, Québec, 4 octobre 1701.

47 ANF, Col., CIIA, vol. 13, f. 384, Callière au ministre, Montréal, 27 octobre 1695.

48 La Potherie, *Histoire*, 2:87. (TN: our translation.)

49 ANF, Col., F3, vol. 8, f. 261, Pourparlez entre [...] Callière [...] et les sauvages [...], 29 juillet 1701. (TN: our translation.)

50 These were the explorer Louis Jolliet and Father Jacques Marquette.

51 Charlevoix, *Histoire*, 1:446.

52 ANF, Col., CIIA, vol. 6, f. 5–7, Montréal, 13ᵉ aoust 1682.

53 Delâge, "War and the French-Indian Alliance," 15; Delâge, "L'alliance franco-amérindienne," 4.

54 See La Potherie, *Histoire*, 2:249; ANF, Col., CIIA, vol. 15, f. 6–7, Relation de ce qui s'est passé [...] automne 1696 [...] automne 1697.

55 Perrot, *Mémoire*, 84.

56 La Potherie, *Histoire*, 3:60; JR, 64:22–38; on the subject of "rebellious children," see Havard, "Empire et métissages," 431–44.

57 See, for example, ANF, Col., CIIA, vol. 12, f. 203, Relation de ce qui s'est passé [...] septembre 1692 [...] départ des vaisseaux 1693. On the robberies, see White, *The Middle Ground*, 75–6; Havard, "Empire et métissages," 445–8.

58 See DCB, 1:12–15; Speck, "Eastern Algonkian Wakanaki Confederacy."

59 Charlevoix, *Histoire*, 2:121; see also Lahontan, *New Voyages*, 1:327–8.

60 Eccles, *Canada under Louis XIV*, 193; ANF, Col., CIIA, vol. 14, f. 132, L'Acadie (mémoire).

61 See La Potherie, *Histoire*, 3:127.

62 Charlevoix, *Histoire*, 2:121; La Potherie, *Histoire*, 3:188–90; Zoltvany, *Vaudreuil*, 41–2.

63 ANF, Col., CIIA, vol. 16, f. 166, Callière au ministre, Québec, 15 octobre 1698; ANF, Col., CIIA, vol. 15, f. 62, Relation de ce qui s'est passé [...] 1695 [...] 1696.

64 On the Amerindians in the mission villages, see Delâge, "Iroquois chrétiens, 1"; Delâge, "Iroquois chrétiens," 11; Grabowski, "The Common Ground"; Grabowski, "Les Amérindiens domiciliés"; Beaulieu, *Les autochtones*; Sawaya, *La fédération des Sept feux*. Cf. Charlevoix, *Histoire*, 2:126; JR, 29:148; JR, 58:74, 248–50. On the protective function of the réductions, see Charlevoix, *Histoire*, 1:436. On the raids against the Iroquois, see La Potherie, *Histoire*, 4:76; ANF, Col., CIIA, vol. 13, f. 13, Frontenac et Champigny au ministre, Québec, 5 novembre 1694.

65 Quoted in ANF, CIIA, vol. 22, f. 265 (TN: our translation). See also Havard, "Empire et métissages," 222–3.

66 See Charlevoix, *Histoire*, 2:126–8, 151, 170–1; Delâge, "Iroquois chrétiens, 11," 39–40.

67 Jennings, ed., *Iroquois Diplomacy*, 38, 116.

68 The image was of a Dutch ship that Amerindians had tied to a tree using a rope.

69 Jennings, ed., *Iroquois Diplomacy*, 116; Jennings, "Evolution of the Covenant Chain," 89; Jennings, *Ambiguous Iroquois Empire*, 54–5.

70 At least, it gradually became silver: see Richter and Merrell, eds., *Beyond the Covenant Chain*, 41–57.

71 Jennings, ed., *Iroquois Diplomacy*, 116; Jennings, *Ambiguous Iroquois Empire*, 167.

72 Jennings, ed., *Iroquois Diplomacy*, 38; Jennings, "Evolution of the Covenant Chain," 91–2.

73 JR, 64:104; NYCD, 4:654, Negotiation of the Commissioners by the Earl of Bellomont to Onondaga, April 1700; Jennings, *Ambiguous Iroquois Empire*, 166.

74 See, for example, Lahontan, *New Voyages*, 1:58–9.

75 Quoted in Jennings, *Ambiguous Iroquois Empire*, xvi; NYCD, 4:1067, Memorial from Mr Livingston about New York, 1703; see also NYCD, 4:505, Bellomont to the Lords of Trade, 17 April 1699.

76 NYCD, 4:1067; see La Potherie, *Histoire*, 3:126.

77 Jennings, "Evolution of the Covenant Chain," 95.

78 Ibid.; see also Lahontan, *New Voyages*, 1:59, 82; ANF, Col., CIIA, vol. 15, f. 32, Relation de ce qui s'est passé [...] 1697 [...] 1698.

79 Havard, "Paix et interculturalité," 15.

80 White, *The Middle Ground*, 28; Havard, "Empire et métissages," 339–41.

81 See Trigger, "The Mohawk-Mahican War," 285.

82 Eccles, *Frontenac*, 77–8.

83 ANF, Col., CIIA, vol. 9, f. 6, Denonville et Champigny au ministre, Québec, 6 novembre 1687; ANF, Col., CIIA, vol. 15, f. 40, Frontenac et Champigny au ministre, Québec, 19 octobre 1697.

84 Charlevoix, *Histoire*, 2:161. (TN: our translation.)

85 They could also have tried to prevent the Iroquois from destroying their allies, but this was no longer a possibility in the 1690s.

86 Lahontan, *New Voyages,* 1:175–6, 396; La Potherie, *Histoire*, 2:166–8, 197; ANF, Col., CIIA, vol. 15, f. 151, Callière au ministre, Québec, 15 octobre 1697.

87 ANF, Col., CIIA, vol. 13, f. 287, Frontenac au ministre, Québec, 4 novembre 1695; La Potherie, *Histoire*, 3:245, 305–6, 308, and 4:16–19, 38, 72.

88 ANF, Col., CIIA, vol. 11, f. 281, Champigny au ministre, Québec, 12 octobre 1691.

89 ANF, Col., CIIA, vol. 9, f. 152, Denonville au ministre, Canada, 1687; ANF, Col., CIIA, vol. 14, f. 61, Relation de ce qui s'est passé [...] départ des vaisseaux 1695 [...] novembre 1696; ANF, Col., CIIA, vol. 14, f. 120, Frontenac et Champigny au ministre, Québec, 26 octobre 1696.

90 ANF, Col., CIIA, vol. 11, f. 149, mémoire de Callière au marquis de Seignelay; Charlevoix, *Histoire*, 1:541–2.

91 ANF, Col., CIIA, vol. 13, f. 108, Callière au ministre, Montréal, 19 octobre 1694. (TN: our translation.)

92 La Potherie, *Histoire*, 3:220, 4:66, 99–100; ANF, Col., F3, vol. 7, f. 341, Relation [...] 1694 [...] 1695.

93 Quoted in Charlevoix, *Histoire*, 1:535–7 (TN: our translation); Lahontan, *New Voyages*, 1:220–5; Goldstein, *French-Iroquois Relations,* 161–3; Fenton, "Kondiaronk," DCB, 2: 320–2.

94 Charlevoix, *Histoire*, 2:156–7; Jennings, *Ambiguous Iroquois Empire*, 79; in the colonial correspondence, see ANF, Col., CIIA, vol. 17, f. 59, Champigny au ministre, Québec, 27 septembre 1699.

95 Delâge, "L'alliance franco-amérindienne," 6, 13.

96 La Potherie, *Histoire*, 4:24.

97 Ibid., 4:21.

98 ANF, Col., CIIA, vol. 13, f. 401, mémoire: commerce du castor de Canada, 1695; Charlevoix, *Histoire*, 2:161; ANF, Col., B, vol. 19.1,

117, Le Roy à Frontenac et Champigny, Versailles, 26 may 1696; ANF, Col., CIIA, vol. 19, f. 7, Callière et Champigny au ministre, Québec, 5 octobre 1701; Eccles, *Frontenac*, 284.

99 Charlevoix, *Histoire*, 1:346.

100 Perrot, *Mémoire*, 85–91, 100–3; La Potherie, *Histoire*, 2:246–7, 303, and 4:34, 49; ANF, Col., CIIA, vol. 18, f. 66, Callière au ministre, Québec, 26 octobre 1700. Only the Ojibwas were periodically at peace with the Sioux. On the question of the Sioux, see Havard, "Empire et métissages," 464–73.

101 ANF, Col., CIIA, vol. 15, f. 130, Champigny au ministre, Québec, 13 octobre 1697. (TN: Our translation.)

102 These territories should not be considered as belonging to the French as they are in many history books. See Eccles, "Fur Trade," 349–50.

103 ANF, Col., CIIA, vol. 16, f. 90, Champigny au ministre, Québec, 3 juillet 1698; La Potherie, *Histoire*, 3:187.

104 ANF, Col., CIIA, vol. 13, f. 343, Champigny au ministre, Montréal, 17 août 1695; La Potherie, *Histoire*, 4:49–50.

105 La Potherie, *Histoire*, 4:29. Was there also a desire on the part of the nations of the west to ally themselves with the strongest party, as they had in 1690?

106 La Potherie, *Histoire*, 2:330–51.

107 See Trelease, *Indian Affairs*, 204–10.

108 NYCD, 4:488, Bellomont to the Lords of Trade, New York, 13 April 1699.

109 Charlevoix, *Histoire*, 1:545 and 2:138; La Potherie, *Histoire*, 4:12.

110 *JR*, 64:142, 258.

111 Jennings, *Ambiguous Iroquois Empire*, 187.

112 Charlevoix, *Histoire*, 1:502.

113 Jennings, *Ambiguous Iroquois Empire*, 188–9.

114 See Aquila, *The Iroquois Restoration*, 136–7.

115 Elisabeth Tooker, "The League of the Iroquois," HNAI, 15:418; Eccles, *Frontenac*, 99.

116 Jennings, *Ambiguous Iroquois Empire*, 34–5.

117 The Senecas, for example, had as many, if not more, warriors than the other four nations together: T.S. Abler and E. Tooker, "Seneca," HNAI, 15:505.

118 Charlevoix, *Histoire*, 1:539; ANF, Col., F3, vol. 7, f. 343, Relation de ce qui s'est passé [...] départ des vaisseaux 1694 [...] novembre 1695, Champigny.

119 Delâge, "Iroquois chrétiens, II," 41.

120 Charlevoix, *Histoire*, 1:376, 2:89, 138.

CHAPTER THREE

1 Lafitau, *Customs*, 2:98; Lahontan, *New Voyages*, 2:434; Charlevoix, *Journal*, 476; ANF, CIIA, vol. 35, f. 222 (Louvigny). (TN: our translation.) For a more detailed – and not rationalistic – interpretation of Native warfare, see Havard, "Empire et métissages," 149–76.

2 Goldstein, *French-Iroquois Relations*, 48–57.

3 Hunt, *Wars of the Iroquois*, 92–104. Other nations, Algonquins and those further to the west, also had to withdraw towards the west (L.M. Stone and D. Chaput, "History of the Upper Great Lakes Area," HNAI, 15:602.

4 Delâge, *Bitter Feast*, 145, 219.

5 Hunt, *Wars of the Iroquois*.

6 Desrosiers, *Iroquoisie* (4 vols.); Trigger, *Children of Aataentsic*, chap. 8; Trigger, "Early Iroquoian Contacts with Europeans," HNAI, 15:352–4; Trigger, *Natives and Newcomers*, chap. 2; Jennings, *Ambiguous Iroquois Empire*, 89, 175; Delâge, *Bitter Feast*, 142; Aquila, *Iroquois Restoration*, 34–42; Starna, "Concerning the Extent of 'Free Hunting' Territory," 243–8. See also the original (French) version of this book, *La Grande Paix de Montréal* (Recherches amérindiennes au Québec, 1992), written in the late 1980s.

7 Trigger, *Children of Aataentsic*; Delâge, *Bitter Feast*; Aquila, *Iroquois Restoration*; Brandão, "Your Fyre."

8 Richter, "War and Culture," 529–41; Viau, *Enfants du néant*; Brandão, "*Your Fyre*"; Delâge, *Bitter Feast*, 226; Jaenen, "Rapport historique," 170.

9 Charlevoix, *Journal*, 466.

10 Ibid. , 466, 519, 523, 745; Margry, *Découvertes*, 5:89 (Cadillac); ANF, CIIA, vol. 122, f. 211–12 (Raudot); Lafitau, *Customs*, 2:171–2. See Chodowiec, "La hantise et la pratique," 55–69; Viau, *Enfant du néant*; E. Désveaux, "Quadratura Americana. Essai d'anthropologie lévi-straussienne" (thèse d'habilitation, EHESS, 1999). See also Havard, "Empire et métissages," 163–7.

11 Charlevoix, *Journal*, 457.

12 ANF, CIIA, vol. 7, f. 180r (Denonville)

13 Eccles, "Report," 5.

14 Brandão and Starna, "Treaties," 224; Starna, "Concerning the Extent of 'Free Hunting' Territory."

15 Richter, *Ordeal of the Longhouse*, 103–4; Beaulieu, in Desrosiers, *Iroquoisie*, xxv; Desrosiers, *Iroquoisie*, 3:42; Goldstein, *French-Iroquois Relations*, 97–8.

16 On the Iroquois in the 1670s and the birth of the Covenant Chain, see Jennings, *Ambiguous Iroquois Empire*, 133–71.

17 Jennings, *Ambiguous Iroquois Empire*, 175; Richter, "War and Culture," 544; Havard, "Empire et métissages," 201.

18 Quoted by Brandão, "*Your Fyre*," 121.

19 Brandão, "*Your Fyre*," 117–29.

20 Beaulieu, in Desrosiers, *Iroquoisie*, xxviii-xxix.

21 Goldstein, *French-Iroquois Relations*, 60.

22 Trigger, *Natives and Newcomers*, chap. 6; Charlevoix, *Histoire*, 1:319; W.N. Fenton and E. Tooker, "Mohawk," HNAI, 15:469.

23 Goldstein, *French-Iroquois Relations*, 138–40; Jennings, *Ambiguous Iroquois Empire*, 184–5.

24 See Goldstein, *French-Iroquois Relations*, 121–2.

25 Beaulieu, in Desrosiers, *Iroquoisie*, xxiv-xxv.

26 Savard, *L'Algonquin Tessouat*, 167–72; Charlevoix, *Histoire*, 1:246–7; see also Jennings, ed., *Iroquois Diplomacy*, 127–53.

27 W.N. Fenton and E. Tooker, "Mohawk," HNAI, 15:468.

28 Goldstein, *French-Iroquois Relations*, 98; Desrosiers, *Iroquoisie*, 3:41–2.

29 Goldstein, *French-Iroquois Relations*, 63–8.

30 See La Potherie, *Histoire*, 4:36, 59, 97; ANF, Col., C11A, vol. 16, f. 3, Frontenac et Champigny au ministre, Québec, 15 octobre 1698.

31 ANF, Col., C11CMA, vol. 13, f. 105, f. 107, Callière au ministre, Montréal, 19 octobre 1694.

32 La Potherie, *Histoire*, 4:160; ANF, Col., C11A, vol. 16, f. 103, Champigny au ministre, Québec, 14 octobre 1698; ANF, Col., C11A, vol. 17, f. 8, Champigny et Callière au ministre, Québec, 20 octobre 1699; ANF, Col., B, vol. 22.4, f. 5–7, le Roy à Callière et Champigny, Versailles, 31 may 1701.

33 Charlevoix, *Histoire*, 1:528–9; Goldstein, *French-Iroquois Relations*, 158–61.

34 W.J. Eccles, "Brisay de Denonville," DCB, 2:102.

35 Ibid., 108; see Garneau, *Histoire du Canada*, 120–5. According to J.A. Dickinson, there were some fifteen civilians killed on 5 August and eighty soldiers killed the next day (see Champagne, ed., *L'histoire du Régime français*, 75–7).

36 Frontenac had already been governor general of the colony, from 1673 to 1682.

37 Of the thirty-six Iroquois deported, Frontenac returned thirteen. The others had probably died. Eccles, "Brisay De Denonville," DCB, 2:102.

38 Goldstein, *French-Iroquois Relations*, 171–2.
39 Ibid., 173–4; Charlevoix, *Histoire*, 1:562–6; La Potherie, *Histoire*, 3:61–74.
40 Brandão, "*Your Fyre*," 125.
41 ANF, Col., CIIA, vol. 12, f. 197–9, Relation de ce qui s'est passé [...] septembre 1692 [...] départ des vaisseaux 1693.
42 ANF, Col., CIIA, vol. 13, f. 104, Callière au ministre, Montréal, 19 octobre 1694; Goldstein, *French-Iroquois Relations*, 181; La Potherie, *Histoire*, 3:191.
43 See La Potherie, *Histoire*, 3:204–18 (quotation, p. 213 [TN: our translation]); Richter, *Ordeal of the Longhouse*, 180–1.
44 See La Potherie, *Histoire*, 3:230–46 (quotation, p. 243 [TN: our translation]); Charlevoix, *Histoire*, 2:141; ANF, Col., CIIA, vol. 13, f. 4–5, Frontenac et Champigny au ministre, Québec, 5 novembre 1694; ANF, Col., F3, vol. 7, f. 170–9; Goldstein, *French-Iroquois Relations*, 184–5.
45 ANF, Col. F3, vol. 7, f. 181–5 (quotation, f. 183v [TN: our translation]); La Potherie, *Histoire*, 3:248–50.
46 ANF, Col., CIIA, vol. 14, f. 178, mémoire sur le Canada, 1695. (TN: our translation.)
47 Ibid.; Richter, *Ordeal of the Longhouse*, 184.

CHAPTER FOUR

1 Peckham, *Colonial Wars*, 52–3.
2 Haan, "Covenant Chain," 58–9.
3 Quoted in Jennings, *Ambiguous Iroquois Empire*, 186, 206.
4 Another English-Dutch report speaks of 130 Mohawk warriors in 1691 (NYCD, 3:815, The Civil and Military Officers to the Commander in chief, Albany, December 30, 1691).
5 NYCD, 4:337, Comparative Population of Albany and of the Indians in 1689 and 1698, April 19, 1698; Jennings, *Ambiguous Iroquois Empire*, 206; Richter, "War and Culture," 542–3, 551; Brandão, "*Your Fyre*," 126, 153–8.
6 Richter, "War and Culture," 551; NYCD, 4:768, Bellomont to the Lords of Trade, New York, October 24, 1700; ANF, Col., CIIA, vol. 19, f. 232, Callière au ministre, Canada, 1701; La Potherie, *Histoire*, 3:44. In comparison, the non-Native population of New France increased from 10,523 to 12,786 between 1688 and 1695 (Eccles, *Canada under Louis XIV*, 201).
7 Richter, "War and Culture," 544–8; JR, 62:184. See the estimate of 1,500 Seneca warriors in 1681 in JR, 62:162. Brandão estimates the

number of Amerindians captured by the Iroquois in the seventeenth century at more than 6,000 (between 6,087 and 6,971) ("*Your Fyre,*" 73).

8 *NYCD*, 4:39, Propositions made by the Maquas Indians to B. Fletcher, June 21, 1693. The lament of the Iroquois also refers to the migrations to New France. See *NYCD*, 4:55, Fletcher to the Committee of Trade, October 9, 1693.

9 Charlevoix, *Histoire*, 2:108.

10 Ibid., 112, 115; *NYCD*, 3:815; Eccles, *Frontenac*, 248–51; ANF, Col., CIIA, vol. 11, f. 97, Callière au ministre, 20 septembre 1692.

11 Goldstein, *French-Iroquois Relations*, 150–3.

12 La Potherie, *Histoire*, 1:323; see also Jennings, *Ambiguous Iroquois Empire*, 205–6. (TN: our translation.)

13 Charlevoix, *Histoire*, 2:126–8; Richter, "War and Culture," 546–7.

14 ANF, Col., CIIA, vol. 14, f. 48–62, Relation de ce qui s'est passé de plus remarquable […] départ des vaisseaux de 1695 […] novembre 1696; La Potherie, *Histoire*, 3:271–3; Charlevoix, *Histoire*, 2:168–75; Eccles, *Frontenac*, 265–7.

15 ANF, Col., CIIA, vol. 14, f. 149, Frontenac au ministre, Québec, 25 octobre 1696; Eccles, *Frontenac*, 266–7; Haan, "Covenant Chain," 62; Aquila, *Iroquois Restoration*, 70–1.

16 Charlevoix, *Histoire*, 2:136. (TN: our translation.)

17 Quoted in La Potherie, *Histoire*, 3:152 (TN: our translation); see also p. 162. Cf. *NYCD*, 4:294, Messrs Schuyler, Dellius and Wessels to Governor Fletcher, Albany, September 28, 1697; see also La Potherie, *Histoire*, 2:195.

18 La Potherie, *Histoire*, 3:132 (TN: our translation); see also ANF, Col., CIIA, vol. 11, f. 49, Relation […] novembre 1689 […] novembre 1690; ANF, Col., CIIA, vol. 12, f. 7, Frontenac et Champigny au ministre, Québec, 15 septembre 1692.

19 Charlevoix, *Histoire*, 2:136. The colonial correspondence also provides many accounts of these raids: see ANF, Col., CIIA, vol. 11, f. 207, journal du Sr de Courtemanche, 1691; ANF, Col., CIIA, vol. 11, f. 234, Frontenac au ministre, Québec, 20 octobre 1691; ANF, Col., CIIA, vol. 11, f. 258, Champigny au ministre, Québec, 10 mai 1691; ANF, Col., CIIA, vol. 11, f. 266, Mémoire instructif sur le Canada, 10 mai 1691; ANF, Col., CIIA, vol. 12, f. 95, Relation de ce qui s'est passé en Canada au sujet de la guerre […] novembre 1691 […] octobre 1692, Champigny. See also Charlevoix, *Histoire*, 2:100, 155; La Potherie, *Histoire*, 3:136.

20 ANF, Col., CIIA, vol. 13, f. 19, Frontenac et Champigny au ministre, Québec, 5 novembre 1694; see also ANF, Col., CIIA, vol. 13, f. 340, Champigny au ministre, Montréal, 11 août 1695; ANF, Col., CIIA, vol. 13, f. 383, Callière au ministre, Montréal, 27 octobre 1695.

21 Charlevoix, *Histoire*, 2:163; La Potherie, *Histoire*, 3:266.

22 ANF, Col., CIIA, vol. 11, f. 24, Frontenac au ministre, Québec, 15 septembre 1692. (TN: our translation.)

23 Quoted in Charlevoix, *Histoire*, 2:112, 199; ANF, Col., CIIA, vol. 15, f. 148, Callière au ministre, Québec, 15 octobre 1697.

24 Aquila, *Iroquois Restoration*, 77.

25 NYCD, 4:648, Robert Livingston's Report of his Journey to Onondaga, April 1700.

26 Jennings, *Ambiguous Iroquois Empire*, 208.

27 JR, vol. 64:62. (TN: our translation.)

28 Delâge, *Bitter Feast*, 88.

29 Jacquin, *Les Indiens blancs*, 84.

30 Charlevoix, *Histoire*, 2:88–91 (TN: our translation); La Potherie, *Histoire*, 3:122, 127; Trelease, *Indian Affairs*, 304–5.

31 NYCD, 4:195, Journal of Major General Winthrop's March from Albany to Wood Creek, N. York, Sept. 18, 1696.

32 JR, 62:66, 100; Haan, "Covenant Chain," 46; Hurley, "Children or Brethren," 17; Aquila, *Iroquois Restoration*, 72.

33 Jennings, *Ambiguous Iroquois Empire*, 196, 205; Trelease, *Indians Affairs*, 314–16; Eccles, *Frontenac*, 267. The inadequacy of English aid is explained in part by the lack of cooperation among the British colonies.

34 Haan, "Covenant Chain," 59.

35 I am simplifying here. The relations of the Iroquois with the Odawas could, in fact, differ greatly from those with the Miamis, for example.

36 Haan, "Covenant Chain," 59.

37 La Potherie, *Histoire*, 3:296.

38 Clastres, *Society against the State*, 189–218.

39 Delâge, *Bitter Feast*, 224–5; Charlevoix, *Histoire*, 1:323.

40 I am here referring to the peace process as the French saw it, that is, as the negotiation of a treaty independent of the English.

41 ANF, Col., CIIA, vol. 16, f. 165, Callière au ministre, Québec, 15 octobre 1698.

42 See La Potherie, *Histoire*, 3:231–4. Two years later the Cayugas came very close to being attacked by the French, since a peace treaty had not been concluded yet (Charlevoix, *Histoire*, 2:174).

43 Haan, "Covenant Chain," 23–5. Beyond their political role, the gifts made it possible to reduce social tensions through a redistribution of wealth.

44 On the problem of factions among the Amerindians, see Fenton, "Locality as a Basic Factor"; Fenton, "Factionalism"; Berkhofer, "New Indian History"; Haan, "Covenant Chain," 22–3, 27; Aquila, *Iroquois Restoration*, 76–7.

45 See Trelease, *Indian Affairs*, 337–40.

46 See Jennings, *Ambiguous Iroquois Empire*, 95.

47 The success of the missionaries – when it occurred – is explained by specific social conditions, not by an outburst of Christian spirituality among the Amerindians. See Delâge, "La religion dans l'alliance."

48 See *JR*, 55:54–64, 58:208.

49 Charlevoix, *Histoire*, 1:236.

50 See Richter, "Iroquois versus Iroquois."

51 *NYCD*, 4:1067, Memorial from Mr Livingston about New York, 1703; ANF, Col., CIIA, vol. 16, f. 70–1, Bellomont à Frontenac, N. York, 13 août 1698; Richter and Merrell, eds., *Beyond the Covenant Chain*, 24.

52 Haan, "Covenant Chain," 47. The situation here is presented in simplified terms. We should not lose sight of the political and social factors underlying the religious issue.

53 Aquila, *Iroquois Restoration*, 77.

54 Haan, "Covenant Chain," 42. The deaths in the 1680s of many Iroquois leaders capable of influencing their compatriots and creating consensus also contributed to the development of factions, and consequently to the deadlock of political institutions. See La Potherie, *Histoire*, 3:151, 208; Haan, "Covenant Chain," 62–3.

55 Aquila, *Iroquois Restoration*, 76; Richter, *Ordeal of the Longhouse*, 257–8.

56 La Potherie, *Histoire*, 2:232.

57 See Charlevoix, *Histoire*, 2:201–2; ANF, Col., CIIA, vol. 15, f. 10–13, Relation de ce qui s'est passé [...] départ des vaisseaux 1696 [...] automne 1697. The war of harassment continued, but on a much smaller scale than in the period from 1689 to 1693.

58 Haan, "Covenant Chain," 60.

59 La Potherie, *Histoire*, 3:285; Charlevoix, *Histoire*, 2:199. (TN: our translation.)

60 Or, at the very least, factions anxious to establish peace.

61 ANF, Col., CIIA, vol. 15, f. 148, Callière au ministre, Québec, 15 octobre 1697 (TN: our translation); Charlevoix, *Histoire*, 2:199–200.

62 There may be some basis for this: ANF, Col., CIIA, vol. 15, f. 11, Relation [...] 1696 [...] 1697: "the Aniers [Mohawk] chiefs charged this savage [from Sault St Louis] with a collar to say to the people of the Sault, their brothers, that they were weary of war, and that they had resolved to come and live with them ... but that this was done in secrecy for fear of being prevented from doing this by the English" (TN: our translation). Subsequent events, however, seem to invalidate this hypothesis: see ANF, Col., CIIA, vol. 15, f. 152, Callière au ministre, Québec, 15 octobre 1697.

63 If so, the purpose of the presence of the two captives would have been not only to make an exchange, but also to ensure the safety of the delegates.

64 ANF, Col., CIIA, vol. 15, f. 10, Relation [...] 1696 [...] 1697.

65 Delâge, "Iroquois chrétiens, II," 41.

66 Charlevoix, *Histoire*, 2:267–8.

67 See, for example, Charlevoix, *Histoire*, 2:142.

68 ANF, Col., CIIA, vol. 16, f. 3, Frontenac et Champigny au ministre, 15 octobre 1698; La Potherie, *Histoire*, 3:243.

69 Quoted in Margry, *Découvertes*, 5:94.

70 Haan, "Covenant Chain," 67–8.

71 Ibid., 30; La Potherie, *Histoire*, 2:24, 4:191.

72 La Potherie, *Histoire*, 4:157.

73 Haan, "Covenant Chain," 69; W.J. Eccles, "Teganissorens," DCB, 2:619–23.

74 The Onondagas had apparently decided to send two delegates, but "the sending of ... collars was diverted by the disagreement of some young people who wanted to avenge the death of an important person of their nation ... and of six others" (La Potherie, *Histoire*, 3:296 [TN: our translation]). Skirmishes continued in various places (most often at the expense of the Iroquois), and it is evident that certain men's desire to make war contributed to the divisions in the Iroquois League. See also ANF, Col., CIIA, vol. 15, f. 150, Callière au ministre, Québec, 15 octobre 1697.

75 ANF, Col., CIIA, vol. 15, f. 149–51, Callière au ministre, Québec, 15 octobre 1697; Haan, "Covenant Chain," 73. (TN: our translation.)

76 It was up to the elements favourable to peace to convince their recalcitrant compatriots.

77 It may also have been to gain time. See Haan, "Covenant Chain," 75–6.

78 ANF, Col., CIIA, vol. 15, f. 12, Relation [...] 1696 [...] 1697; ANF, Col., CIIA, vol. 15, f. 151–2, Callière au ministre, Québec, 15 octobre 1697.

79 ANF, Col., CIIA, vol. 15, f. 22–3, Relation [...] départ des vaisseaux de 1697 [...] 20e octobre 1698. (TN: our translation.)

80 Haan, "Covenant Chain," 76.

81 ANF, Col., CIIA, vol. 15, f. 24–5, Relation [...] 1697 [...] 1698.

82 ANF, Col., CIIA, vol. 16, f. 165, Callière au ministre, Québec, 15 octobre 1698.

83 With the exception, however, of the Great Lakes nations, who, depending on the tribes and factions, still combined war and negotiation on the western frontier.

84 ANF, Col., B, vol. 20.1, p. 53, Le ministre à Frontenac, Versailles, 12 mars 1698; Haan, "Covenant Chain," 77–8; see Charlevoix, *Histoire*, 2:201.

85 Trelease, *Indian Affairs*, 336.

86 See ANF, Col., CIIA, vol. 16, f. 63, Frontenac et Champigny au ministre, Québec, 25 octobre 1698; ANF, Col., CIIA, vol. 16, f. 167, Callière au ministre, Québec, 15 octobre 1698.

87 Haan, "Covenant Chain," 106.

88 Commissaries were appointed on both sides to solve the problem of the borders of Iroquoia.

89 Bellomont was governor of New York from 1698 to 1701.

90 ANF, Col., CIIA, vol. 16, f. 166, Callière au ministre, Québec, 15 octobre 1698; Charlevoix, *Histoire*, 2:226.

91 ANF, Col., CIIA, vol. 16, f. 66–7, Bellomont à Frontenac, New York, 22 avril 1698.

92 ANF, Col., CIIA, vol. 16, f. 66, Frontenac à Bellomont, Québec, 8 juin 1698. It was traditional for the French to assert the "right of discovery" to justify sovereignty or possession of a territory. A memoirist thus stated categorically in 1698 that "the sovereignty of the King over the Iroquois is very ancient and dates back to about the year 1504" (ANF, Col., CIIA, vol. 16, f. 194, mémoire, souveraineté du Roy sur les Iroquois [TN: our translation]; see ANF, Col., CIIA, vol. 16, f. 167–70, Callière au ministre, Québec, 15 octobre 1698). Imagine the reverse: A Native person crossing the Atlantic in 1500, landing in Brittany, and declaring it his by virtue of the "right of discovery." The "right of conquest," traditionally invoked by the English (see Charlevoix, *Histoire*, 2:235), was also used on occasion by the French: see, for example, ANF, Col., CIIA, vol. 19, f. 40–2, acte de prise de possession du païs des Iroquois dit sonnontouans, 19 juillet 1687. For more on these issues, see Hurley, "Children or Brethren," 252–67.

93 Charlevoix, *Histoire*, 2:227–8 (TN: our translation); see Hurley, "Children or Brethren," 235–42.

94 ANF, Col., CIIA, vol. 16, f. 166, Callière au ministre, Québec, 15 octobre 1698; ANF, Col., CIIA, vol. 15, f. 25, Relation [...] 1697 [...] 1698. (TN: our translation.)

95 ANF, Col., CIIA, vol. 15, f. 26, Relation [...] 1697 [...] 1698.

96 ANF, Col., CIIA, vol. 15, f. 30–1, Relation [...] 1697 [...] 1698 (TN: our translation); ANF, Col., CIIA, vol. 16, f. 168, Callière au ministre, Québec, 15 octobre 1698; La Potherie, *Histoire*, 3:98–100.

97 Peter Wraxall, *An Abridgement of the Indian Affairs Contained in Four-Folio Volumes, Transacted in the Colony of New York, From Year 1678 to Year 1751* (Cambridge: Harvard University Press, 1915), 29; ANF, Col., CIIA, vol. 16, f. 169, Callière au ministre, Québec, 15 octobre 1698; Charlevoix, *Histoire*, 2:228–9; Haan, "Covenant Chain," 83–5; Trelease, *Indian Affairs*, 340.

98 Charlevoix, *Histoire*, 2:231; Trelease, *Indian Affairs*, 341; Haan, "Covenant Chain," 87.

99 ANF, Col., CIIA, vol. 16, f. 170, Callière au ministre, Québec, 15 octobre 1698; ANF, Col., CIIA, vol. 15, f. 36, Relation [...] 1697 [...] 1698.

100 Trelease, *Indian Affairs*, 341; Haan, "Covenant Chain," 90. Note Trelease's error, p. 342; he seems to confuse English statements with French actions. In addition, the Mohawks, who were very attached to Albany, had already refused to make such a journey to Montreal.

101 D.H. Corkhran, "Ohonsiowanne," DCB, 2:502; D.J. Horton, "Le Moyne de Maricourt," DCB, 2:404; NYCD, 4:492–3, Propositions by the Sachems of Onondaga and Oneida, Albany, February 3, 1699; Haan, "Covenant Chain," 91.

102 Frontenac had died the previous November, and Callière, the governor of Montreal, had replaced him at the negotiations. He was officially appointed governor general the following September.

103 The Senecas, Mohawks, and Cayugas were not part of this delegation.

104 Quoted in La Potherie, *Histoire*, 4:115–18; ANF, Col. F3, vol. 8, f. 143–4, Parolles adressées à Callière [...] par trois députés iroquois, 8 mars 1699 (TN: our translation); Charlevoix, *Histoire*, 2:237–8.

105 C. Colden, quoted in Fenton, *The Great Law and the Longhouse*, 322.

106 La Potherie, *Histoire*, 4:118–20. (TN: our translation.) See also ANF, Col., F3, vol. 8, f. 144–6, réponse faite par Callière aux paroles [des Iroquois]; ANF, Col., F3, vol. 8, f. 137, Callière [...] aux dix nations outaouaises, Montréal, 12 juillet 1699; ANF, Col., CIIA, vol. 17, f. 25–6, Callière au ministre, Montréal, 2 mai 1699; ANF, Col., CIIA,

vol. 17, f. 29–30, Callière au ministre, Montréal, 2 juin 1699. The inclusion of the allies in the peace was a leitmotiv in French policy during these years, contrary to what is said by Haan, "Covenant Chain," 93.

107 And also because there would not have been time to inform these nations.

108 La Potherie, *Histoire*, 4:121; Charlevoix, *Histoire*, 2:258.

109 Haan, "Covenant Chain," 94–6; Wraxall, *Abridgement*, 32; Jennings, ed., *Iroquois Diplomacy*, 164.

110 La Potherie, *Histoire*, 4:123–6; ANF, Col., F3, vol. 8, f. 140, Parolles des Iroquois à Callière, 20 septembre 1699; ANF, Col., CIIA, vol. 17, f. 38, Callière au ministre, 20 octobre 1699.

111 Quoted in La Potherie, *Histoire*, 4:126–31; ANF, Col., F3, vol. 8, f. 141, Réponses de Callière aux Iroquois, 22 septembre 1699.

CHAPTER FIVE

1 La Potherie, *Histoire*, 1:225; Delâge, *Bitter Feast*, 145.

2 See Havard, "Empire et métissages," 433–4.

3 *NYCD*, 4:735, Conference of the Earl of Bellomont with the Indians, Albany, August 29, 1700; *NYCD*, 4:501, Memorial of Robert Livingston Recommending a Trade with the Western Indians, 1699. See also Jennings, *Ambiguous Iroquois Empire*, 133–76; Richter, *Ordeal of the Longhouse*, 133–50.

4 Quoted by Brandão and Starna, "Treaties," 218.

5 Beaulieu and Lavoie, "La Grande Paix de Montréal." On the League legend, see Fenton, *The Great Law and the Longhouse*, 51–103; on the Tree of Peace, ibid., 103 (quotation), 308.

6 Charlevoix, *Histoire*, 1:407. (TN: our translation.)

7 *JR*, 60:211.

8 Charlevoix, *Histoire*, 1:502, 513, 521; La Potherie, *Histoire*, 2:201; ANF, Col., CIIA, vol. 9, f. 21–2, Denonville au ministre, Montréal, 8 juin 1687.

9 La Potherie, *Histoire*, 2:302.

10 See La Potherie, *Histoire*, 2:231–43, 300–2, and 3:63–4, 100; Charlevoix, *Histoire*, 1:563, 566–70, and 2:57, 61–2; Havard, "Empire et métissages," 436–9; Wallace, "Origins of Iroquois Neutrality," 226–8.

11 ANF, Col., CIIA, vol. 13, f. 105–7, Callière au ministre, Montréal, 19 octobre 1694; ANF, Col., CIIA, vol. 13, f. 44. De ce qui s'est passé pendant l'année [...] 1694.

12 See La Potherie, *Histoire*, 2:316–23 (quotation p. 318 [TN: our translation]).

13 Delâge, "L'alliance franco-amérindienne," 6.

14 La Potherie, *Histoire*, 3:260–7; ANF, Col., CIIA, vol. 14, f. 40–6, Relation [...] 1695 [...] 1696; ANF, Col., CIIA, vol. 14, f. 119, Frontenac et Champigny au ministre, Québec, 26 octobre 1696; ANF, Col., CIIA, vol. 14, f. 154, Frontenac au ministre, Québec, 25 octobre 1696; Charlevoix, *Histoire*, 2:156–7, 163; see La Potherie, *Histoire*, 4:14–30, 48–73.

15 See, for example, ANF, Col., CIIA, vol. 15, f. 151, Callière au ministre, Québec, 15 octobre 1697, which reports a war between the Ojibwas and the Miamis in which the Odawas were ready to join on the side of the Ojibwas. See also La Potherie, *Histoire*, vol. 2, which provides detailed accounts of the tensions and wars in the Great Lakes.

16 La Potherie, *Histoire*, 4:38–9.

17 From an economic point of view, the French were a very mediocre partner for the Amerindians. We have already noted that English prices were much more competitive than French prices (ANF, Col., CIIA, vol. 9, f. 149, Lagny, Canada, 1687; ANF, Col., CIIA, vol. 10, f. 343, Différences de traittes avec les sauvages entre Montréal en Canada et Orange [Albany] a la nouvelle angleterre, 1689; see also ANF, Col., CIIA, vol. 14, f. 99, Relation [...] 1694 [...] 1695). Albany also seemed to attract the Amerindians of the west because they expected that it would be easier to buy brandy there, whereas the missionaries living in their midst sought to keep them from drinking (La Potherie, *Histoire*, 4:78).

18 Especially the prospect of hunting without risk (La Potherie, *Histoire*, 1:226–7).

19 La Potherie, *Histoire*, 4:16–20.

20 Ibid., 54.

21 ANF, Col., CIIA, vol. 13, f. 296, Frontenac au ministre, Québec, 10 novembre 1695 (TN: our translation); see also La Potherie, *Histoire*, 2:301. The Miamis nevertheless also had positive contacts with the Covenant Chain, since the English, "through the Loups [Mahicans]," sent them gifts to encourage them to bring their trade to Albany (TN: our translation) (cf. ANF, CIIA, vol. 12, f. 202–3, Relation [...] 1693 [...] 1694; La Potherie, *Histoire*, 3:186).

22 La Potherie, *Histoire*, 4:15; see also ANF, Col., CIIA, vol. 13, f. 292, Frontenac au ministre, Québec, 4 novembre 1695.

23 Perrot, *Mémoire*, 143–5. (TN: our translation.)

24 La Potherie, *Histoire*, 1:226–7; La Potherie, *Histoire*, 2:319, 353, and 3:260–7, 288; La Potherie, *Histoire*, 3:240. It should be noted that the factions among the Odawas were not in any way generated or aggravated by missionary action, which was very limited there. In general, the Amerindians of the west who negotiated with the Iroquois at the end of the seventeenth century were from around Michilimackinac (La Potherie, *Histoire*, 4:52). On the Fox factions, see La Potherie, *Histoire*, 2:314–15 ("The son of the great chief of the Outagamis [Foxes] came to [Green] Bay, where he had secret discussions with a Frenchman ... people of his nation did what they could to prevent him" [TN: our translation]).

25 ANF, Col., F3, vol. 8, f. 4, Relation de ce qui s'est passé en Canada au sujet de la guerre depuis le départ des vaisseaux de l'année 1696 jusqu'au mois d'octobre 1697, Champigny, 18 octobre 1697; Charlevoix, *Histoire*, 2:213. "Thirty families" is approximately 150 people, quite a large number. See, however, ANF, Col., CIIA, vol. 15, f. 11, Relation de ce qui s'est passé de plus remarquable [...] 1696 [...] 1697, where the reference is to "thirty Hurons" and not "thirty families."

26 La Potherie, *Histoire*, 4:97.

27 La Potherie, *Histoire*, 3:299; ANF, Col., CIIA, vol. 15, f. 14, Relation [...] 1696 [...] 1697; ANF, Col., CIIA, vol. 15, f. 39, Frontenac et Champigny au ministre, Québec, 19 octobre 1697.

28 ANF, Col., CIIA, vol. 18, f. 79–80, Callière, 21 juin 1700. (TN: our translation.)

29 *NYCD*, 4:691, Messrs Groenendyke and Provost to Commissioners for Indian Affairs, Albany, June 16, 1700; *NYCD*, 4:694–5, Propositions of the Five Nations to the Commissioners of Indian Affairs, Albany, June 30, 1700; *NYCD*, 4:691; Brandão and Starna, "Treaties," 217–18; Richter, *Ordeal of the Longhouse*, 202; Haan, "Covenant Chain," 110–11.

30 Dechêne, *Habitants and Merchants*, 75.

31 Since 1681, the governor and the intendant had granted twenty-five congés or trading permits a year, each authorizing three men, with one canoe, to go trade in the West. This edict was easily circumvented, Frontenac usually doubling the manpower for departures for the Great Lakes. See W.J. Eccles, "Bochart de Champigny," *DCB*, 2:76–7.

32 ANF, Col., B, vol. 19.1, p. 105–6, Declaration du Roy [...] Versailles le 23 may 1696; ANF, Col., B, vol. 19.1, p. 117, le Roy à Frontenac et Champigny, Versailles, 26 may 1696.

33 ANF, Col., CIIA, vol. 14, f. 123, Frontenac et Champigny au ministre, Québec, 26 octobre 1696; see also ANF, Col., CIIA, vol. 14, f. 158, Frontenac au ministre, Québec, 25 octobre 1696. (TN: our translation.)

34 ANF, Col., B, vol. 19.3, p. 71–2, Ordonnance pour la conservation des postes [...] Versailles, 28 avril 1697.

35 ANF, Col., F3, vol. 8, f. 25, Ordonnance du Roy portant deffenses [...] de faire la traitte avec les sauvages dans la profondeur des bois, Versailles, 28 avril 1697. For further information on this, see Eccles, *France in America*, 99; William J. Eccles, "A Belated Review of Harold Adams Innis' *The Fur Trade in Canada*," in *Essays on New-France* (Toronto: Oxford University, 1987), 64–5; Zoltvany, "New-France and the West," 301–5.

36 ANF, Col., CIIA, vol. 16, f. 219, Observations sur la ferme des castors de Canada, Québec, 27 octobre 1698.

37 ANF, Col., CIIA, vol. 15, f. 151, Callière au ministre, Québec, 15 octobre 1697.

38 Quoted in La Potherie, *Histoire*, 3:302; ANF, Col., CIIA, vol. 15, f. 15, Relation [...] 1696 [...] 1697. (TN: our translation.)

39 La Potherie, *Histoire*, 3:302.

40 ANF, CIIA, vol. 10, f. 67, Denonville au ministre, Québec, 10 août 1688. (TN: our translation.)

41 See, for example, ANF, Col., CIIA, vol. 17, f. 6–8, Callière et Champigny au Ministre, Québec, 20 octobre 1699.

42 Several conferences of this kind were held either in Montreal or Quebec between 1695 and 1701. In 1695 Frontenac met with representatives of the Ojibwas, the Sable Odawas, and the Sioux in July; with delegates of the nations of Green Bay (the Potawatomis, Sauks, Menominees, Foxes, and Miamis of Maramek) in August; and with delegates of the Sable Odawas and the Miamis of St Joseph River in September. A little later he held a conference with Huron-Petuns, Sinago Odawas, Kiskakons, and Nipissings. In September 1697, Potawatomi, Kiskakon, and Fox ambassadors travelled to the colony to meet with Frontenac. In July 1698 delegates of the Kiskakons, Sinago Odawas, and Sable Odawas came to parley with New France. A year later, Callière held a conference in Montreal with ten Great Lakes nations. Another conference was held in June 1700 with Odawas, and finally, in September 1700 and July-August 1701, conferences took place for a general peace.

43 ANF, Col., CIIA, vol. 18, f. 259, Champigny au ministre, Montréal, 12 septembre 1700; Charlevoix, *Histoire*, 1:513.

44 On New France's use of the chief's role, see White, *The Middle Ground*, 38–9, 177–85; Clifton, *Prairie People*, 55–62, 119–21; Havard, "Empire et métissages," 403–17.

45 ANF, Col., C11A, vol. 14, f. 216, Callière au ministre, Québec, 20 octobre 1696.

46 ANF, Col., C11A, vol. 14, f. 216, Callière au ministre, Québec, 20 octobre 1696; ANF, Col., C11A, vol. 14, f. 158, Frontenac au ministre, Québec, 25 octobre 1696.

47 La Potherie, *Histoire*, 3:263, 4:36, 59.

48 See *supra*, p. 56

49 ANF, Col., C11A, vol. 15, f. 17, Relation [...] 1696 [...] 1697.

50 As that might jeopardize New France's ability to make peace with the Iroquois, which it considered absolutely essential.

51 La Potherie, *Histoire*, 4:70.

52 ANF, Col., C11A, vol. 16, f. 166–8, Callière au ministre, Québec, 15 octobre 1698; La Potherie, *Histoire*, 4:94–7.

53 ANF, Col., F3, vol. 8, f. 137, Callière aux dix nations outaouaises [...], le 12 juillet 1699. (TN: our translation.)

54 La Potherie, *Histoire*, 4:66. (TN: our translation.)

55 Quoted in La Potherie, *Histoire*, 4:19. (TN: our translation.)

56 For an analysis of war among the Central Algonquians, see Havard, "Empire et métissages," 167–71.

57 Both in the HNAI, vol. 15 (*Northeast*), and in Eccles, *Canada under Louis XIV*, 201, and *Frontenac*, 266–7, Frontenac's expedition against the Onondagas and the Oneidas is presented as the principal explanation for Iroquois acceptance of the peace treaty. In keeping with this view, there is no mention of the fighting on the Great Lakes frontier.

58 Lahontan took part in Denonville's expedition against the Senecas in 1687.

59 Lahontan, *New Voyages*, 1:120.

60 Ibid., 1:271.

61 Charlevoix, *Histoire*, 2:198. (TN: our translation.) This short phrase effectively refutes the argument of many studies that Frontenac's expedition was a major factor in the peace of 1701.

62 ANF, Col., C11A, vol. 16, f. 6, Frontenac et Champigny au ministre, Québec, 15 octobre 1698. (TN: our translation.)

63 La Potherie, *Histoire*, 3:262. (TN: our translation.)

64 That of an Onondaga chief too old to run away.

65 See ANF, Col., CIIA, vol. 14, f. 121, Frontenac et Champigny au ministre, Québec, 26 octobre 1696: this source gives fifty-one dead and thirty-four prisoners.

66 ANF, Col., CIIA, vol. 16, f. 166, Callière au ministre, Québec, 15 octobre 1698.

67 Charlevoix, *Histoire*, 2:282.

68 Perrot, *Mémoire*, 97–9. (TN: our translation.) This was the first stage in the retreat of the Iroquois from the Great Lakes, which is certainly linked to the epidemic that struck them that year. See Tanner, ed., *Atlas*, 31; La Potherie, *Histoire*, 2:64.

69 According to G. Copway, the Amerindians of the west engaged in these battles because the Iroquois had broken treaties, blocked trade with the European colonies, and threatened their territories. See George Copway, *The Traditional History and Characteristic Sketches of the Ojibway Nation* (Toronto: Coles, 1972), 83, 87, 93. See also Warren, *History of the Ojibway People*, 146; Eid, "The Ojibwa-Iroquois War"; Schmalz, *Ojibwa of Southern Ontario*, 18–30; Jennings, *Ambiguous Iroquois Empire*, 207, 209; Smith, "Important evidence."

70 Brandão and Starna, "Treaties," 237.

71 See MacLeod, "Anishnabeg Point of View."

72 ANF, Col., CIIA, vol. 15, f. 13, Relation [...] 1696 [...] 1697; Charlevoix, *Histoire*, 2:214.

73 ANF, Col., CIIA, vol. 15, f. 96, Frontenac au ministre, Québec, 15 octobre 1697; La Potherie, *Histoire*, 3:299; see also NYCD, 4:294, Messrs Schuyler, Dellius and Wessels to Governor Fletcher, Albany, September 28, 1697.

74 ANF, Col., CIIA, vol. 16, f. 97, Champigny au ministre, Québec, 12 juillet 1698; Charlevoix, *Histoire*, 2:224.

75 Bellomont, quoted in Charlevoix, *Histoire*, 2:230. See also the figures in ANF, Col., F3, vol. 8, f. 49, f. 54, Relation [...] départ des vaisseaux 1697 [...] octobre 1698.

76 NYCD, 4:488, Bellomont to the Lords of Trade, New York, April 13, 1699. NYCD, 4:505, Bellomont to the Lords of Trade, April 17, 1699; Brandão and Starna, "Treaties," 219.

77 Quoted in La Potherie, *Histoire*, 4:125. Five Senecas were reported to have been killed "near their Castle" at the end of the summer of 1699 (TN: our translations) (see Jennings, *Ambiguous Iroquois Empire*, 209).

78 NYCD, 4:597, Message from Onondaga to the Commissioners for Indian Affairs.

79 The future site of Detroit. ANF, Col., CIIA, vol. 18, f. 78, Callière, 21 juin 1700.

80 ANF, Col., CIIA, vol. 18, f. 317, Louvigny au Conseil souverain de Québec, 1700.

81 ANF, Col., CIIA, vol. 18, f. 146, La Potherie au ministre, Québec, 11 août 1700.

82 Charlevoix, *Histoire*, 2:244; see also NYCD, 4:693–4, Propositions of the Five Nations to the Commissioners of Indian Affairs, Albany, June 30, 1700. The Senecas were reported to have lost forty people during the spring of 1700.

83 Quoted in Wraxall, *Abridgement*, 33–4; see also NYCD, 4:729, Conference of the Earl of Bellomont with the Indians, Albany, August 27, 1700; NYCD, 4:493, Propositions by the Sachems of Onondaga and Oneida, Albany, February 3, 1699.

84 Charlevoix (*Histoire*, 2:241) mentions a victorious raid against the Miamis in 1699. See also Brandão, "*Your Fyre*," 97, 126–7.

85 Cited in Richter, "The Ordeal of the Longhouse," 599. This figure of 1,400 seems more realistic than that of 1,230 given by another report from Albany in April 1698.

86 For the "echo" that persisted a quarter-century later, see NYCD, 5:725, Conference between the Massachusetts Commissioners and the Six Nations of Indians, Albany, September 16, 1724.

CHAPTER SIX

1 See Richter, *Ordeal of the Longhouse*, 257–8.

2 Haan, "Covenant Chain," 105.

3 Their identity is not certain. They were either two Senecas, two Onondagas, or one Seneca and one Onondaga.

4 ANF, Col., CIIA, vol. 18, f. 166, Parolles de deux Iroquois à Callière, le 12ᵉ mars; ANF, Col., CIIA, vol. 18, f. 167, Réponse de Callière aux deux Iroquois; ANF, Col., F3, vol. 8, f. 153–4; La Potherie, *Histoire*, 4:133–5; Aquila, *Iroquois Restoration*, 47.

5 Aquila, *Iroquois Restoration*, 48–9.

6 See NYCD, 4:694, Propositions of the Five Nations to the Commissioners of Indian Affairs, Albany, June 30, 1700. At the conference in June 1700 in Albany, the Iroquois delegates – including Teganissorens – told the English that it had not been possible to prevent certain chiefs from going to Montreal. This seems to prove that there were schisms within the League, unless the two delegations of June and July to Albany and

Montreal were acting together. It also became apparent at the conference in Albany that if the English did not take action to persuade the French to stop the war waged by their allies in the west, all the Iroquois would decide to deal separately with the French. Consensus was therefore not far from being established within the League.

7 The Mohawks were clearly excluded from the negotiation process. The French accepted this situation without difficulty, since they knew that the Mohawks had become very weak (see ANF, Col., C11A, vol. 18, f. 148, La Potherie au ministre, Québec, 11 août 1700).

8 ANF, Col., C11A, vol. 18, f. 81–3, Parolles des Iroquois [...] Réponses de [...] Callière, juillet 1700; ANF, Col., C11A, vol. 18, f. 146–8, La Potherie au ministre, Québec, 11 août 1700; La Potherie, *Histoire*, 4:135–48.

9 Richter, "Ordeal of the Longhouse," 390.

10 Y.F. Zoltvany, "Chabert de Joncaire," *DCB*, 2:125.

11 C.J. Jaenen, "Bruyas," *DCB*, 2:106–8.

12 Richter, *Ordeal of the Longhouse*, 198.

13 La Potherie, *Histoire*, 4:148 (TN: our translation). On the Onondaga conference of August 1700, see La Potherie, *Histoire*, 4:148–64; ANF, Col., C11A, vol. 18, f. 150–2; La Potherie au ministre, Québec, 15 octobre 1700; Charlevoix, *Histoire*, 2:245–50.

14 The presence of the Mohawks is reported by La Potherie, *Histoire*, 4:151.

15 Richter, "Ordeal of the Longhouse," 391–2.

16 La Potherie, *Histoire*, 4:154. (TN: our translation.)

17 ANF, Col., C11A, vol. 18, f. 86.

18 Quoted in La Potherie, *Histoire*, 4:154 (TN: our translation); Aquila, *Iroquois Restoration*, 52–3; Richter, "Ordeal of the Longhouse," 392–3.

19 La Potherie, *Histoire*, 4:159. (TN: our translation.)

20 Richter, "Ordeal of the Longhouse," 393–4.

21 Fenton, *The Great Law and the Longhouse*, 343.

22 La Potherie, *Histoire*, 4:150.

23 Ibid., 156–8.

24 Ibid., 157. (TN: our translation.)

25 Ibid., 163.

26 Charlevoix, *Histoire*, 2:249. The attitude of the Oneidas may seem surprising when we consider that it was they who had set the peace process in motion in 1697. Was the difference in 1700 because they did not feel the pressure of the war as much as their western brothers? Did they also want to keep their prisoners at any price?

27 Wraxall, *Abridgement*, 33–4.

28 See Richter, "Ordeal of the Longhouse," 397–403; Richter, *Ordeal of the Longhouse*, 206–7.

29 For this conference, see ANF, Col., CIIA, vol. 18, f. 84–8; La Potherie, *Histoire*, 4:164–75.

30 La Potherie, *Histoire*, 4:164 (TN: our translation); ANF, Col., CIIA, vol. 18, f. 84. According to D.K. Richter (*Ordeal of the Longhouse*, 207), Teganissorens was present in Montreal, but this is not indicated in the French sources.

31 La Potherie, *Histoire*, 4:167.

32 The Kiskakons, Sable Odawas, Sinago Odawas, and Nassauaketons.

33 ANF, Col., CIIA, vol. 18, f. 85.

34 Richter, "Ordeal of the Longhouse," 395.

35 Quoted in ANF, Col., CIIA, vol. 18, f. 85. (TN: our translation.)

36 Ibid. (TN: our translation.)

37 Ibid.

38 Ibid.

39 Quoted in ANF, Col., CIIA, vol. 18, f. 87. (TN: our translation.)

40 Quoted in ANF, Col., CIIA, vol. 18, f. 158, La Potherie au ministre, Québec, 16 octobre 1700 (TN: our translation); La Potherie, *Histoire*, 4:172–3.

41 ANF, Col., CIIA, vol. 18, f. 88; La Potherie, *Histoire*, 4:174. It was an Onondaga delegate who undertook to represent the Mohawks.

42 ANF, Col., CIIA, vol. 18, f. 3, Callière et Champigny au ministre, Québec, 18 octobre 1700.

43 ANF, Col., CIIA, vol. 18, f. 67, Callière au ministre, Québec, 16 octobre 1700. With respect to religion, Callière was apparently mistaken (see Richter, "Ordeal of the Longhouse," 399). In any event, the main issue was that of neutrality.

44 ANF, Col., CIIA, vol. 18, f. 67.

45 Y.F. Zoltvany, "Laumet dit Cadillac," DCB, 2:351–6; ANF, Col., CIIA, vol. 17, f. 101–3, mémoire du Sieur [...] Cadillac [...] et sentiments de Champigny, Québec, 20 octobre 1699.

46 Richter, "Ordeal of the Longhouse," 403–4.

47 ANF, Col., CIIA, vol. 18, f. 64, Callière au ministre, Québec, 16 octobre 1700. (TN: our translation.)

48 ANF, Col., CIIA, vol. 18, f. 66, Callière au ministre, Québec, 16 octobre 1700.

49 See La Potherie, *Histoire*, 4:223–5; ANF, Col., CIIA, vol. 18, f. 87.

50 ANF, Col., CIIA, vol. 19, f. 114v, Callière au ministre, Québec, 4 octobre 1701. (TN: our translation.)

51 A party of Huron-Petuns including Chief Quarante Sols, had recently left Michilimackinac for the St Joseph River.

52 Just as for the Odawas, the term *nation* should be used with caution. Unquestionably, the Illinois were divided into various groups.

53 ANF, Col., CIIA, vol. 19, f. 114–16, Callière au ministre, Québec, 4 octobre 1701; Charlevoix, *Histoire*, 2:273–4. Father Enjalran returned to Montreal on 23 June with two Iroquois captives. Courtemanche had to stay in Michilimackinac until 5 July "both to wait for the delegates who had not arrived yet and to deal with the problems that troublemakers among the Outaouais [Odawas] were causing in order to avoid bringing their Iroquois prisoners, some intending to use the prisoners to make peace with them themselves, and others to confuse the situation, saying there was sickness in Montreal." ANF, Col. CIIA, vol. 19, f. 116 (TN: our translation).

54 Reported in ANF, Col., CIIA, vol. 19, f. 114–15, Callière au ministre, Québec, 4 octobre 1701.

55 ANF, Col., F3, vol. 8, f. 262–3, Pourparlez entre [...] Callière [...] et les sauvages descendus à Montréal pour parvenir à la rattiffication de la paix, 29 juillet 1701; ANF, Col., CIIA, vol. 19, f. 116, Callière au ministre, Québec, 4 octobre 1701; La Potherie, *Histoire*, 4:201.

56 Ibid.

57 La Potherie, *Histoire*, 4:224, 245. The Mississaugas were at that time probably in talks with the Iroquois (La Potherie, *Histoire*, 4:179).

58 ANF, Col., CIIA, vol. 19, f. 115, Callière au ministre, Québec, 4 octobre 1701; JR, 65:100.

59 La Potherie, *Histoire*, 4:224.

60 ANF, Col., CIIA, vol. 19, f. 116, Callière au ministre, Québec, 4 octobre 1701.

61 La Potherie, *Histoire*, 4:175. This is the same problem encountered among the Iroquois.

62 Ibid., 224.

63 Ibid., 225–6. (TN: our translation.)

64 Ibid., 224. (TN: our translation.)

65 In May, probably. ANF, Col., CIIA, vol. 19, f. 115, Callière au ministre, 4 octobre 1701.

66 La Potherie, *Histoire*, 4:175, 225. (TN: our translation.)

67 ANF, Col., F3, vol. 8, f. 266, Pourparlez [...] du 1er août. (TN: our translation.)

68 Charlevoix, *Histoire*, 2:277.

69 La Potherie, *Histoire*, 4:177–8, 224; Charlevoix, *Histoire*, 2:268; NYCD, 4:768, Bellomont to the Lords of Trade, New York, October 24, 1700.

70 Richter, "Ordeal of the Longhouse," 405–9; Haan, "Covenant Chain," 119.

71 La Potherie, *Histoire*, 4:178–80; ANF, Col., F3, vol. 8, f. 230, Parolles de Tsioueouy et Tieugonentagueté [...] à Callière [...] Québec, 2 mars 1701.

72 La Potherie, *Histoire*, 4:181–3; ANF, Col., F3, vol. 8, f. 230, Réponses de Callière.

73 Haan, "Covenant Chain," 118; Richter, "Ordeal of the Longhouse," 405.

74 La Potherie, *Histoire*, 4:187.

75 ANF, Col., F3, vol. 8, f. 231–2, Parolles que Teganissorens et les autres chefs [...] le 25e may [...] à Callière; Richter, "Ordeal of the Longhouse," 410–11.

76 Richter, "Ordeal of the Longhouse," 413; quotation from ANF, Col., F3, vol. 8, f. 231–3, Réponses de Calliere [...] 26 may 1701 (TN: our translation).

77 La Potherie, *Histoire*, 4:186.

78 Richter, "Ordeal of the Longhouse," 413.

79 NYCD, 4:893, Journal of Messrs Bleeker and Schuyler's visit to Onondaga, Albany, June 1700.

80 Ibid.

81 Ibid., 894; La Potherie, *Histoire*, 4:190.

82 La Potherie, *Histoire*, 4:190. (TN: our translation.)

83 Beaulieu and Lavoie, "La Grande Paix de Montréal." Teganissorens's speech follows the Iroquois political tradition. It is similar to the one Kiotseaeton, a Mohawk orator, delivered in Trois Rivières in July 1645, as reported by a Jesuit father: "... and thereupon he turned around, and caught the Frenchman and Algonquin by their two arms, holding them so closely that he seemed unwilling ever to let them go" (JR 27:261 [TN: our translation]). I am indebted to A. Beaulieu for pointing this out to me.

84 Richter, *Ordeal of the Longhouse*, 210.

85 Quoted in La Potherie, *Histoire*, 4:191. (TN: our translation.)

86 Haan, "Covenant Chain," 127–8.
87 Charlevoix, *Histoire*, 2:272.
88 La Potherie, *Histoire*, 3:101–3.

CHAPTER SEVEN

1 La Potherie, *Histoire*, 4:241.
2 Ibid., 195; Charlevoix, *Histoire*, 2:273.
3 La Potherie, *Histoire*, 4:266 (first quote); Charlevoix, *Histoire*, 2:285; ANF, Col., CIIA, vol. 19, f. 125, Callière au ministre, Québec, 31 octobre (second quote). (TN: our translations.)
4 From 12 to 21 July, the English and the Iroquois held a conference in Albany. See chapter 9.
5 La Potherie, *Histoire*, 4:216, 229–30.
6 ANF, Col., CIIA, vol. 19, f. 43.
7 Richter, "Ordeal of the Longhouse," 417.
8 La Potherie, *Histoire*, 4:200. According to Charlevoix (*Histoire*, 2:274), there were only 150 canoes. Thirty apparently gave up along the way because of disease.
9 La Potherie, *Histoire*, 4:219.
10 Ibid., 197.
11 We find the names of certain nations in the reports of the talks, but have been unable to identify them among all the pictographs. We have, in fact, only been able to clearly identify thirty of the thirty-eight or thirty-nine signatures. See Appendix 1.
12 La Potherie, *Histoire*, 4:211.
13 Ibid., 214, 246.
14 La Potherie, *Histoire*, 4:222.
15 Ibid., 225.
16 For the identification of the Illinois nations, see C. Callender, "Illinois," *HNAI*, 15:673.
17 ANF, Col., F3, vol. 8, f. 262, f. 270; La Potherie, *Histoire*, 4:212, 255.
18 La Potherie, *Histoire*, 4:224.
19 Ibid. The Gokapatagans were apparently Kickapoos.
20 ANF, Col., F3, vol. 8, f. 270; ANF, Col., CIIA, vol. 19, f. 41.
21 La Potherie, *Histoire*, 4:247.
22 Ibid., 4:248.
23 Ibid., 207; ANF, Col., F3, vol. 8, f. 263. The Miamis, unlike the Odawas, did not use canoes. There were in fact six Miami groups or nations in the

seventeenth century: the Atchatchakangouens, Kilatikas, Mengakonkias, Pepikokias, Piankashaws, and Ouiatenons (or Weas). See C. Callender, "Miami," HNAI, 15:681; La Potherie, *Histoire*, 4:54–72. At the treaty conference, Chichicatalo was the main chief for all the Miami nations.

24 La Potherie, *Histoire*, 4:245.

25 Ibid., 219. The Nipissings arrived during the conference with the Algonquins.

26 Ibid., 204.

27 Ibid.

28 Ibid. It should be noted that Elaouesse, like Kinongé, Kileouiskingié, and Outaliboi (or Outaoualiboi), had signed the treaty of the previous year, in September in Montreal. The same pictographs are found on both treaties.

29 Ibid., 215.

30 Ibid., 4:207.

31 ANF, Col., F3, vol. 8, f. 263.

32 La Potherie, *Histoire*, 4:208.

33 The Winnebagos were Sioux-speakers. They lived in the area of Green Bay (or the Bay des Puants) in the western Lake Michigan region. The French name for them, the "Puants," simply means Sioux in Algonquian (see Wilson, *Ojebway Language*, 353). The pictograph on the treaty represents a thunderbird. Winnebago, in Sioux, is *Ho-Tan-Ka*, which means "the big voice," or the voice of thunder (see Riggs, *Dakota-English Dictionary*, 155).

34 Charlevoix, *Histoire*, 2:276–7.

35 La Potherie, *Histoire*, 4:201.

36 Ibid., 202–4.

37 Ibid., 231. It should be noted that on this date Kondiaronk was no longer alive.

38 Ibid., 256–7.

39 Ibid., 259–60. The other important Amerindian figures at this conference were Hassaki, a Kiskakon chief; Quarante Sols, a Huron-Petun chief; and Chichicatalo, a Miami chief (ibid., 256, 260–1).

40 Ibid., 258. (TN: our translation.)

41 Charlevoix, *Histoire*, 2:281.

42 The Abenakis, according to their orator Haouatchouath, had been at peace with the Iroquois since 1697 (La Potherie, *Histoire*, 4:251–2). Some of them were from "Saint François" (ibid.), that is, from Odanak, a village of Amerindians on the south bank of the St Lawrence between Montreal and Trois-Rivières. But there were likely also chiefs from Acadia; the words *abenakis delacadie* appear under the signature of Mesk-

ouadoue (ANF, CIIA, vol. 19, f. 43). Chiefs of the "Abenaguis de Lacadie" were also present in Montreal in September 1700 (La Potherie, *Histoire*, 4:170). The Abenakis had maintained strong links with the Wabanaki Confederacy. See ANF, Col., CIIA, vol. 18, f. 85. According to Wabanaki oral tradition, this eastern league made peace with the Mohawks under the supervision of the Odawas. Until the mid-nineteenth century, the Odawas, probably on behalf of the Great Lakes nations, presided over a system of alliances that also included the nations settled in the colony (the Seven Nations) and the members of the Wabanaki Confederacy. This vast network, which was based and kept its "fire" in Kahnawake – where its members met every three years for various rituals and festivities lasting several weeks – existed at least in the second half of the eighteenth century. Given that the Iroquois League and the Wabanaki Confederacy were no longer at war in the eighteenth century, and that it was the Odawas who, with their diplomatic title of "father," were most likely the founders of that confederacy, it is possible that discussions among all these parties began during the negotiation of the Great Peace of Montreal. Thus the Abenakis could have spoken for the entire Wabanaki Confederacy in 1701. See Delâge, "Iroquois chrétiens, II," 46–7; Speck, "Eastern Algonkian Wabanaki Confederacy," 492–508.

43 La Potherie, *Histoire*, 4:249–51. Note that the signatories of the treaty were not L'Aigle and Tsahouanhos, but Haronhiateka, a "chief from the Sault," and Mechayon, a "chief from La Montagne" (ANF, Col., CIIA, vol. 19, f. 43). These settled Iroquois, who were signatories of the 1701 treaty as well as of the treaty of September 1700, were thus making a de facto affirmation of their sovereignty despite the fact that they lived in the colony.

44 For their participation in the wars, see La Potherie, *Histoire*, 4:7; on the July 1700 conference, see ANF, Col., CIIA, vol. 18, f. 81–3, Parolles des Iroquois [...] Réponses de [...] Callière, juillet 1700; ANF, Col., CIIA, vol. 18, f. 146–8, La Potherie au ministre, Québec, 11 août 1700; La Potherie, *Histoire*, 4:135–48.

45 Delâge, "Iroquois chrétiens, II," 46–7.

46 ANF, Col. CIIA, vol. 16, f. 112, Champigny au ministre, Québec, 14 octobre 1698; CIIA, vol. 13, f. 234, relation [...] 1695; ANF, Col., CIIA, vol. 17, f. 37, Callière au ministre, 20 octobre 1699; Perrot, *Mémoire*, 139–41; La Potherie, *Histoire*, 2:182, 194–7, 218–19, 245, 266, 268; Anderson, *Kinsmen of Another Kind*, 34–5.

47 ANF, Col., CIIA, vol. 21, f. 74, Vaudreuil aux sauvages hurons, le 14 juillet 1703. See also ANF, Col., CIIA, vol. 21, f. 66, Réponse de

Vaudreuil au Parolles du Pesant, Outaouais, le 17 juillet 1703. (TN: our translation.)

48 ANF, Col., CIIA, vol. 19, f. 58, Callière au ministre, Québec, octobre 1701.

49 La Potherie, *Histoire*, 4:196, 199.

50 Ibid., 194. (TN: our translation.)

51 Ibid., 194–5. (TN: our translation.)

52 Ibid., 195. (TN: our translation.)

53 Ibid., 196.

54 Ibid., 197–8 (TN: our translation); Fenton, "Kondiaronk," DCB, 2:322.

55 La Potherie, *Histoire*, 2:14–19 (TN: our translation); see Perrot, *Mémoire*, 100; Lahontan, *New Voyages*, 1:75–6, 402, and 2:423–4; Therrien, *Parole et pouvoir*, 141.

56 La Potherie, *Histoire*, 4:197. (TN: our translation.)

57 Ibid., 200–1 (TN: our translation); Jennings, ed., *Iroquois Diplomacy*, 19.

58 Dechêne, *Habitants and Merchants*, 10.

59 ANF, Col., CIIA, vol. 19, f. 117, Callière au ministre, Québec, 4 octobre 1701.

60 Dechêne, *Habitants and Merchants*, 7.

61 It is the second figure that is undoubtedly most relevant. It should be noted that the island of Montreal is about fifty kilometres long, and the Amerindian delegates stayed close to the town. The comparison throws a very interesting light on the power relationship between the French and the Native people at the time. For the population figures, see Dechêne, *Habitants and Merchants*, 297.

62 Grabowski, "The Common Ground," 283.

63 Dechêne, *Habitants et marchands*, 31–2.

64 La Potherie, *Histoire*, 4:200. (TN: our translation.)

65 Ibid., 227–8. Note that Maricourt was always compensated for this service to the governor (D.J. Horton, "Le Moyne de Maricourt," DCB, 2:402).

66 La Potherie, *Histoire*, 4:200–5. He said further: "The fair was held along the palisade, with the huts of the savages on one side and on the other the stalls of the many merchants, who eagerly awaited this opportunity to present their wares" (ANF, Col., F3, vol. 2, f. 263 [TN: our translation]).

67 La Potherie, *Histoire*, 1:364–5 (first quotation); Lahontan, *New Voyages*, 1:94; ANF Col., F3, vol. 2, f. 263 (La Potherie's words on the interpreters).

68 Dechêne, *Habitants et marchands*, 32.

69 ANF, Col., CIIA, vol. 19, f. 117, Callière au ministre, Québec, 4 octobre 1701.

70 JR, 62:100, 67:38; ANF, Col., CIIA, vol. 21, f. 241, Mémoire touchant la vente et le commerce de l'eau-de-vie aux sauvages, 1703; Charlevoix, *Journal*, 542, 646 ("These barbarians know themselves that drunkenness ruins and destroys them" [TN: our translation]). However, there is no consistent Amerindian position on the negative effects of alcohol, as they often blamed the Europeans for their excesses. See Havard, "Empire et métissages," 556–61.

71 La Potherie, *Histoire*, 4:204. (TN: our translation.)

72 ANF, Col., CIIA, vol. 21, f. 240–2, Memoire touchant la vente et le commerce de l'eau-de-vie aux sauvages, 1703.

73 Successor to Champigny in 1702.

74 ANF, Col., CIIA, vol. 20, f. 64, Callière et Beauharnois au ministre, Québec, 3 novembre 1702.

75 Ibid., 225. (TN: our translation.)

76 ANF, Col., F3, vol. 8, f. 262, pourparlez [...] 29 juillet 1701. La Potherie (*Histoire*, 4:203) quotes Outoutagan's speech as follows: "We have destroyed and eaten all the land. There are few beavers now, and we can only hunt for Bears, Cats, and other humble Pelts." (TN: our translations.)

77 La Potherie, *Histoire*, 4:207. (TN: our translation.)

78 Delâge, "L'alliance franco-amérindienne," 6–7.

79 La Potherie, *Histoire*, 4:203 (TN: our translation). Many delegates from the west complained about the high prices of French goods (La Potherie, *Histoire*, 4:200; ANF, Col., F3, vol. 8, f. 262, Pourparlez [...] 29 juillet 1701).

80 Delâge, "L'alliance franco-amérindienne," 6.

81 La Potherie, *Histoire*, 4:203, 211. (TN: our translations.)

82 ANF, Col., CIIA, vol. 19, f. 9, Callière et Champigny au ministre, Québec, 5 octobre 1701; ANF, Col., CIIA, vol. 19, f. 62, Champigny au ministre, octobre 1701; La Potherie, *Histoire*, 4:254.

83 La Potherie, *Histoire*, 4:205; ANF, Col., F3, vol. 8, f. 264.

84 La Potherie, *Histoire*, 4:207; ANF, Col., F3, vol. 8, f. 263.

85 ANF, Col., CIIA, vol. 19, f. 117, Callière au ministre, Québec, 4 octobre 1701.

86 Charlevoix, *Histoire*, 2:274. (TN: our translation.)

87 La Potherie, *Histoire*, 4:201–2. (TN: our translation.)

88 Ibid., 232.

89 Callière spoke of "the deaths of the nine main Huron and Miami leaders who were closest to us" (ANF, Col., CIIA, vol. 19, f. 117, Callière au ministre, 4 octobre 1701). The quotation of the Kiskakon chief is in ANF, Col., F3, vol. 8, f. 266v, Pourparlez entre mr. le chevalier de Callière et les sauvages [...] 2ᵉ aoust. A number of chiefs died in the days or weeks following the conference, including the Miami Chichicatalo (La Potherie, *Histoire*, 4:262), the Sinago Chingouessi (Margry, *Découvertes*, 5:277), and the Potawatomi Onanguicé, who "died while he was bringing [Callière's] word back to the Illinois" (ANF, Col., F3, vol. 8, f. 312, Parolles des Kiskakons, sakis, poux et puants dessendus a Montreal le 23 juillet 1702 [TN: our translations]).

90 La Potherie, *Histoire*, 4:239. (TN: our translation.)

91 Charlevoix, *Histoire*, 2:279–80. (TN: our translation.)

92 The association between epidemics and the "black robes" was made by the Hurons as early as the 1630s. See Delâge, *Bitter Feast*, 171–2; Delâge, "La religion dans l'alliance," 64–5.

93 La Potherie, *Histoire*, 4:233. (TN: our translation.)

94 Charlevoix, *Histoire*, 2:280. (TN: our translation.)

95 Ibid., 276–7. (TN: our translation.)

96 La Potherie, *Histoire*, 4:223–5. (TN: our translation.)

97 Charlevoix, *Histoire*, 2:277. (TN: our translation.)

98 La Potherie, *Histoire*, 4:225. (TN: our translation.)

99 Ibid., 228.

100 Charlevoix, *Histoire*, 2:278. (TN: our translation.)

101 La Potherie, *Histoire*, 4:229. (TN: our translation.)

102 Ibid., 229–31. (TN: our translation.)

103 Bély, *Espions et Ambassadeurs*, 372–3, 392, 680.

104 Ibid., 400.

105 La Potherie, *Histoire*, 4:219, 222.

106 One element, however, was not typical of Amerindian diplomatic tradition: the answers were usually given the same day as the questions, which may perhaps be explained by the extraordinary nature of the conference.

107 La Potherie, *Histoire*, 4:234. (TN: our translation.)

108 According to La Potherie (ibid., 228), Kondiaronk had been converted by the Jesuits, but Charlevoix qualified this: "His esteem for Father de Carheil [a missionary at Michilimackinac] was undoubtedly what made him decide to become a Christian, or at least to live in a manner in conformity with the Gospel" (Charlevoix, *Histoire*, 2:277–8 [TN: our translation]).

109 La Potherie, *Histoire*, 4:234–6. (TN: our translation.)

110 For another analysis, see White, *The Middle Ground*, 144–5. See also Havard, "Empire et métissages," 395–6.

111 La Potherie, *Histoire*, 4:234–6; Charlevoix, *Histoire*, 2:278–9 (TN: our translation); W.N. Fenton, "Kondiaronk," DCB, 2:323. Kondiaronk's funeral was not the only one held. La Potherie wrote: "We also marked the death of Houatsaranti, the greatest of the Huron nation, after Le Rat. His funeral took place without quite the same ceremony. Many others also died." (*Histoire*, 4:239 [TN: our translation].)

112 La Potherie, *Histoire*, 4:239. (TN: our translation.)

113 Personal communication from Laurence Johnson, 2000.

114 La Potherie, *Histoire*, 4:240 ("People of quality ..."); Charlevoix, *Histoire*, 2:280 ("in a very orderly fashion"); ANF, Col., CIIA, vol. 19, f. 117, Callière au ministre, Québec, 4 octobre 1701. (TN: our translations.)

115 La Potherie, *Histoire*, 4:240–2; Charlevoix, *Histoire*, 2:281.

116 ANF, Col., CIIA, vol. 19, f. 41. (TN: our translation.)

117 La Potherie, *Histoire*, 4:242.

118 Ibid., 240–1; Charlevoix, *Histoire*, 2:280–1. This figure of thirty-one is given by La Potherie, *Histoire*, 4:240, but there were thirty-eight or thirty-nine signatures on the treaty. This may be an error by La Potherie, or perhaps Callière did not distribute wampum belts to the absent Illinois nations.

119 Charlevoix, *Histoire*, 2:281. (TN: our translation.)

120 *JR*, 55:216. (TN: our translation.)

121 La Potherie, *Histoire*, 4:241–2. (TN: our translation.)

122 Charlevoix, *Histoire*, 2:282. (TN: our translation.)

123 La Potherie, *Histoire*, 4:248. (TN: our translation.)

124 Charlevoix, *Histoire*, 2:281–2. (TN: our translation.)

125 Ibid., 282; La Potherie, *Histoire*, 4:247. (TN: our translation.)

126 Charlevoix, *Histoire*, 2:282.

127 Ibid. (TN: our translation); see Havard, "Paix et interculturalité," 8–9.

128 See Havard, "Empire et métissages," 712–20.

129 Charlevoix, *Histoire*, 2:283. See Appendix 1.

130 La Potherie, *Histoire*, 4:252 (TN: our translation), 208; Charlevoix, *Histoire*, 2:275, 283; ANF, Col., CIIA, vol. 19, f. 41.

131 La Potherie, *Histoire*, 4:253–4. (TN: our translation.)

132 Charlevoix, *Histoire*, 2:283. (TN: our translation.)

133 La Potherie, *Histoire*, 4:253–4.

134 Ibid., 254; Charlevoix, *Histoire*, 2:283. It should be noted that the distribution of presents was selective; La Potherie reported regarding the meeting on 6 August: "The presents, which consisted of powder, musket balls, caps decorated with laces of gold braid, were distributed. They were given in particular to those who had shown the most attachment to our interests" (*Histoire*, 4:255–6 [TN: our translations]).

135 La Potherie, *Histoire*, 4:201–2. The courtyard was located between two buildings (a residence and a barn) that Callière had had built between 1695 and 1697 (personal communication, Laurence Johnson, 2000).

136 Ibid., 214–15.

137 Charlevoix, *Histoire*, 2:275–6. (TN: our translation.)

138 La Potherie, *Histoire*, 4:231–8.

139 Ibid., 254–6; Charlevoix, *Histoire*, 2:283–4.

CHAPTER EIGHT

1 La Potherie, *Histoire*, 4:257. (TN: our translation.)

2 Ibid., 247.

3 Ibid., 170.

4 Ibid., 247.

5 Ibid., 140, 144, 151, 166, 168, 173, 177, 178, 182, 250, 260; ANF, Col., CIIA, vol. 18, f. 157, La Potherie au ministre, Québec, 16 octobre 1700; ANF, Col., CIIA, vol. 18, f. 84–5. (TN: our translation.)

6 Jennings, ed., *Iroquois Diplomacy*, 122.

7 La Potherie, *Histoire*, 4:249–51. (TN: our translation.)

8 Ibid., 256. (TN: our translation.)

9 Ibid., 260. (TN: our translation.)

10 ANF, Col., CIIA, vol. 19, f. 41–2, Ratification de la Paix. (TN: our translation.)

11 Brandão and Starna, "Treaties." See also Brandão, "*Your Fyre*"; Starna, "Concerning the Extent of 'Free Hunting' Territory." The analysis of Starna and Brandão is based in part on that of Wallace ("Origins of Iroquois Neutrality," 233–5). See also Miquelon, *New France*, 23.

12 ANF, Col., CIIA, vol. 122, f. 206v, Mémoire de Raudot; ANF, Col., CIIA, vol. 19, f. 116, Callière au ministre, Québec, 4 octobre 1701. (TN: our translations.) See also Havard, "Empire et métissages," 159–62.

13 Brandão and Starna, "Treaties," 230; Starna, "Concerning the Extent of 'Free Hunting' Territory," 57.

14 Brandão and Starna, "Treaties," 218, 229; Starna, "Concerning the Extent of 'Free Hunting' Territory," 25, 57.

15 Eccles, "Report," 18, 13. For Eccles, the hunting grounds of the Iroquois "were south of Lakes Ontario and Erie, mainly in the Ohio valley, east of the Miamis" (p. 13). However, he does not prove this assertion.

16 Eccles, "Report," 23–5.

17 La Potherie, *Histoire*, 4:259–60, 264, 242, 256, 266; ANF, Col., CIIA, vol. 19, f. 41 (cf. Callière's speech: "… recommending to you when you will meet each other that you treat each other as brothers, and you agree together to hunt in a manner that no quarrels occur between you"). Similarly, in March 1701 Callière had told some Iroquois delegates that the Amerindians of the west and those of the Five Nations should "consider each other as brothers" and "reach agreement concerning the hunt since peace has been made and the land is united" (ANF, Col., F3, vol. 8, f. 230v [TN: our translations]).

18 Catalogne, "Recuil de ce qui s'est passé en Canada," 245–6; AFF, Col., CIIA, vol. 31, f. 95v, Reponse de mr le marquis de Vaudreuil aux colliers des sauvages onnontaguez, 29 janvier 1710. (TN: our translation.)

19 Conseil adressé à John Campbell, Kahnawake, 7 octobre 1791, NA, RG10, bob. C-10999, vol. 8, p. 8202, quoted in Sawaya, *La fédération des Sept Feux*, 41. Personal communication from D. Delâge, 2000.

20 Starna, "Concerning the Extent of 'Free Hunting' Territory," 64, 72 (see also Brandão and Starna, "Treaties," 228). It appears that Starna, eager to find territorial guarantees to the Iroquois, confuses the Montreal agreements with the Albany Agreements concluded the same year between the Iroquois and the British. The Albany Deed stipulated that a very large portion of the Great Lakes region – supposedly corresponding to the hunting territories of the Iroquois – was placed under the protection of New York. See also Wallace, "Origins of Iroquois Neutrality," 235 ("Thus, in regard to the beaver country, in 1701, the French agreed to Iroquois possession of it"); Tanner, ed., *Atlas*, 34 ("As a result of the agreements in 1701, the Iroquois could hunt in Canada"); Dickason, *Canada's First Nations*, 155; Fenton, *The Great Law and the Longhouse*, 346 ("The Iroquois hunters might hunt now in Michigan").

21 La Potherie, *Histoire*, 4:179; ANF, Col., F3, vol. 8, f. 230v, Parolles de Tsioueouy et de Tiengonentaguete, deputez des iroquois a […] callières, Québec […] le 2 mars 1701 ("When we were assembled to go hunting in the area around Fort Catarakouy, eight Mississaugas came and

warned us that the Crees and other nations had malicious intentions"
[TN: our translations]).

22 Ambassadors of the Onondagas asked Governor Vaudreuil in 1710 to
intercede on their behalf on the same matter. According to them, the
Odawas and the Abenakis had "taken over ... [their] hunting territories" (the Iroquois had started using those territories regularly in the
1650s); "may the Outaouais [Odawas] return to hunting in their ancient land on the side of the setting sun, and the Abenakis hunt on the
other side of the great river if they do not want to return to their ancient
land" (ANF, Col., CIIA, vol. 31, f. 91rv, Parolles des sauvages onnontaguez a mr le marquis de Vaudreuil 28 janvier 1710). It is likely that
the game resources in the regions north of Lake Ontario had been re-
plenished since the mid-seventeenth century. (TN: our translations.)

23 ANF, Col., F3, vol. 8, f. 231, Parolles que Teganissorens et les autres
chefs des Iroquois [...] a montreal le 25e de may [...] 1701; ANF, Col.,
F3, vol. 8, f. 231v, reponses de mr le chevalier de calliere, le 26 may
1701. Callière mentioned Detroit during the meeting of 7 August 1701
with the Iroquois (La Potherie, *Histoire*, 4:264). (TN: our translation.)

24 Margry, *Découvertes*, 5:216; La Potherie, *Histoire*, 4:22; see Havard,
"Paix et interculturalité," 5–6. (TN: our translation.)

25 La Potherie, *Histoire*, 4:205–6. (TN: our translation.)

26 Ibid., 207, 233–4; ANF, Col., CIIA, vol. 19, f. 41–3; ANF, Col., CIIA,
vol. 19, f. 117, Callière au ministre, Québec, 4 octobre 1701. According
to La Potherie (F3, vol. 2, f. 265), "each nation [of the west] forced ...
the slaves to leave with them whether they liked it or not" (TN: our
translations.)

27 La Potherie, *Histoire*, 4:216, 225, 244, 246. (TN: our translation.)

28 It should be noted that the Oneidas did not bring any (La Potherie, *Histoire*, 4:219).

29 ANF, Col., F3, vol. 8, f. 278–9, 7 août; ANF, Col., F3, vol. 8, f. 264–5;
ANF, Col., CIIA, vol. 19, f. 117, Callière [...]; ANF, Col., CIIA, vol. 19,
f. 42.

30 La Potherie, *Histoire*, 4:216–17. La Potherie, who resented Callière for
excluding him from the negotiations, accused him of being responsible
for the behaviour of the Iroquois: "The truth is that ... Callières gave
no order to ... Maricourt to ask for the allies ... Callières was convinced that if he pushed the Iroquois too hard to bring back the prisoners of our allies he could not be successful in the peace for which he
wanted all the glory, and if he returned to them even a few of their people, which he was sure that the allies would bring, the Iroquois would

have reason to be pleased with him. Moreover, he did not trouble himself as to whether all the allies would be content or not with the conduct of the Iroquois, because he believed that by appeasing only a few specific nations such as the Hurons and the Outaouais [Odawas] of Michilimackinac he could avoid lasting consequences." (ANF, Col., F3, vol. 2, f. 266v–267r [TN: our translations]).

31 Ibid., 216–19.

32 ANF, Col., F3, vol. 8, f. 265. (TN: our translation.)

33 ANF, Col., F3, vol. 2, f. 266, La Potherie au ministre. (TN: our translation.)

34 See ANF, Col., F3, vol. 8, f. 264.

35 ANF, Col., CIIA, vol. 19, f. 117, Callière [...]

36 ANF, Col., F3, vol. 2, f. 266. (TN: our translation.)

37 La Potherie, *Histoire*, 4:217, 236–7; ANF, Col., F3, vol. 8, f. 267v, Pourparlez entre mr le chevalier de callière et les sauvages [...] 3ᵉ aoust; Charlevoix, *Histoire*, 2:277; Richter, "Ordeal of the Longhouse," 425. (TN: our translation.)

38 ANF, Col., F3, vol. 8, f. 271v, Répliques des nations [...], 6 aôut 1701. (TN: our translation.)

39 La Potherie, *Histoire*, 4:263–4. (TN: our translation.)

40 ANF, Col., CIIA, vol. 19, f. 124–5, Callière au ministre, Québec, 31 octobre 1701; La Potherie, *Histoire*, 4:263–4; Charlevoix, *Histoire*, 2:284; NYCD, 4:918, Report of Messrs Bleeker and Schuyler's Visit to Onondaga, Albany, September, 1701.

41 Magry, *Découvertes*, 5:262–5, conseil tenu dans le fort du détroit avec les Iroquois, 7 décembre 1701 (TN: our translation); ibid., 219, le père Mermet à Cadillac, rivière st Joseph, 19 avril 1702. See also ibid., 274, 275; ANF, Col., F3, vol. 8, f. 315. In 1702 the Mohawks were still reluctant to return their captives (ANF, Col., F3, vol. 8, f. 308, Parolles des trois Agniers a mr le chevalier de Calliere [...] 4 juillet 1702).

42 ANF, Col., CIIA, vol. 18, f. 67, Callière au ministre, Québec, 16 octobre 1700 (first quotation); ANF, Col., CIIA, vol. 19, f. 112v, Callière au ministre, Montréal, 6 août 1701 (second quotation [TN: our translations]); ANF, Col., CIIA, vol. 19, f. 116, Callière au ministre, Québec, 4 octobre 1701.

43 La Potherie, *Histoire*, 4:265–6 (TN: our translation); ANF, Col., F3, vol. 8, f. 278–9, 7 août. Richter ("Ordeal of the Longhouse," 424; *Ordeal of the Longhouse*, 218) and Haan ("Covenant Chain," 141) talk about neutrality extending to all the Amerindians, at the request of the Iroquois. There is no evidence in the French sources to support this.

44 La Potherie, *Histoire*, 4:266; ANF, Col., F3, vol. 8, f. 278–9. (TN: our translation.)

45 Richter, *Ordeal of the Longhouse*, 362; see also Eccles, *France in America*, 106; Jennings, ed., *Iroquois Diplomacy*, 39.

46 Goldstein, *French-Iroquois Relations*, 159–60; Richter, *Ordeal of the Longhouse*, 153; Fenton, *The Great Law and the Longhouse*, 261, 281.

47 Charlevoix, *Histoire*, 2:248.

48 ANF, Col., F3, vol. 8, f. 260v, Instruction pour le pere Bruyas [...], 15 juin 1701 (TN: our translation); see also Jennings, ed., *Iroquois Diplomacy*, 22; Haan, "Covenant Chain," 144.

49 ANF, Col., F3, vol. 8, f. 316v, Parolles des sonnontouans, onontagués et goyogouins a calliere, 23 aoust 1702. (TN: our translation.)

50 ANF, Col., CIIA, vol. 19, f. 41, Ratification [...] (TN: our translation); La Potherie, *Histoire*, 4:260, 264.

51 Delâge, "L'alliance franco-amérindienne," 14.

52 ANF, Col., F3, vol. 8, f. 270v–271, Assemblée [...] le 6 aoust 1701. (TN: our translation.)

53 La Potherie, *Histoire*, 4:209. (TN: our translation.)

54 Ibid., 210. (TN: our translation.) The slave referred to was perhaps a Pawnee. This episode also reveals, if we believe La Potherie's report, the existence of factions among the Sauks. Their chief Ouabiskamon had refused to go to the conference, and the Sauk delegates present in Montreal went out of their way to discredit him in the eyes of Callière. They were eager to confirm the French alliance for economic and military reasons and for personal motives that had to do with their political prestige within their nation. Another point of friction between the French and their allies was revealed during the conference when the Odawas told Callière that they intended "to plunder the alcohol that arrived at Michilimackinac" (see ibid., 259 [TN: our translation]).

55 Ibid., 214–16.

56 Ibid., 216.

57 Ibid., 255. (TN: our translation.)

58 ANF, Col., F3, vol. 8, f. 270v, Assemblée [...] 6 aoust 1701. (TN: our translation.)

59 ANF, Col., CIIA, vol. 19, f. 119v, Callière au ministre, Montréal, 6 août 1701. (TN: our translation.)

60 La Potherie, *Histoire*, 4:247. (TN: our translation.)

61 ANF, Col., F3, vol. 8, f. 266, 2 août 1701; ANF, Col., CIIA, vol. 19, f. 58, Callière au ministre, Québec, octobre 1701; ANF, Col., CIIA,

vol. 19, f. 119, Callière [...]; ANF, Col., CIIA, vol. 19, f. 123–4, Callière [...] 31 octobre 1701.

62 ANF, Col., CIIA, vol. 19, f. 118–19, Callière au ministre, Québec, 4 octobre 1701.

63 Callière told the Iroquois ambassadors that when they went "to the fort of Detroit," they would be "well received" and find "merchandise at reasonable prices," and also noted that "if there occur any disputes when you are both hunting in that region, without having the trouble because of the distance to come and find me, the Commander that I place there should be able to protect you, and accommodate you, reporting to me ... so that it may be a means to maintain the Peace" (La Potherie, *Histoire*, 4:264 [TN: our translation]).

64 Ibid., 266. In September 1701 the Jesuit father François Vaillant, who had just met with some Iroquois on Lake Ontario, told Cadillac: "We did not find them very opposed to your establishment. Some even express joy to me that in going to Lake Erie for the hunt, they will find at Detroit everything they need for the skins of deer, stags and does" (Margry, *Découvertes*, 5:213 [TN: our translation]).

65 ANF, Col., CIIA, vol. 19, f. 119, Callière au ministre, octobre 1701. The Seneca nation at that time was dominated by the chiefs in the pro-French faction (Aouenano, Tonatakout, La Grande Terre, and Oronyatez) who had played a decisive role in the peace process (ANF, Col., CIIA, vol. 21, f. 60–1, Parolles du chef nommé Oronyatez Sonnontouan a Mr de vaudreuil le 26 octobre 1703). Aouenano declared to Cadillac in October 1701, during a council held at Fort Pontchartrain: "We regard this fire here ... as the highest of all the fires, where all the nations will come to talk of matters." Detroit, he noted, "will settle all our disputes if any occur" (Margry, *Découvertes*, 5:262–4 [TN: our translation]).

66 ANF, Col., CIIA, vol. 19, f. 4, Callière et Champigny au ministre, Québec, 5 octobre 1701; ANF, Col., CIIA, vol. 19, f. 119, Callière [...]

67 La Potherie, *Histoire*, 4:265.

68 Ibid., 254.

69 ANF, Col., F3, vol. 8, f. 271, Assemblée faite par Callière [...] de tous les chefs de sauvages de chaque nation d'en haut [...] Montréal, 6 août 1701; JR, 65:250.

70 La Potherie, *Histoire*, 4:227.

71 ANF, Col., F3, vol. 8. f. 272, Assemblée [...]

72 JR, 65:250; Charlevoix, *Histoire*, 2:291–2; ANF, Col., F3, vol. 8, f. 310–11, Montréal, juillet 1702. See Havard, "Empire et métissages,"

235–6. It was also decided, at the request of Chichicatalo, to assemble all the Miamis on the St Joseph River (La Potherie, *Histoire*, 4:208, 255; ANF, Col., F3, vol. 8, f. 271, Assemblée [...] 6 aoust).

CHAPTER NINE

1 As D.K. Richter explains (*Ordeal of the Longhouse*, 362), "The term 'Grand Settlement' was coined by Anthony F. C. Wallace, who first noted the connections between the Albany and Montreal Treaties." See Wallace, "Origins of Iroquois Neutrality."

2 Richter, "Ordeal of the Longhouse," 418; Richter, *Ordeal of the Longhouse*, 211; Brandão and Starna, "Treaties," 223.

3 NYCD, 4:899, Conference of Nanfan with the Indians, July 1701; Brandão and Starna, "Treaties."

4 And also: "if the French make any attempts or come into our country to delude us, wee desire you to send men of wisdom and understanding to countermine them, for they [are] to subtile and cunning for us"; "wee have not power to resist such a Christian enemy, therefore wee must depend upon you Brother Corlaer to take this case in hand" (NYCD, 4:905–6; Richter, *Ordeal of the Longhouse*, 212; Brandão and Starna, "Treaties," 225–7).

5 NYCD, 4:905; Richter, *Ordeal of the Longhouse*, 212.

6 NYCD, 4:905, 908–11; Brandão and Starna, "Treaties," 225–7.

7 Brandão and Starna, "Treaties," 228, 232; Richter, *Ordeal of the Longhouse*, 362. See also Wallace, "Origins of Iroquois Neutrality," 233–5; Haan, "Covenant Chain," 135.

8 Jennings, *Ambiguous Iroquois Empire*, 212 (see also 10–24). Trelease (*Indian Affairs*, 362) explains that the deed "was symbolic ... The French naturally refused to recognize it, and the English were no more able to exercise control in that vast area than before the deed was executed. The Indians, moreover, had no intention of opening it to English settlement or of surrendering their hunting rights there – far from it. They merely offered the king the dubious privilege of protecting it." See also Kent, *Historical Report*, 42–3. Richter (*Ordeal of the Longhouse*, 362) disagrees with Jennings's analysis: "the thrust of his argument is correct, but it is placed a quarter century too early ... [B]y 1726 no copy of it [the deed] could be found in the province."

9 Eccles, "Report," 35–40.

10 Even if, as Richter writes, "the previous decade of experience had disabused them of any illusions about New York martial value" (Richter, *Ordeal of the Longhouse*, 212).

11 In the autumn of 1703, the Seneca chief Oronyatez asked for the protection of the French governor: "We make you master of our land and this is something we have never done but for you; therefore my father if any accident happens to us look upon us as your children and give us your help." This speech calls for several observations. First of all, it contradicts the Albany Deed of 1701; thus – if the deed has an Iroquois origin – it reveals the divisions within the League (Oronyatez was a pro-French leader, while Onucheranorum represented the pro-English faction in Albany in 1701). It also shows that the Iroquois regularly called on the protection of the European colonies: Oronyatez did not want to surrender Seneca territory to the French colonists, but rather preferred to consolidate the alliance with Onontio – hence the Treaty of Montreal of 1701 (ANF, Col., CIIA, vol. 21, f. 60, Parolles [...] Oronyatez [...] 26 octobre 1703 [TN: our translation]).

12 *NYCD*, 4905. The issue of missionaries was not raised at the Montreal conference (Charlevoix, *Histoire*, 2:284).

13 Richter, "Ordeal of the Longhouse," 419.

14 Jennings, *Ambiguous Iroquois Empire*, 211–12.

15 Trelease, *Indian Affairs*, 362–3.

16 *NYCD*, 4:1068, Memorial from Mr Livingston about New York, 1703.

17 Starna, "Concerning the Extent," 63.

18 Jennings, *Ambiguous Iroquois Empire*, 211; Charlevoix, *Histoire*, 2:303, 313, 328; ANF, Col., CIIA, vol. 21, f. 73, Reponse de monsieur de vaudreuil aux parolles de Teganissorens a Quebec le 31 octobre 1703.

19 Eccles, *Frontenac*, 332–3; Eccles, "Teganissorens," DCB, 2:619–23; Eccles, *Canada under Louis XIV*, 244; Eccles, *France in America*, 100–1; Eccles, "Report," 17–19; see also Trelease, *Indian Affairs*, 363.

20 Brandão and Starna, "Treaties"; Starna, "Concerning the Extent of 'Free Hunting' Territory."

21 Wallace, "Origins of Iroquois Neutrality"; Haan, "Covenant Chain"; Richter, *Ordeal of the Longhouse*.

22 *NYCD*, 5:724.

23 Haan, "Covenant Chain," 102–3.

24 Richter, *Ordeal of the Longhouse*, 427–31.

25 Starna, "Concerning the Extent of 'Free Hunting' Territory," 61–2; Brandão and Starna, "Treaties," 232.

26 Dickason, *Canada's First Nations*, 155.

27 Brandão and Starna, "Treaties," 217; Starna, "Concerning the Extent of 'Free Hunting' Territory," 20; see also Brown, ed., *The Illustrated History of Canada*, 145–6.

28 Starna, "Concerning the Extent of 'Free Hunting' Territory," 26.

29 Jennings, *Ambiguous Iroquois Empire*, 210; Jennings, ed., *Iroquois Diplomacy*, 39.

30 Dickason, *Canada's First Nations*, 155; Starna, "Concerning the Extent of 'Free Hunting' Territory," 72; see also Brandão and Starna, "Treaties," 232, 209.

31 ANF, Col., CIIA, vol. 19, f. 232, Callière, 1701 (TN: our translation); see also ANF, Col., CIIA, vol. 19, f. 3, Callière et Champigny au ministre, Québec, 5 octobre 1701; ANF, Col., CIIA, vol. 19, f. 232, Callière au ministre, Canada, Projets sur la Nouvelle Angleterre, 1701.

32 ANF, Col., CIIA, vol. 20, f. 159, Callière au ministre, Québec, 4 novembre 1702; ANF, Col., B, vol. 23.1, p. 116, Le ministre à Callière, Versailles, 6 mai 1702; ANF, Col., B, vol. 23.2, p. 41, Le Roy à Callière et Beauharnois, 1703; ANF, Col., CIIA, vol. 19, f. 232, Callière au ministre, Canada, Projets sur la Nouvelle Angleterre, 1701; Haan, "The Problem of Iroquois Neutrality," 319–20; Jennings, ed., *Iroquois Diplomacy*, 39; Zoltvany, *Vaudreuil*, 34. The diplomats back in France even suggested, rather unrealistically, a military alliance with the Iroquois against the British.

33 ANF, Col., CIIA, vol. 19, f.118 (TN: our translation); Zoltvany, *Vaudreuil*, 35; Richter, *Ordeal of the Longhouse*, 217.

34 ANF, Col., CIIA, vol. 24, f. 11v, Vaudreuil au ministre, Québec, 30 avril 1706; ANF, CIIA, vol. 22, f. 238, Vaudreuil au Ministre, Québec, 5 mai 1705 ("the Iroquois whom I regard as the only nation that it is important for me to conserve" [TN: our translation]); ANF, Col., CIIA, vol. 24, f. 3, Vaudreuil au ministre, Québec, 28 avril 1706; ANF, Col., CIIA, vol. 24, f. 14, Vaudreuil au ministre, Québec, 4 novembre 1706; ANF, Col., CIIA, vol. 22, f. 8–9, Vaudreuil et Beauharnois au ministre, 17 novembre 1704; ANF, Col., CIIA, vol. 22, f. 235v, Vaudreuil au ministre, Québec, 19 octobre 1705; ANF, Col., CIIA, vol. 28, f. 104v, Vaudreuil au ministre, Québec, 5 novembre 1708; ANF, Col., CIIA, vol. 28, f. 8v, 36v, Vaudreuil et Raudot au ministre, Québec, 14 novembre 1708. See also White, *The Middle Ground*, 150–1; Miquelon, *New France*, 38–9.

35 See Vaugeois, ed., *Les Hurons de Lorette*, 180–1, 264.

36 *JR*, 65:222. (TN: our translation.)

37 Lahontan, *New Voyages*, 1:394.

38 Trigger, "Mohawk-Mahican War," 285–6.

39 ANF, Col., B, vol. 19.1, pp. 111, 116, Le Roy à Frontenac et Champigny, Versailles, 26 may 1696; Jennings, *Ambiguous Iroquois Empire*, 211; Jennings, ed., *Iroquois Diplomacy*, 39.

40 Trigger, "Mohawk-Mahican War," 286.

41 Jennings, *Ambiguous Iroquois Empire*, 211.

42 Callière showed a great deal of confidence in his military possibilites: "This Peace," he wrote, "… prevents the Iroquois from joining with the English in the event of a break [with the French] if they did otherwise, all the other savages would join together to make war on the Iroquois who would soon be destroyed by the multitude. The Five Iroquois nations cannot assemble more than twelve hundred warriors at the most, it would be easy to make a corps of six thousand men of the other savages which joined with a detachment of five hundred men from our troops would annihilate the Iroquois for ever" (ANF, Col., CIIA, vol. 19, f. 232v, Callière, 1701 [TN: our translation]).

43 See ANF, Col., CIIA, vol. 21, f. 6v-7r, Beauharnois et Vaudreuil au ministre, Québec, 15 novembre 1703.

44 ANF, Col., CIIA, vol. 19, f. 232v, Callières, 1701. (TN: our translation.)

45 The Abenakis of Acadia, who had economic links with New England, in 1701 reaffirmed their alliance with New France. In the War of the Spanish Succession, Callière and his successor, Vaudreuil, urged them to fight the British. See ANF, Col., CIIA, vol. 21, f. 13–14, Beauharnois et Vaudreuil au ministre, Québec, 15 novembre 1703; ANF, Col., CIIA, vol. 21, f. 51v, Vaudreuil au ministre, Québec, 14 novembre 1703; Zoltavany, *Vaudreuil*, 41–2, 45–6, 48–51; Miquelon, *New France*, 25–31, 40–1.

46 ANF, Col., F3, vol. 2, f. 267v. (TN: our translation.)

47 Charlevoix, *Histoire*, 2:267.

48 ANF, Col., F3, vol. 8, f. 263, Pourparlez […] pour parvenir a la rattiffication de la paix, 29 juillet 1701.

49 ANF, Col., F3, vol. 8, f. 267, Pourparlez entre mr le chevalier de callière et les sauvages […] 2e aoust 1701.

50 Louisiana was founded in 1699 by Le Moyne d'Iberville. It was dynastic rivalries that induced Louis XIV to sanction this new colony. The king of Spain, Charles II, who died in November 1700 without an heir, had bequeathed all his Spanish possessions to Philip of Anjou, the

grandson of Louis XIV. The Sun King accepted the will of his brother-in-law Charles II, thus incurring the wrath of the Austrian monarchy and the maritime powers; by colonizing Louisiana, he wanted to create a protective bond between New France and New Spain. See Lebrun, *Le XVIIᵉ siècle*, 249, 317–20; Y.F. Zoltvany, "Callière," *DCB*, 2:116; Eccles, *Canadian Frontier*, 130.

51 Starna, "Concerning the Extent of 'Free Hunting' Territory," 72; Eccles, "Report," 26.

52 La Potherie, *Histoire*, 4:224; Charlevoix, *Histoire*, 2:273, 276, 279.

53 ANF, Col., CIIA, vol. 19, f. 9r, Callière et Champigny au ministre, Québec, 5 octobre 1701. (TN: our translation.)

54 Havard, "Empire et métissages," 232–6.

55 ANF, Col., B, vol. 19.3, p. 37, Le Roy à Frontenac et Champigny, Versailles, 27 avril 1697.

56 ANF, Col., CIIA, vol. 21, f. 81 (remarques de Champigny). (TN: our translation.)

57 Delâge, "Les Iroquois chrétiens, II," 43. (TN: our translation.)

58 Ibid., 41–2.

59 This "contraband" for fiscal reasons was against the interests of the colony (ANF, Col., B, vol. 23.1, p. 134, Mémoire pour servir d'instruction au Sieur Beauharnois intendant, 6 may 1702), but it benefited the Montreal merchants, who in exchange for the furs from the Great Lakes received English textile products at an excellent price, which they used in trade with the Amerindians of the west: "More furs therefore came down from the Great Lakes to Montreal; consequently, fewer had to go through Iroquoia" (Delâge, "Les Iroquois chrétiens, II," 43 [TN: our translation]; see also Richter, "Ordeal of the Longhouse," 433–4).

60 The expression "la grande alliance" is used by La Potherie, *Histoire*, 4:252.

61 Eccles, "Report," 44.

62 ANF, Col., F3, vol. 2, f. 267v. (TN: our translation.)

63 ANF, Col., CIIA, vol. 22, f. 54, Parolles des Sonnontouans [...] 30 may 1704 (TN: our translation); Richter (*Ordeal of the Longhouse*, 218) also speaks of the death in 1704 of five Oneidas during a skirmish.

64 ANF, Col., CIIE, vol. 14, f. 188, mémoire de m. de la mothe Cadillac touchant l'établissement du Détroit [avec les remarques de Pontchartrain], Québec, 14 novembre 1704 (TN: our translation); Richter, *Ordeal of the Longhouse*, 219.

65 Richter, *Ordeal of the Longhouse*, 214–16, 223. The strategy of attracting the nations of the west to the Albany market did not always win

unanimous support from the League in the short term. In 1702, for example, some Senecas barred the way to a group of Amerindians from Detroit who had gone to trade with the English (ANF, Col., CIIA vol. 20, f. 65, Callière, Champigny et Beauharnois au ministre, Québec, 3 novembre 1702).

66 ANF, Col., CIIA, vol. 28, f. 211, Parolles des folles avoines a mr le gouverneur general [...] 23 juillet 1708. (TN: our translation.)

67 ANF, Col., CIIA, vol. 30, f. 86v, Reponse de mr de Vaudreuil aux sauvages outtaois [...] 29 juillet 1709. (TN: our translation.)

68 ANF, Col., CIIA, vol. 31, f. 99–100, Parolles des Iroquois sonnontouans et onnontaguez a mr le marquis de Vaudreuil 8 aout 1710. (TN: our translation.)

69 Richter, *Ordeal of the Longhouse*, 237.

70 See also ANF, Col., CIIA, vol. 21, f. 62v, Parolles des Sonnontouans et onontaguez a monsieur de Vaudreuil le 12 juin 1703.

71 Quoted by Lytwyn, "Historical Research Report," 44.

72 ANF, Col., CIIA, vol. 20, f. 100v, Callière au ministre, Québec, 4 novembre 1702 (on the Sauks-Foxes against the Ojibwas); Margry, *Découvertes*, 5:327, Lamothe Cadillac à Pontchartain, 31 aoust 1703 (on war between the Ojibwas and the Sauks-Menominees); ANF, Col., CIIA, vol. 30, f. 86, 89–92, Reponse de mr de Vaudreuil aux sauvages outtaois [...] 29 juillet 1709 (mediation of the Sauks between the Foxes and Ojibwas); ANF, Col., CIIA, vol. 31, f. 26–7, Vaudreuil et Raudot au ministre, Québec, 2 novembre 1710 (the Ojibwas against the Potawatomis); Havard, "Empire et métissages," 466.

73 Zoltvany, *Vaudreuil*, 81–4; White, *The Middle Ground*, 82–90.

74 White, *The Middle Ground*, 150–75; C. Callender, "Fox," *HNAI*, 15:643; Havard, "Empire et métissages," 473–6; Edmunds and Peyser, *Fox Wars*.

75 See ANF, Col., CIIA, vol. 20, f. 100, 156, Callière au ministre, Québec, 4 novembre 1702.

76 The aboriginal societies of Canada were "stateless" societies and inherently military in the sense that "the role of war in the reproduction of social relationships and the value system [was] predominant ... [in them]" ("Guerre," in Bonte, Izard, *Dictionnaire de l'ethnologie*, 315 [TN: our translation]).

77 Charlevoix, *Journal*, 528–9, 475; Perrot, *Mémoire*, 147 (TN: our translation); Havard, "Empire et métissages," 152–6; Richter, *Ordeal of the Longhouse*, 224.

78 La Potherie, *Histoire*, 1:303; ANF, Col., CIIA, vol. 22, f. 207, mémoire de Raudot. (TN: our translations.)

79 This did not perhaps have unanimous support among the Iroquois, but apart from the fact that it was objectively necessary for them, they could not really avoid it.

80 Quotation in Richter, *Ordeal of the Longhouse*, 237–9 (quotation on p. 237); Aquila, *Iroquois Restoration*, 205–32. Richter (*Ordeal of the Longhouse*, 237) quotes another document from 1707, written by an English interpreter: "Most of the [young men of the] five Nations were out against the Flatheads … they brought in a great many prisoners."

81 ANF, Col., CIIA, vol. 21, f. 74, Parolles des sauvages hurons a monsieur de Vaudreuil le 14 juillet 1703. (TN: our translation.)

82 ANF, Col., F3, vol. 87, f. 271 (on the Quapaw); ANF, Col., CIIA, vol. 21, f. 75v, reponse de mr de Vaudreuil aux sauvages hurons; Richter, *Ordeal of the Longhouse*, 237–8.

83 Haan, "The Problem of Iroquois Neutrality," 323–4; Richter, *Ordeal of the Longhouse*, 224–30.

84 ANF, Col., CIIA, vol. 31, f. 90, Parolles des sauvages onontaguez a mr le marquis de Vaudreuil a Montreal, 28 janvier 1710 (TN: our translation); see also ANF, Col., CIIA, vol. 21, f. 72–3, Parolles du chef nommé Teganissorens au nom des Cinq Nations a Montreal le 24 octobre 1703.

85 For the traditional interpretation, see Wallace, "Origins of Iroquois Neutrality," 223–35; E. Tooker, "The League of the Iroquois: Its History, Politics, and Rituals," HNAI, 15:432–4. For the revisionist perspective, see Haan, "The Problem of Iroquois Neutrality," 317–27; Richter, *Ordeal of the Longhouse*, 362 (first quotation), 215 (second quotation); Aquila, *Iroquois Restoration*, 68–9.

86 During the War of the Austrian Succession, except for the Mohawks, the League remained neutral. During the Seven Years' War (1756–63), which the English colonists called the "French and Indian War" (1754–60), the Iroquois were split between the two camps: the Mohawks sided with the English, while the Senecas remained pro-French. See Haan, "The Problem of Iroquois Neutrality"; Richter, *Ordeal of the Longhouse*, 225–30; Aquila, *Iroquois Restoration*, 85–128; Tooker, "The League of the Iroquois," 433–4.

CHAPTER TEN

1 Eccles, *Essays on New France*, 82; Miquelon, *New France*, 1, 14–15.

2 In the British colonies, the year 1701 was marked by the Albany conference, but also by the conference held in Philadelphia (in May) under the

auspices of William Penn, the founder of Pennsylvania (see Richter, *Ordeal of the Longhouse*, 436; Jennings, *Ambiguous Iroquois Empire*, 244, 250).

3 Aquila, *Iroquois Restoration*, 112; Richter, *Ordeal of the Longhouse*, 235. The Treaty of Utrecht affirmed that the Iroquois were British subjects. This declaration had no real effect, since the Five Nations maintained their policy of neutrality between the two empires.

4 ANF, Col., CIIA, vol. 19, f. 232, Callière, 1701. (TN: our translation.)

5 These figures are from 1706. See Trocmé and Rovet, *Naissance de l'Amérique moderne*, 67. In 1700 the French population of Canada was 14,000. In 1754 New France had 70,000 colonists as against 1,850,000 in the Thirteen Colonies.

6 ANF, Col., CIIA, vol. 28, Vaudreuil et Raudot au ministre, Québec, 14 novembre 1708; ANF, Col., F3, vol. 7, f. 178, 252–3.

7 NYCD, 5:726–33, Mr Colden's Memoir on the Fur Trade, Nov. 10, 1724.

8 Bougainville, *Ecrits*, 83, 96, 30, 166, 253. (TN: our translation.)

9 ANF, Col., CIIA, vol. 36, f. 107v, Vaudreuil au comte de Toulouse, février 1716. (TN: our translation.)

10 ANF, Col., CIIA, vol. 99, f. 391v-392, quoted by Delâge, "Les Iroquois chrétiens, II," 44.

APPENDIX ONE

1 Part of this section is taken from my article "Paix et interculturalité en Nouvelle-France au temps de Louis XIV," *RAQ* 27, no. 2:3–18.

2 Bély, *Espions et ambassadeurs*, 436. (TN: our translation.)

3 ANF, Col., CIIA, vol. 37, f. 324. (TN: our translation.)

4 Havard, "Paix et interculturalité," 10. Wampum belts had a referential value in intercultural diplomacy that was as important as that of treaties and their signatures. According to the oral tradition of the Hurons of Quebec, the "Lorette collar" symbolizes one of the agreements of 1701 and was presented at the conference by Kondiaronk (Delâge, "L'alliance franco-amérindienne," 9).

5 Jennings, ed., *Iroquois Diplomacy*, 86. Inconsistencies between the oral and the written were quite frequent in negotiations between the French and the Natives. For example, the scathing colonial speech found in the minutes of the French-Iroquois treaty of 1665, in which Amerindians are relegated to the status of subject, undoubtedly reflects neither the tone nor content of the discussions, and even less the intentions of the Iroquois ambassadors. But this discrepancy did not have

serious consequences, because the transfer of territories was not involved (Delâge, "Les Sept feux," 4–8).

6 The French practices were different from those of the Americans, for example, who in the nineteenth century would sometimes bribe chiefs to get them to sign a treaty, particularly when it involved giving up land. "It even happened," notes J. Pictet, "that they forged their signatures or got them drunk" (Pictet, *L'Épopée des Peaux Rouges*, 34 [TN: our translation]).

7 Havard, "Paix et interculturalité," 12–13.

8 ANF, Col., CIIA, 19, f. 44, 117; ANF, Col., CIIA, 18, f. 64, 88, 157; La Potherie, *Histoire*, 4:254. (TN: our translation.)

9 Charlevoix, *Journal*, 553. (TN: our translation.)

10 ANF, Col., CIIA, vol. 19, f. 41–4, Ratification de la Paix.

11 Lévi-Strauss, *Totemism*, 18–23.

12 Seven signatures could not be identified. The French word *dessant*, however, which is found near the last three pictographs, may come from the Algonquian term *Odessan*, which means, roughly, "the one who represents" (personal communication from Denys Delâge, 1989).

13 *HNAI*, 15: 649; Warren, *History*, 47, 88; ANF, Col., CIIA, vol. 19, f. 41–44, Ratification de la Paix.

14 ANF, Col., CIIA, 19, f. 44; *HNAI*, 15:615–16, 693; Callender, *Social Organisation*.

15 La Potherie, *Histoire*, 4:262.

16 ANF, Col., CIIA, 18, f. 88; CIIA, 19, f. 43.

17 Wogan, "Perceptions of European Literacy"; De Francis, *Visible Speech*, 3–7, 35–58.

18 Bossu, *Nouveaux Voyages*, 102–3, 76, 134, 158 (TN: our translation); Lafitau, *Customs*, 1:196–200.

19 Lahontan, *New Voyages*, 2:510–11; Lafitau, *Customs*, 1:200; ANF, Col., CIIA, vol. 2, f. 264–7.

20 Desveaux, "De l'interdit de dire au besoin de peindre," 208, 220; Dewdney and Kidd, *Indian Rock Paintings*.

21 Charlevoix, *Journal*, 685–6 (TN: our translation); Tooker, *An Ethnography of the Huron Indians, 1615–1649*, 21.

APPENDIX TWO

1 P.N. Moogk, "Aouenano," *DCB*, 2:20; La Potherie, *Histoire*, 4:135, 229–30, 252.

2 La Potherie, *Histoire*, 4:84, 135.

3 B.G. Trigger, "Aradgi," *DCB*, 2:21.

4 T. Charland, "Bigot, Vincent," *DCB*, 2:64–5.

5 C.J. Jaenen, "Bruyas, Jacques," *DCB*, 2:106–8.

6 Y.F. Zoltvany, "Laumet, Antoine, *dit* de Lamothe Cadillac," *DCB*,
   2:351–6; Havard, "Empire et métissages," 333–5.

7 François de Callières, *De la manière de négocier avec les souverains, de
   l'utilité des négociations, du choix des ambassadeurs et des envoyez, et
   des qualitez necessaires pour réussir dans ces employs* (Paris: M. Brunet,
   1716).

8 ANF, Col., CIIA, vol. 14, f. 67–73; Charlevoix, *Histoire*, 2:276.

9 ANF, Col., CIIA, vol. 13, f. 108; Eccles, *Canada under Louis XIV*, 190;
   Fenton, *The Great Law and the Longhouse*, 267.

10 Charlevoix, *Histoire*, 2:287–8 (TN: our translation); Y.F. Zoltvany,
   "Callière, Louis-Hector de," *DCB*, 2:112–17.

11 ANF, Col., CIIA, vol. 17, f. 64.

12 ANF, Col., CIIA, vol. 19, f. 117.

13 W.J. Eccles, "Bochart de Champigny, Jean," *DCB*, 2:71–80.

14 La Potherie, *Histoire*, 4:207. (TN: our translation.)

15 Ibid., 208.

16 Ibid., 260–2.

17 Ibid., 262.

18 Ibid., 207–8, 283, 260–2; D.J. Horton, "Chichikatelo," *DCB*, 2:143–4.

19 La Potherie, *Histoire*, 4:23.

20 Ibid., 94–8. (TN: our translation.)

21 Quoted in ibid., 233 (TN: our translation); D.J. Horton, "Chingouessi,"
   DCB, 2:144.

22 Margry, *Découvertes*, 5:277

23 Charlevoix, *Histoire*, 2:93, 100.

24 Ibid., 133, 156.

25 Ibid., 273–4. (TN: our translation.)

26 "Le Gardeur de Courtemanche, Augustin," *DCB*, 2:383–4.

27 J.P. Donnely, "Enjalran, Jean," *DCB*, 2:217–18.

28 W.J. Eccles, "Buade de Frontenac et de Palluau, Louis de," *DCB*,
   1:133–42.

29 Charlevoix, *Histoire*, 2:60, 133.

30 ANF, Col., CIIA, vol. 11, f. 130–1, Parolle qui doit estre ditte a l'outaouacs [...] 1690; Lahontan, *New Voyages*, 1:228; an Iroquois chief in
   1703 spoke of Frontenac as "our great father Onontio" (ANF, Col.,
   CIIA, vol. 21, f. 62v, Parolles des Sonnontouans et Onontaguez a
   Monsieur de Vaudreuil le 12 juin 1703 [TN: our translation]).

31 La Potherie, *Histoire*, 1:245; Hennepin, *Description*, 298–9. (TN: our translation.)

32 ANF, Col., CIIA, vol. 6, f. 7v, Paroles échangées entre Frontenac et les alliés hurons, outaouais et miamis, Montréal, août 1682. It was with Frontenac that the title "Onontio" became indissociable from the term "father." The Iroquois chief Otreouti spoke of Onontio in 1684 as his "father for the past ten years" (quoted in Dubé, *La Nouvelle-France*, 225 [TN: our translation]); see also Leclercq, *Etablissement*, 2:383.

33 See Havard, "Paix et interculturalité," 9; Havard, "Empire et métissages," 411–13; Desrosiers, *Iroquoisie*, 3:118.

34 Charlevoix, *Histoire*, 1:543, 562–3. (TN: our translation.)

35 Quoted in Charlevoix, *Histoire*, 2:278. (TN: our translation.)

36 L. Pouliot, "Garnier, Julien," DCB, 2:237–8.

37 La Potherie, *Histoire*, 4:140.

38 La Potherie, *Histoire*, 3:249.

39 Y.F. Zoltvany, "Chabert de Joncaire, Louis-Thomas," DCB, 2:125–7.

40 D. Chaput, "Kinongé," DCB, 2:317–18; ANF, Col., CIIA, vol. 6, f. 231–9, Daniel Greysolon Dulhut à La Barre, Michilimackinac, 12 avril 1684; La Potherie, *Histoire*, 3:225, 4:31.

41 W.N. Fenton, "Kondiaronk," DCB, 2:320–3. According to Lahontan (*New Voyages*, 1:220), Kondiaronk was forty years old in 1689, which means he died at fifty-two, although the Sulpicians of Montreal stated on his death certificate that he was seventy-five (personal communication from Denys Delâge, 2000). That latter figure seems overstated, since Kondiaronk, as a war leader, had led an expedition against the Iroquois in 1697 on Lake Erie.

42 Charlevoix, *Histoire*, 1:535–6. (TN: our translation.)

43 Ibid.; La Potherie, *Histoire*, 4:228 (TN: our translation). As mentioned above (chapter 7, note 108), Kondiaronk is also presented as an Amerindian convert to Catholicism.

44 On Sastaretsi, see ANF, Col., F3, vol. 7, f. 178; Tooker, "Wyandot," HNAI, 15:405.

45 Charlevoix, *Histoire*, 2:214.

46 Charlevoix, *Histoire*, 1:536–7; La Potherie, *Histoire*, 4:171.

47 Ibid., 277. (TN: our translation.)

48 Lahontan, *New Voyages*, 1:xiv, 7, and 2:519–618.

49 La Potherie, *Histoire*, 3:240. (TN: our translation.)

50 ANF, Col., CIIA, vol. 6, f. 7. (TN: our translation.)

51 Perrot, *Mémoire*, 143, 145. (TN: our translation.)

52 La Potherie, *Histoire*, 3:240, 4:23–4.

53 La Potherie, *Histoire*, 3:299; Charlevoix, *Histoire*, 2:214 (TN: our translation).

54 Quoted in La Potherie, *Histoire*, 4:172–3. (TN: our translation.)

55 Charlevoix, *Histoire*, 2:276–7. (TN: our translation.)

56 ANF, Col., CIIA, vol. 18, f. 85–8; D. Chaput, "Koutaoiliboe," *DCB*, 2:323–4; Havard, "Empire et métissages," 403, 405. This chief should not be confused with the Sinago Odawa signatory of the Montreal peace treaties of 1700 and 1701 who was named Outaliboi (or Outaoualiboi).

57 L. Pouliot, "Le Roy de La Potherie, *dit* Bacqueville de La Potherie (La Poterie), Claude-Charles," *DCB*, 2:421–3; La Potherie, *Histoire*.

58 Charlevoix, *Histoire*, 2:156.

59 La Potherie, *Histoire*, 3:94–103, 222–3, 226.

60 Charlevoix, *Histoire*, 2:156.

61 Ibid., 213.

62 Ibid.

63 La Potherie, *Histoire*, 4:16–27, 50–1; Charlevoix, *Histoire*, 2:156, 162–3, 213–14; ANF, Col., CIIA, vol. 14, f. 86.

64 Fenton, *The Great Law and the Longhouse*, 293–4.

65 D.J. Horton, "Le Moyne de Maricourt, Paul," *DCB*, 2:403–5; W.J. Eccles, "Teganissorens," *DCB*, 2:619–23; La Potherie, *Histoire*, 3:207.

66 D.J. Horton, "Ounanguissé," *DCB*, 2:504.

67 Charlevoix, *Histoire*, 2:215. (TN: our translation.)

68 La Potherie, *Histoire*, 3:302–3. (TN: our translation.)

69 Leclercq, *Etablissement*, 2:198–9; Clifton, *The Prairie People*, 82, 120.

70 La Potherie, *Histoire*, 4:58–60. (TN: our translation.)

71 Quoted in Charlevoix, *Histoire*, 2:215. (TN: our translation.)

72 La Potherie, *Histoire*, 4:224–6. (TN: our translation.)

73 Ibid., 212.

74 Ibid., 260.

75 We encounter his successor in Detroit in the 1720s, a "Man of merit, and completely in our interests," according to Charlevoix (*Journal*, 541, 543 [quote on 534; TN: our translation]).

76 Clifton, *The Prairie People*, 20, 24, 89; Margry, *Découvertes*, 1:539, Relation des descouvertes et des voyages du sieur de La Salle [...]; Margry, *Découvertes*, 2:154, La Salle, relation du voyage [...] 1680 [...] 1681.

77 ANF, Col., CIIA, vol. 34, f. 284v, Vaudreuil au ministre, Québec, 16 septembre 1714.

78 La Potherie, *Histoire*, 3:265–6.

79 D.J. Horton, "Ouenemek," *DCB*, 2:503–4; ANF, Col., CIIA, vol. 22, f. 263r, Parolles de Ouilamek chef poutouatamy a mr le gouverneur,

4 aout 1705; ANF, Col., C11A, vol. 31, f. 86–7, Parolles de mr le gouverneur general aux sauvages descendus d'en hault; ANF, Col., C11A, vol. 33, f. 51–2, Vaudreuil au ministre, Québec, 6 novembre 1712; Charlevoix, *Journal*, 645.

80 La Potherie, *Histoire*, 4:202. (TN: our translation.)

81 Quoted in ibid., 69–70. (TN: our translation.)

82 Charlevoix, *Histoire*, 2:276. (TN: our translation.)

83 La Potherie, *Histoire*, 4:203, 212, 258. (TN: our translation.)

84 P.N. Moogk, "Outoutagan," DCB, 2:504–6.

85 C. Perrault, "Perrot, Nicolas," DCB, 2:516–20.

86 Charlevoix, *Histoire*, 2:291.

87 Ibid., 308. (TN: our translation.)

88 Quoted in La Potherie, *Histoire*, 4:24. (TN: our translation.)

89 Quoted in ibid., 3:305. (TN: our translation.)

90 Quoted in ibid., 4:213. (TN: our translation.)

91 Ibid., 222, 236.

92 Ibid., 256, 258.

93 Charlevoix, *Histoire*, 2:292, 308.

94 W.J. Eccles, "Teganissorens," DCB, 2:619–23; La Potherie, *Histoire*, 4:204–18; Charlevoix, *Histoire*, 2:136, 289.

95 La Potherie, *Histoire*, 4:156.

96 "Tekanoet," DCB, 2:623–5; La Potherie, *Histoire*, 4:156, 200, 216, 258.

97 Tonatakout is mentioned in the sources in 1734, but it was perhaps not the same person (DCB, 2:631; La Potherie, *Histoire*, 4:135–47, 229–30).

98 Y.F. Zoltvany, "Rigaud de Vaudreuil, Philippe de," DCB, 2 565–74.

Glossary of the Names of Native Peoples

Every human group is known by a variety of names. As the American anthropologist John H. Moore states, "The people English-speakers call Germans … are called Allemands by the French, Duitser by the Dutch, and Niemicki by the Poles, while the Germans call themselves Deutsch" (*The Cheyenne* [Malden: Blackwell Publishers, 1999], 13). The names of Amerindian nations either were made up by the colonizers or are transcriptions of the Native names. The Foxes (*Renards* in French), a group from the Great Lakes, were given that name by seventeenth-century French explorers; they were also called the Outagamis ("people of the other shore") by their Ojibwa neighbours; and they called themselves Muskwakiwuk ("the Red Earth People"). The name *Huron* comes from the French *hure*, or "boar's head," derived either from the way the men wore their hair or from a pejorative slang term meaning "ruffian," "knave," or "lout." The real name of the Hurons is Wendats, meaning "islanders" or "peninsula dwellers." According to the French sources of the second half of the seventeenth century, they were also called the Tionontatis after they joined with the Petuns. Another example is the Sioux, whose name is a contraction of *Naud-o-wa-se-wug* (or, in French, *Nadouessioux*), which literally means "like adders," the term the Ojibwas used for their enemies. The colonizers also preserved the names that the Amerindians used for themselves. When the French coureurs de bois asked them their name, the Illinois answered "Illinois," which meant "the people" in their language. This type of name ("men," "true men," "human beings," etc.) is found in many Native groups.

The glossary provides (1) the English/American name, (2) the French name, (3) the aboriginal name, i.e., what the group called itself. Some of the self-designations are still hypothetical. In a few cases, notably where a little-known (to the Europeans) group ceased to exist as a distinct ethnic entity during the colonial period (the Susquehannocks, the Wenros, the Neutrals), we do not know the Aboriginal name. What is given here is not the modern technical "phonemicization" of words from living languages but the popular English form and the form used by modern First Nations rather than the historic form (although the latter is sometimes mentioned). For example, several related Algonquian-speaking groups – Algonkins, Ojibwa, Odawa, and Potawatomi – currently identify themselves as Anishinabe or Anishinabeg ("The Real People") (W.C. Sturtevant, ed., *Handbook of North American Indians*, vol. 6, *Subarctic* and vol. 15, *Northeast* [Washington DC: Smithsonian Institute, 1981, 1978]; D.R. Snow, *The Iroquois* [Cambridge, MA: Blackwell, 1996]).

English/American	French	Aboriginal
Abenakis	Abénaquis	Wabanakis ("People of the Dawnland")
Algonquins (or Algonkins)	Algonquins	Anishinabe
Amikwas (Ojibwa sub-group)	Amikoués, Amikois ("Les gens du castor")	Anishinabe
Caughnawagas, Kahnawakes	Gens du Sault	Kahnawakero':non
Cayugas (Iroquois nation)	Oiogouens, Goyogouins	Kayohkhono
Coiracoentanons (Illinois nation)	Coiracoentanons	
Crees	Cris, Cristinaux, Kilistinons	Eeyou[1]
Eries	Ériés, nation du Chat ("Raccoon nation")	
Flatheads	Têtes Plates	
Foxes	Renards, Outagamis	Mesquakie ("the Red Earth People")
	Gens des terres ("inlanders") (Crees or Naskapis or Attikamekw)	
Hurons of Lorette	Hurons de Lorette	Huron-Wendat, Wendat
Illinois	Illinois	Ilini ("The People")[2]
Iroquois	Iroquois	Haudenosaunee ("People of the Longhouse")

English/American	French	Aboriginal
Iroquois of the Mountain	Gens de la Montagne	Kanehsata'kehro':non.
Kaskakias (Illinois nation)	Kaskakias	Cascakia(sq), Cascakiaki
Kickapoos	Kicapous, Kikabous	Kiikaapoa
Kiskakons (Odawa sub-group)	Kiskakons, "Culs Coupez" (Cutting Tails)	Odawa, Anishnabe
Mahicans	Mohicans, Loups ("Wolves"), Mahingans ("Wolves" in Algonquin)	
Maliseets	Malécites	
Maroas, Tamaroas (Illinois subgroup)	Tamarois	
Mascoutens	Mascoutens, Mascoutins	
Menominees	Malominis, Folles avoines ("Wild Oats")	
Miamis, Twicktwigs	Miamis, Oumamis	Miamia
Mi'kmaq or Micmac	Micmacs	Mi'kmaq
Mississaugas (Ojibwa nation)	Mississagués	Anishinabe
Mohawks (Iroquois nation), Maquas	Agniers	Kanyenkehaka ("People of the Place of Crystals" or "People of the Place of Flint")[3]
Moingwenas (Illinois subgroup)	Monisgouenars, Les Moines	
Montagnais	Montagnais	Innu (sq.), Innuat (pl.)
Nassouakouetons (Odawa subgroup)	Nassauaketons, "nation de la fourche"	Odawa, Anishinabe
Neutrals	Neutres	
Nipissings	Népissingues	Anishinabe
Odawas (or Ottawas)	Outaouais	Odawa, Anishinabe
Ojibwas (Chippewas)	Ojibwés, Saulteurs	Ojebway, Ocipwe, Anishinabe
Oneidas (Iroquois nation)	Onneiouts	Oneyoteaka ("The people of the Erected Stone")
Onondagas (Iroquois nation)	Onontagués	Onontakeka ("People of the Hill")
Ouiatanons, Weas (Miami subgroup)	Ouiatanons	
Passamaquoddys	Passamaquodys	
Penobscots	Pentagouets	
Peorias (Illinois subgroup)	Peorias, Peouarea	

English/American	French	Aboriginal
Petuns (Tobacco nation)	nation du Pétun, Gens du pétuns	
Piankashaws (Miami sub-group)	Peanguichias, Peouanguichias	Peangishia
Potawatomis	Poutéouatamis	Potewatmi, anishinabe
Sable Odawas	Outaouais du Sable	Odawa, Anishinabe
Sauks	Sakis, Ousakis	Asaakiiwaki ("People of the Inlet")
Senecas (Iroquois Nation)	Tsonnontouans	Onontowaka ("People of the Big Hill")
Shawnees	Chaouanons	shawanwa ("Person of the South")
Sinagos (Odawa sub-group)	Outaouais Sinago	Odawa, Anishinabe
Sioux	Sioux	Dakota ("men" or "allies")[4]
Susquehannocks, Conestogas	Andastes	
Tapouaros (Illinois subgroup)	Tapouarouas, Raparouas	
Timiskamings	Témiscamingues	Anishinabe
Wenros	Ouaroronons	
Winnebagos	Puants ("Stinkards")	Otchagras ("People of the Parent Speech")
Wyandots	Huron-Petuns (Tionontatés, Tionontatis, Hurons)	Wendat

1 Term used by the Grand Council of the Crees in Quebec. There were many Cree groups and each had its own self-designation; see J.G.E. Smith, "Western Woods Cree," in vol. 6, *Subarctic*, 167–8 of W.C. Sturtevant, ed., *Handbook of North American Indians* (Washington DC: Smithsonian Institute, 1981).

2 JR59: 124

3 The gloss "People of the Place of the Crystals" is Snow's hypothesis; see Snow, *The Iroquois*, 86.

4 The Sioux with whom the French were in contact in the seventeenth century were Dakota, but the term Sioux refers in fact to three linguistic subgroups, the Dakota, the Nakota, and the Lakota.

Bibliography

The list of documents consulted is divided into two parts: first the primary sources, then historical studies. Included under the primary sources are historical works published in the seventeenth and eighteenth centuries, as well as collections of the oral tradition from the nineteenth and twentieth centuries.

PRIMARY SOURCES

Manuscript Sources

Archives nationales de France (Paris), Fonds des colonies
Série B: correspondance générale: dépêches du roi, du ministre de la Marine et du Conseil d'Etat aux administrateurs des colonies.
Série C I IA: correspondance générale: lettres, mémoires, etc., envoyés en France par les administrateurs du Canada et autres personnes.
Série C I IE: correspondance des limites et postes.
Série F3: Collection Moreau de Saint-Méry: copies de documents faisant partie des séries C I IA et B et d'autres pièces qui ont disparu depuis.
Archives de la Marine (Paris)
Série 2JJ: papiers personnels de géographes et d'hydrographes des XVIIe-XIXe siècles. In particular: Le Sueur, *Mémoire* (2JJ no. 56, vol. 115, Livre X, no. 9: Claude Delisle, "Mémoires de Mr Le Sueur, 1699–1702," 94 folios).

Published

Archives nationales de France (Paris) (ANF), Fonds des colonies: série B.

Boucher, Pierre. *Histoire véritable et naturelle des moeurs et productions du pays de la Nouvelle-France vulgairement dite le Canada* (1664). Société historique de Boucherville, 1964.

Bougainville, Louis-Antoine. *Ecrits sur le Canada: Mémoires-Journal-Lettres*. Pelican/Klincksiek, 1993.

Breteuil, Baron de. *Mémoires*. Edited by Evelyne Lever. Paris: François Bourrin, 1992.

Callières, François de. *De la manière de négocier avec les souverains, de l'utilité des négociations, du choix des ambassadeurs et des envoyez, et des qualitez necessaires pour réussir dans ces employs*. Paris: M. Brunet, 1716. English translation: *On the Manner of Negotiating with Princes: On the Uses of Diplomacy, the Choice of Ministers and Envoys, and the Personal Qualities Necessary for Success in Missions Abroad*. Translated by A.F. Whyte. Boston: Houghton Mifflin, 1919.

Catalogne, Gédéon de. "Recuil (*sic*) de se qui s'est passé en Canada au suyet (*sic*) de la guerre tant des anglois que des iroquois depuis l'année 1682." In Robert Le Blant, *Histoire de la Nouvelle-France: les sources narratives du début du XVIIIe siècle*. Dax: P. Pradeu, 1948.

Charlevoix, P. François Xavier de. *Histoire et description générale de la Nouvelle-France, avec le journal historique d'un voyage fait par ordre du Roi dans l'Amérique septentrionale*. Ottawa: Éditions Élysée, 1976 (1744). 3 Vols.

– *Journal d'un voyage fait par ordre du roi dans l'Amérique septentrionale*. Edited by Pierre Berthiaume. 2 vols. Collection Bibliothèque du Nouveau Monde (Écrits de la Nouvelle-France). Montréal: Presses de l'Université de Montréal, 1994 (1744).

Colden, Cadwallader. *The History of the Five Indian Nations Depending on the Province of New-York in America, 1727–1747*. Ithaca, N.Y.: 1958.

Deliette, Pierre Charles. *Mémoire (Memoir of De Gannes Concerning the Illinois Country)*. Collections of the Illinois Historical Library, 23: 302–95.

Documents Relative to the Colonial History of the State of New-York (NYCD). Edited by Edmund B. O'Callaghan. 15 vol. Albany: A. Weed, 1853–77.

Dubé, Pauline, ed. *La Nouvelle-France sous Joseph-Antoine de La Barre, 1682–1685, Lettres, mémoires, instructions et ordonnances*. Sillery, Québec: Septentrion, 1993.

Furetière, Antoine. *Dictionnaire universel.* 3 vols. La Haye, Rotterdam: A. et R. Leers, 1690.

Hennepin, Louis. *Description de la Louisiane, nouvellement découverte au Sud Ouest de la Nouvelle-France par ordre du Roy.* Paris: Veuve Sébastien Huré, 1683.

Illinois Historical Library Collections (IHC). Vol. 23, *The French Foundations, 1680–1693.* Edited by Pease T.C. and R.C. Werner. Springfield: Illinois, 1934.

The Jesuit Relations and Allied Documents: Travels and Explorations of the Jesuit Missionaries in New-France, 1610–1791. Edited by Reuben Gold Thwaites. 73 vols. Cleveland, Ohio, 1896–1901.

Kalm, Pehr. *Peter Kalm's Travels in North America.* Translated and edited by Adolph B. Benson. New York: Dover Publications, 1966.

Lafitau, J.-F. Lafitau, J.-F. *Customs of the American Indians Compared with the Customs of Primitive Times.* Edited and translated by William N. Fenton and Elizabeth L. Moore (*Moeurs des sauvages américains*). 2 vols. Toronto: Champlain Society, 1974–77 (1724).

Lahontan, Louis Armand de Lom d'Arce, baron de. *New Voyages to North-America.* Edited by Reuben Gold Thwaites. Chicago: A.C. McClurg and Co., 1905.

– *Œuvres complètes.* 2 vols. Édition établie par R. Ouellet et A. Beaulieu. Montréal: Presses de l'Université de Montréal, 1990.

– *Voyages du Baron de La Hontan dans l'Amérique septentrionale.* Montréal: Éditions Élysée, 1974 (1705).

– *Mémoires de l'Amérique septentrionale ou la suite des voyages de Mr le Baron de La Hontan.* Montréal: Éditions Élysée, 1974 (1705).

La Potherie, Claude-Charles Le Roy, dit Bacqueville de. *Histoire de l'Amérique septentrionale.* 4 vols. Paris: Brocas, 1753 (1722).

Le Blant, Robert. *Histoire de la Nouvelle-France: les sources narratives du début du XVIIIe siècle et le recueil de Gédéon de Catalogne,* vol. 1. Dax: P. Pradeu, 1948.

Le Clercq, Chrestien. *Premier établissement de la Foy dans la Nouvelle-France.* 2 vols. Paris: Amable Auroy, 1691.

Louis XIV. *Mémoires de Louis XIV.* Edited by J. Longnon. Paris: Tallandier, 1978.

Margry, Pierre, ed. *Découvertes et Etablissement des Français dans l'Ouest et dans le Sud de l'Amérique Septentrionale, 1614–1754, Mémoires et documents originaux.* 6 vols. Paris: D. Jouaud, 1876–86.

Perrot, Nicolas. *Mémoire sur les moeurs, coustumes et relligion des sauvages de l'Amérique septentrionale.* Montréal: Éditions Élysée, 1973 (1864).

Radisson, Pierre-Esprit. *Voyages of Pierre-Esprit Radisson, being a Account of his Travels and Experiences among the North American Indians, from 1652 to 1684.* Edited by G.D. Scull. New York: Burt Franklin Boston, 1885.

Rapport de l'Archiviste de la Province de Québec (RAPQ).

Raudot, Antoine-Denis. *Relation par lettres de l'Amérique septentrionale, 1709–1710.* Texte établi et présenté par Camille de Rochemonteix. Paris: Letouzey et Ané, 1904.

Sagard, Gabriel. *Le Grand Voyage du pays des Hurons, suivi du Dictionnaire de la langue huronne.* Edited by Jack Warwick. Collection Bibliothèque du Nouveau Monde (Écrits de la Nouvelle-France). Montréal: Les Presses de l'Université de Montréal, 1998.

Troyes, Pierre Chevalier de. *Journal de l'expédition du chevalier de Troyes à la baie d'Hudson en 1686.* Edited by Ivanhoe Caron. Beauceville: La Cie de l'Éclaireur, 1918.

Wraxall, Peter. *An Abridgement of the Indian Affairs Contained in Four-folio Volumes, Transacted in the Colony of New York, From Year 1678 to Year 1751.* Edited by Charles H. McIlwain. Cambridge: Harvard University Press, 1915.

Sources for the Oral Traditions

Barbeau, C. Marius. *Huron and Wyandot Mythology; with an appendix containing earlier published records.* Ottawa, Government Printing Bureau, 1915.

Copway, George. *The Traditional History and Characteristic Sketches of the Ojibwa Nation.* Toronto: Coles, 1972 (1850).

Kohl, Johann Georg. *Kitchi-gami, Life Among The Lake Superior Ojibway.* St Paul: Minnesota Historical Society Press, 1985 (1860).

Speck, Frank. "The Eastern Algonkian Wabanaki Confederacy." In *Northern Algonquian Source Book: Papers by Frank G. Speck.* Edited by Edward S. Rogers, 492–508. New York and London: Garland Publishing, 1985.

Warren, William. *History of the Ojibway People* (1885). St Paul: Minnesota Historical Society Press, 1984.

HISTORICAL STUDIES

Anderson, Gary Clayton. *Kinsmen of Another Kind: Dakota-White Relations in the Upper Mississippi Valley, 1650–1862.* Lincoln: University of Nebraska Press, 1984.

Apostolidès, Jean-Marie. *Le Roi-machine: spectacle et politique au temps de Louis XIV.* Paris: Éditions de Minuit, 1981.

Aquila, Richard. *The Iroquois Restoration: Iroquois Diplomacy on the Colonial Frontier, 1701–1754.* Detroit: Wayne State University Press, 1983.

Axtell, James. "Ethnohistory of Early America: A Review Essay." *William and Mary Quarterly* 35, no. 3 (1979): 110–44.

– "Ethnohistory: An Historian's Viewpoint." *Ethnohistory* 26 (1978): 1–13.

– *The European and the Indian: Essays in the Ethnohistory of Early America.* Oxford: Oxford University Press, 1981.

– *The Invasion Within: The Contest of Cultures in Colonial North America.* New York: Oxford University Press, 1985.

– *After Columbus: Essays in the Ethnohistory of Colonial North America.* New York: Oxford University Press, 1988.

– *Beyond 1492: Encounters in Colonial North America.* New York: Oxford University Press, 1992.

Bailey, A.G. *The Conflict of European and Eastern Algonkian Cultures, 1504–1700: A Study in Canadian Civilization.* St John: New Brunswick Museum, 1937.

Balandier, Georges. *Political Anthropology.* Translated by A.M. Sheridan Smith (*Anthropologie politique*). New York: Pantheon Books, 1970.

Beaulieu, Alain. *Convertir les fils de Caïn: Jésuites et Amérindiens nomades en Nouvelle-France, 1632–1642.* Québec: Nuit Blanche, 1994.

– *Les autochtones du Québec.* Montréal: Musée de la civilisation et Editions Fides, 1997.

Beaulieu, Alain, and Michel Lavoie. "La Grande Paix de Montréal (1701) et l'Arbre de Paix iroquois." Paper presented at the 53rd conference of the Institut d'histoire de l'Amérique française, Montreal, 19–21 October 2000.

Bély, Lucien. *Espions et ambassadeurs au temps de Louis XIV.* Paris: Fayard, 1990.

– ed. *Dictionnaire de l'Ancien Régime.* Paris: Presses Universitaires de France, 1996.

– ed. *L'invention de la diplomatie: Moyen Age-Temps modernes.* Paris: Presses Universitaires de France, 1998.

Bercé, Yves Marie, ed. *Les monarchies.* Paris: Presses Universitaires de France, 1997.

Berkhofer, Robert J., Jr. "The Political Context of a New Indian History." *Pacific Historical Review* 40 (1971): 357–82.

Black-Rogers, Mary. "Varieties of Starving: Semantics and Survival in the Subartic Fur Trade, 1750–1850." *Ethnohistory* 33, no. 4:353–83.

Bonte, Pierre, and Michel Izard, eds. *Dictionnaire de l'ethnologie et de l'anthropologie*. Paris: Presses Universitaires de France, 1991.

Brandão, J.A. *"Your Fyre shall burn no more": Iroquois Policy toward New France and Its Native Allies to 1701*. Lincoln and London: University of Nebraska Press, 1997.

Brandão, J.A., and William A. Starna. "The Treaties of 1701: A Triumph of Iroquois Diplomacy." *Ethnohistory* 43, no. 2 (1996): 209–44.

Brown, Craig, ed. *The Illustrated History of Canada*. Toronto: Lester Publishing, 1991.

Callender, Charles. *Social Organisation of the Central Algonquian Indians*. Milwaukee Public Museum, Publications in Anthropology 7. Milwaukee Public Museum, 1962.

Carmack, Robert M. "Ethnohistory: A Review of Its Development, Definitions, Methods, and Aims." *Annual Review of Anthropology* 1 (1972): 227–46.

Carpin, Gervais. "Les Amérindiens en guerre (1500–1650)." RAQ 26, nos. 3–4: 99–113.

Champagne, André, ed. *L'histoire du Régime français*. Montréal: Septentrion/Radio Canada, 1996.

Chaunu, Pierre. *Les Amériques, 16ᵉ – 17ᵉ – 18ᵉ siècles*. Paris: Armand Colin, 1976.

Chodowiec, Urszula. "La hantise et la pratique: le cannibalisme iroquois." *Nouvelle Revue de Psychanalyse* 6 (1972): 55–69.

Clastres, Pierre. *Society against the State: Essays in Political Anthropology*. Translated by Robert Hurley in collaboration with Abe Stein (*La société contre l'Etat*). New York: Zone Books, 1987.

– *Recherches d'anthropologie politique*. Paris: Éditions du Seuil, 1980.

Cleland, Charles E. *Rites of Conquest: The History and Culture of Michigan's Native Americans*. Ann Arbor: University of Michigan Press, 1992.

Clifton, James A. *The Prairie People: Continuity and Change in Potawatomi Culture, 1665–1965*. Lawrence: Regents Press of Kansas, 1977.

Constant, Monique. "Les traités: validité, publicité." In Bély, ed., *L'invention de la diplomatie*, 235–48.

Cornette, Joël. *Le Roi de guerre: essai sur la souveraineté dans la France du Grand Siècle*. Paris: Payot, 1993.

– ed. *La France de la monarchie absolue, 1610–1715*. Paris: L'Histoire/Seuil, 1997.

Couture, Yvon H. *Les Algonquins: Racines amérindiennes*. Val d'Or: Editions Hyperborée, 1983.

Creagh, Ronald, ed. *Les Français des Etats-Unis d'hier à aujourd'hui*. Montpellier: Actes du colloque international sur les Français des Etats-Unis, 1994.

Day, Gordon M. "Oral Tradition as Complement." *Ethnohistory* 19, no. 2 (1972): 99–108.

Dechêne, Louise. *Habitants and Merchants in Seventeenth-Century Montreal*. Translated by Liana Vardi (*Habitants et marchands de Montréal au XVIIe siècle*). Montreal and Kingston: McGill-Queen's University Press, 1992.

Delâge, Denys. "L'alliance franco-amérindienne, 1660–1701." *RAQ* 19, no. 1 (1989): 3–15.

– "Les Iroquois chrétiens des réductions, 1667–1770, I: Migration et rapports avec les Français." *RAQ* 21, nos. 1-2 (1991): 59–70.

– "Les Iroquois chrétiens des réductions, 1667–1770, II: Rapports avec la Ligue iroquoise, les Britanniques et les autres nations autochtones." *RAQ* 21, no. 3 (1991): 39–50.

– "La religion dans l'alliance franco-amérindienne." *Anthropologie et Sociétés* 15, no. 1 (1991): 55–87.

– "War and the French-Indian Alliance." *European Review of Native American Studies* 5, no. 1 (1991): 15–20.

– "L'influence des Amérindiens sur les Canadiens et les Français au temps de la Nouvelle-France." *Lekton* 2, no. 2 (1992): 103–91.

– "Les premiers contacts selon un choix de récits amérindiens publiés aux XIXe et XXe siècles." In *RAQ* 22, nos. 2–3 (1992): 101–16.

– "Les premiers contacts dans *History of the Ojibway People* de William Warren, un récit de transition entre l'oral et l'écrit." In *RAQ* 22, no. 4 (1992): 49–60.

– *Bitter Feast: Amerindians and Europeans in Northeastern North America, 1600–64*. Translated by Jane Brierley. Vancouver: University of British Columbia Press, 1993.

– "Les principaux paradigmes de l'histoire amérindienne et l'étude de l'alliance franco-amérindienne aux XVIIe et XVIIIe siècles." *Revue internationale d'études canadiennes* 12 (automne 1995): 51–67.

– "Les Hurons de Lorette dans leur contexte historique en 1760." In *Les Hurons de Lorette*. Edited by D. Vaugeois, 97–131. Montréal: Septentrion, 1996.

– et al. "Les Sept Feux, les alliances et les traités: Autochtones du Québec dans l'histoire." Rapport soumis à la Commission royale d'enquête sur les peuples autochtones, 30 juillet 1996.

Delanoë, Nelcya. *L'entaille rouge, terres indiennes et démocratie américaine, 1776–1980*. Paris: Maspero, 1982.

De Francis, John. *Visible Speech: The Diverse Oneness of Writing Systems.* Honolulu: University of Hawaii Press, 1989.

Dennis, Matthew, *Cultivating a Landscape of Peace: Iroquois-European Encounters in Seventeenth-Century America.* Ithaca: Cornell University Press, 1993.

Desrosiers, Léo-Paul. *Iroquoisie.* 4 vols. Montréal: Septentrion, 1998.

Désveaux, Emmanuel. *Sous le signe de l'ours: Mythes et temporalité chez les Ojibwa septentrionaux.* Paris: Edition de la Maison des Sciences de l'Homme, 1988.

– "Les forêts du Nord-Est et les plaines: le figuratif et le géométrique." In *Le Grand Atlas de l'art,* 2:370–1. Encyclopedia Universalis, 1993.

– "Les Grands lacs et les plaines." In *Papers of the 24th Algonquian Conference,* edited by W. Cowan, 104–12. Ottawa: Carleton University, 1993.

– "De l'interdit de dire au besoin de peindre, l'art iconique ojibwa." In *Mémoire de la tradition,* edited by Aurore Becquelin and Antoinette Molinié, 203–25. Nanterre: Société d'ethnologie, 1993.

– "Les Indiens écrivent en dépit de l'histoire." *Critique* 565–6 (1994): 494–520.

– "Parenté, rituel, organisation sociale: le cas des Sioux." *JSA* 83 (1997): 111–40.

– "Quadratura Americana: Essai d'anthropologie lévi-straussienne." Thèse d'habilitation. Paris: École des Hautes Études en Sciences Sociales, 1999.

Dewdney, S., and K.E. Kidd. *Indian Rock Paintings of the Great Lakes.* Toronto: University of Toronto Press, 1962.

Dickason, Olive P. *Canada's First Nations.* Toronto: McClelland and Stewart, 1992.

Dickinson, John A. "Annaotaha et Dollard vus de l'autre côté de la palissade." *Revue d'histoire de l'Amérique française* 35, no. 2 (1981): 163–78.

Dickinson, John A., and Lucien-René Abénon. *Les Français en Amérique.* Lyon: Presses Universitaires de Lyon, 1993.

Dictionnaire biographique du Canada (DBC). Presses de l'Université Laval. Vols. 1 (1966) and 2 (1969).

Dictionary of Canadian Biography (DCB). University of Toronto Press. Vols. 1 (1966) and 2 (1969).

Driver, Harold E. *Indians of North America.* Chicago: University of Chicago Press, 1969.

Dubant, Bernard. *Sitting Bull, "le dernier Indien."* Paris: Guy Trédaniel, 1982.

– *Crazy Horse, Chamane et guerrier*. Paris: Guy Trédaniel, 1990.

Dupuis, Renée. *La question indienne au Canada*. Montréal: Boréal, 1991.

Eccles, William J. *Frontenac, the Courtier Governor*. Toronto: McClelland and Stewart, 1959.

– *Canada under Louis XIV, 1663–1701*. Toronto: McClelland and Stewart, 1964.

– *France in America*. New York: Harper and Row, 1972.

– *The Canadian Frontier, 1534–1760*. Albuquerque: University of New Mexico Press, 1983 (1969).

– "The Fur Trade and Eighteenth-Century Imperialism." *WMQ* 40, no. 3 (1983): 341–62.

– *Essays on New-France*. Toronto: Oxford University Press, 1987.

– "Report for the Ontario Ministry of Natural Resources: MNR's Action in Support of *R. v. Decaire*." 1995.

Edmunds, David R. *The Potawatomis, Keepers of the Fire*. Norman: University of Oklahoma Press, 1978.

Edmunds, David R., and Joseph L. Peyser. *The Fox Wars: The Mesquakie Challenge to New France*. Norman: University of Oklahoma Press, 1993.

Eid, Leroy V. "The Ojibwa-Iroquois War: The War the Five Nations Did Not Win." *Ethnohistory* 26, no. 4 (1979): 297–324.

Fenton, William N. "Locality as a Basic Factor in the Development of Iroquois Social Structure." In *Symposium on Local Diversity in Iroquois Culture*, edited by W.N. Fenton, 39–54. Bureau of American Ethnology, Bulletin 149. Washington, 1951.

– "Factionalism in American Indian Society." In *Actes de IVe congrès international des sciences anthropologiques et ethnologiques* (Vienna, 1955) 2:330–40.

– "Ethnohistory and Its Problems." *Ethnohistory* 9, no. 1 (1962).

– *The Great Law and the Longhouse: A Political History of the Iroquois Confederacy*. Norman: University of Oklahoma Press, 1998.

Flandrin, Jean-Louis. *Families in Former Times: Kinship, Household, and Sexuality*. Translated by Richard Southern (*Familles: Parenté, maison, sexualité dans l'ancienne société*). Cambridge, England; New York: Cambridge University Press, 1979.

Foster, Michael, Jack Campisi, and Marianne Mithun, eds. *Extending the Rafters: Interdisciplinary Approaches to Iroquoian Studies*. Albany, N.Y.: State University of New York Press, 1984.

Fournier, Martin. *Pierre-Esprit Radisson, coureur de bois et homme du monde (1652–1685)*. Québec: Nuit blanche éditeur, 1996.

Fregault, Guy. *La civilisation de la Nouvelle-France, 1713–1744*. Bibliothèque québécoise, 1990 (1969).

Garneau, François-Xavier. *Histoire du Canada*. Vol. 3, 8th ed. Montréal: Éditions de l'Arbre, 1944.

Gélinas, Claude. "La nature des attaques iroquoises contre Ville-marie, 1642–1667." *RAQ* 24, nos. 1–2 (1994): 119–27.

Girard, Camil, and Édith Gagné. "Première alliance interculturelle: Rencontre entre Montagnais et Français à Tadoussac en 1603." *RAQ* 25, no. 3 (1995): 3–14.

Goldstein, Robert A. *French-Iroquois Diplomatic and Military Relations, 1609–1701*. The Hague, Paris: Mouton, 1969.

Grabowski, Jan. "The Common Ground: Settled Natives and French in Montreal, 1667–1760." PhD dissertation, Département d'histoire, Université de Montréal, 1993.

– "Les Amérindiens domiciliés et la 'contrebande' des fourrures en Nouvelle-France." *RAQ* 24, no. 3 (1994): 45–52.

– "Le petit commerce entre les Trifluviens et les Amérindiens en 1665–1667." *RAQ* 28, no. 1 (1998): 105–21.

Groulx, Lionel. *Histoire du Canada français*. Vol. 1, *Le régime français*. Montréal: Editions Fides, 1960.

Gruzinski, Serge, and Nathan Wachtel, eds. *Le Nouveau Monde: mondes nouveaux. L'expérience américaine*. Paris: École des Hautes Études en Sciences Sociales, 1996.

Haan, Richard L. "The Covenant Chain: Iroquois Diplomacy on the Niagara Frontier, 1697–1730." PhD dissertation, University of California, Santa Barbara, 1976.

– "The Problem of Iroquois Neutrality: Suggestions for Revision." *Ethnohistory* 27, no. 4 (1980): 317–30.

Handbook of North American Indians (HNAI). Vol. 15, *Northeast*, edited by B.G. Trigger. Vol. 6, *Subarctic*, edited by June Helm. Washington: Smithsonian Institution, 1978.

Handbook of North American Indians. Vol. 4, *History of Indian-White Relations*, edited by Wilcomb Washburn. Washington: Smithonian Institution, 1988.

Harris, R. Cole, ed. *Historical Atlas of Canada, I: From the Beginnings to 1800*. Toronto: University of Toronto Press, 1987.

Havard, Gilles. "Paix et interculturalité en Nouvelle-France au temps de Louis XIV." *RAQ* 27, no. 2 (1997): 3–18.

– "Empire et métissages: la naissance du Pays d'en Haut, une région franco-amérindienne." Thèse soutenue à l'Université Paris VII, 2000.

Hunt, George T. *The Wars of the Iroquois: A Study in Intertribal Trade Relations*. Madison: University of Wisconsin Press, 1960 (1940).

Hurley, J.D. "Children or Brethren: Aboriginal Rights in Colonial Iroquoia." PhD dissertation, University of Cambridge, 1985.

Jacquin, Philippe. *Histoire des Indiens d'Amérique du Nord*. Paris: Payot, 1976.

– *Les Indiens blancs: Français et Indiens en Amérique du Nord, XVIe–XVIIIe siècles*. Paris: Payot, 1987.

Jaenen, Cornelius J. *Friend and Foe: Aspects of French-Amerindian Cultural Contact in the Sixteenth and Seventeenth Centuries*. New York: Columbia University Press, 1976.

– "Les relations franco-amérindiennes en Nouvelle-France et en Acadie." Ottawa: Affaires indiennes et du nord Canada, 1985.

– "French Sovereignty and Native Nationhood during the French Regime." In *Sweet Promises: A Reader on Indian-White Relations in Canada*, edited by J.R. Miller, 19–42. Toronto: University of Toronto Press, 1991.

– ed. *Les Franco-Ontariens*. Ottawa: Presses de l'université d'Ottawa, 1993.

– "La présence française dans le Pays d'en-Haut." In *Les Français des Etats-Unis d'hier à aujourd'hui*, edited by R. Creagh, 11–24. Actes du colloque international sur les Français des Etats-Unis. Montpellier, 1994.

– "Colonisation compacte et colonisation extensive aux XVIIe et XVIIIe siècles en Nouvelle-France." In *Colonies, territoires, sociétés: l'enjeu français*, edited by A. Saussol and J. Zitomersky, 15–22. Paris: L'harmattan, 1996.

– "Rapport historique de la nation huronne-wendat." In *Les Hurons de Lorette*, edited by D. Vaugeois, 61–253. Montréal: Septentrion, 1996.

Jennings, Francis. "The Constitutional Evolution of the Covenant Chain." *Proceedings of the American Philosophical Society* 115, no. 2 (1971): 88–96.

– *The Invasion of America: Indians, Colonialism, and the Cant of Conquest*. Williamsburg: University of North Carolina Press, 1975.

– "A Growing Partnership: Historians, Anthropologists and American Indian History." *Ethnohistory* 29, no. 1 (1982): 21–34.

– *The Ambiguous Iroquois Empire: The Covenant Chain Confederation of Indian Tribes with English Colonies from Its Beginnings to the Lancaster Treaty of 1744*. New York: Norton, 1984.

– *Empire of Fortune: Crowns, Colonies and Tribes in the Seven Years War in America*. New York: Norton, 1988.

– ed. *The History and Culture of Iroquois Diplomacy: An Interdiscplinary Guide to the Treaties of the Six Nations and Their League*. Syracuse, N.Y.: Syracuse University Press, 1985.

Jetten, Marc. *Enclaves amérindiennes: les "réductions" du Canada 1637–1701*. Montréal: Septentrion, 1994.

Kent, Donald H. *The Iroquois Indians*. Vol. 2, *Historical Report on the Niagara River and the Niagara River Strip to 1759*. New York and London: Garland Publishing, 1974.

Lanctôt, Gustave. *Histoire du Canada*. Montréal: Librairie Beauchemin, 1963. Vol. 2.

Lanoue, Guy, "When Is a Turtle a Turtle? Representations of Social Solidarity in Rock Art." *JSA* 76 (1990): 7–31.

Lebrun, François. *Le XVIIᵉ siècle*. Paris: A. Colin, Collection "U," 1967.

Lévi-Strauss, Claude. *Totemism*. Translated by Rodney Needham *(Le totémisme aujourd'hui)*. Boston: Beacon Press 1963 (1962).

– *The Savage Mind. (La pensée sauvage)*. Chicago: University of Chicago Press, 1966.

– *The Origin of Table Manners*. Translated by John and Doreen Weightman (*Les origines des manières de table*). New York: Harper & Row, 1979.

Lintvelt, Jaap, Real Ouellet, and Hubert Hermans, eds. *Culture et colonisation en Amérique du Nord / Culture and Colonization in North America: Canada, United States, Mexico*. Sillery, Québec: Septentrion, 1994.

Lurie, Nancy O. "Ethnohistory: An Ethnological Point of View." *Ethnohistory* 8, no. 1 (1961): 78–92.

Lytwyn, Victor P. "Historical Research Report on the Treaty Rights and Geographical Extent of Watha Mohawks Resource Harvesting." 1995.

MacLeod, D. Peter. "The Anishnabeg Point of View: The History of the Great Lakes to 1800 in Nineteenth-Century Mississauga, Odawa, and Ojibwa Historiography." *CHR* 73, no. 2 (1992): 194–210.

Marienstras, Elise. "Problèmes d'historiographie américaine: le champ amérindien." *Annales, Economies, Sociétés, Civilisations* (1978): 408–26.

– *La Résistance indienne aux États-Unis du XVIᵉ au XXᵉ siècle*. Paris: Gallimard/Julliard, 1980.

Marin, Louis. *Portrait of the King*. Translated by Martha Houle (*Le Portrait du Roi*). Minneapolis: University of Minnesota Press, 1988.

Martin, Calvin. *Keepers of the Game: Indian-Animal Relationships and the Fur Trade*. Berkeley: University of California Press, 1978.

– ed. *The American Indian and the Problem of History*. New York, 1987.

Mathieu, Jacques. *La Nouvelle-France: Les Français en Amérique du Nord, XVIᵉ–XVIIIᵉ siècle*. France: Belin; Sainte-Foy, Québec: Presses de l'Université Laval, 1991.

Mauro, Frédéric. *L'expansion européenne (1600–1870)*. Paris: Presses Universitaires de France, 1996.

Merrell, James H. *The Indians' New World: Catawbas and Their Neighbours from European Contact through the Era of Removal*. Chapel Hill: University of North Carolina Press, 1989.

– "Some Thoughts on Colonial Historians and American Indians." *WMQ* 46, no. 3 (1989): 94–119.

Merrell, James H., and Daniel K. Richter, eds. *Beyond the Covenant Chain*. Syracuse: Syracuse University Press, 1987.

Miquelon, Dale. *New France, 1701–1744: A Supplement to Europe*. Toronto: McClelland and Stewart, 1989.

Moore, John H. *The Cheyenne*. Malden: Blackwell Publishers, 1999.

Morin, Michel. *L'usurpation de la souveraineté autochtone: Le cas des peuples de la Nouvelle-France et des colonies anglaises de l'Amérique du Nord*. Montréal: Boréal, 1997.

Ouellet, Réal, ed. *Rhétorique et conquête missionnaire: le jésuite Paul Lejeune*. Québec: Septentrion, 1993.

Peckham, Howard H. *The Colonial Wars, 1689–1762*. Chicago: University of Chicago Press, 1967 (1964).

Pictet, Jean. *L'Épopée des Peaux-Rouges*. Paris: Favre, 1988.

Pilette, Marie-Laure. "Un dilemme iroquois: combattre pour s'allier et s'allier pour combattre." *RAQ* 21, nos. 1–2 (1991): 71–78.

Prucha, Francis Paul. *American Indian Treaties: The History of a Political Anomaly*. Berkeley, Los Angeles, London: University of California Press, 1994.

Ray, Arthur, and D.J. Freeman. *"Give us good mesure": An Economic Analysis of Relations between the Indians and Hudson's Bay Company before 1763*. Toronto: University of Toronto Press, 1978.

Richefort, Isabelle. "Présents diplomatiques et diffusion de l'image de Louis XIV." In Bély, ed., *L'invention de la diplomatie*, 263–79.

Richter, Daniel K. "War and Culture: The Iroquois Experience." *WMQ* 40, no. 4 (1983): 528–9.

– "The Ordeal of the Longhouse: Change and Persistence on the Colonial Frontier, 1609–1720." PhD dissertation, Columbia University, 1984.

– "Iroquois versus Iroquois: Jesuit Missions and Christianity in Village Politics, 1642–1686." *Ethnohistory* 32, no. 1 (1985): 1–16.

– *The Ordeal of the Longhouse: The Peoples of the Iroquois League in the Era of European Colonization*. Chapel Hill: University of North Carolina Press, 1992.

Riggs, Stephen R. *Dakota-English Dictionary.* Minneapolis: Ross & Haines, 1968 (1852).

Sahlins, Marshall. *Stone Age Economics.* Chicago, Aldine-Atherton, 1972.

Salone, Emile. *La colonisation de la Nouvelle-France: Etude sur les origines de la nation canadienne française.* Paris: E. Guilmoto Editeur, 1970 (1905).

Saussol, Alain, and Joseph Zitomersky. *Colonies, territoires, sociétés: l'enjeu français.* Paris: L'harmattan, 1996.

Savard, Rémi. *L'Algonquin Tessouat et la fondation de Montréal: Diplomatie franco-indienne en Nouvelle-France.* Montréal: L'Hexagone, 1996.

Sawaya, Jean Pierre. "Les Sept Nations du Canada: Traditions d'alliances dans le Nord-Est, XVIIIᵉ-XIXᵉ siècles." Mémoire de maitrise, Québec, Université Laval, 1994.

– *La fédération des Sept feux de la vallée du Saint-Laurent, XVIIe–XIXᵉ siècle.* Québec: Septentrion, 1998.

Schmalz, Peter S. *The Ojibwa of Western Ontario.* Toronto: University of Toronto Press, 1991.

Simard, Jean-Jacques. "White Ghosts, Red Shadows: The Reduction of North American Natives." In *The Invented Indian: Cultural Fictions and Government Policies,* edited by J. A. Clifton, 333–69. New Brunswick, N.J.: Transaction Publishers, 1990.

Sioui, Anne-Marie. "Les onze portraits d'Indiens du 'Codex canadiensis.'" *RAQ* 11, no. 4 (1981): 281–96.

Sioui, Georges E. *For an Amerindian Autohistory: An Essay on the Foundations of a Social Ethic.* Translated by Sheila Fischman. Montreal and Kingston: McGill-Queen's University Press, 1992.

Huron-Wendat: The Heritage of the Circle. Translated by Jane Brierley (*Les Wendats, une civilisation méconnue*). Vancouver: University of British Columbia Press, 1999.

Smith, Donald B. "Who Are the Mississauga?" *Ontario History* 67, no. 4 (1975): 211–22.

– "Important Evidence: Nineteenth Century Anishnabeg Perspectives on the Algonquin-Iroquois Wars in Seventeenth Century Southern Ontario." Presented at Eight North American Fur Trade Conference, 26 May 2000.

Snow, Dean, and Kim M. Lanphear. "European Contact and Indian Depopulation in the Northeast: The Timing of the First Epidemics." *Ethnohistory* 35, no. 1 (1988): 15–32.

Snyderman, George S. "The Functions of Wampum." *Proceedings of the American Philosophical Society* 98, no. 6 (1954): 469–94.

Speck, Frank G. "The Eastern Algonkian Wakanaki Confederacy." In *Northern Algonquian Source Book: Papers by Frank G. Speck*, edited by Edward S. Rogers, 492–508. New York and London: Garland Publishing, 1985.

Starna, William A. "Concerning the Extent of 'Free Hunting' Territory under the Treaty of 1701 between the Five Nations Confederacy and the British Sovereign, and the Harvesting Activities Protected under that Treaty." Ontario Native Affairs, 1994.

Sturtevant, William C. "Anthropology, History, and Ethnohistory." *Ethnohistory* 13, nos. 1–2 (1966): 1–51.

Tanner, Helen H., ed. *Atlas of Great Lakes Indian History.* Norman: University of Oklahoma Press, 1987.

Therien, Gilles, ed. *Figures de l'Indien.* Montréal: Typo, 1995.

Therrien, Jean-Marie. *Parole et pouvoir: figure du chef amérindien en Nouvelle-France.* Montréal: Hexagone, 1986.

Thorne, Tanis C. *The Many Hands of My Relations: French and Indians in the Lower Missouri.* Columbia and London: University of Missouri Press, 1996.

Thornton, Russel. *American Indian Holocaust and Survival: A Population History Since 1492.* Norman: University of Oklahoma Press, 1987.

Todorov, Tzvetan. *La Conquête de l'Amérique: la question de l'autre.* Paris: Seuil, 1982.

Tooker, Elisabeth. *An Ethnography of the Huron Indians, 1615–1649.* Syracuse, N.Y.: Syracuse University Press, 1991.

Trelease, Allen W. *Indian Affairs in Colonial New York: The Seventeenth Century.* Ithaca, N.Y.: Cornell University Press, 1960.

Trigger, Bruce G. "The Mohawk-Mahican War (1624–1628): The Establishment of a Pattern." *CHR* 52 (1971): 276–86.

– *The Children of Aataentsic: A History of the Huron People to 1660.* 2 vols. Montreal and Kingston: McGill-Queen's University Press, 1976.

– "Pour une histoire plus objective des relations entre les colonisateurs et les autochtones en Nouvelle-France." *RAQ* 11, no. 3 (1981): 199–204.

– "Ethnohistory: Problems and Prospects." *Ethnohistory* 29, no. 1 (1982): 1–19.

– *Natives and Newcomers: Canada's "Heroic Age" Reconsidered.* Montreal and Kingston: McGill-Queen's University Press, 1985.

- "Ethnohistory: The Unfinished Edifice." *Ethnohistory* 33, no. 3 (1986): 253–67.

Trocmé, Hélène, and Jeanine Rovet. *Naissance de l'Amérique moderne, XVIe-XIXe siècle.* Paris: Hachette supérieur, 1997.

Turgeon, Laurier, Denys Delâge, and Réal Ouellet, eds. *Transferts culturels et métissages, Amérique/Europe, XVIe-XXe siècle / Cultural Transfer, America and Europe: 500 years of Interculturation.* Québec: Presses de l'Université Laval, 1996.

Vachon, André. *Éloquence indienne.* Ottawa: Editions Fides, 1968.

- "Colliers et ceintures de porcelaine chez les Indiens de la Nouvelle-France." *Cahier des dix* 35 (1970): 251–78.

- "Colliers et ceintures de porcelaine dans la diplomatie indienne." *Cahier des dix* 36 (1971): 179–92.

Vastokas, J.M., and R.K. Vastokas. *Sacred Art of the Algonquians.* Peterborough: Mansard Press, 1973.

Vaugeois, Denis. *La fin des alliances franco-indiennes: Enquête sur un sauf-conduit devenu un traité en 1990.* Montréal: Boréal, 1995.

- , ed. *Les Hurons de Lorette.* Québec: Septentrion, 1996.

Viau, Roland. *Enfants du néant et mangeurs d'âmes: Guerre, culture et société en Iroquoisie ancienne.* Montréal: Boréal, 1997.

Vincens, Simone. *Madame de Montour et son temps.* Montréal: Québec/Amérique, 1979.

Wallace, Anthony F.C. "Origins of Iroquois Neutrality: The Grand Settlement of 1701." *Pennsylvania History* 24 (1957): 223–35.

Washburn, Wilcomb. "Ethnohistory: History 'in the Round.'" *Ethnohistory* 8 (1961): 31–48.

White, Richard. *The Middle Ground: Indians, Empires and Republics in the Great Lakes Region, 1650–1815.* Cambridge: Cambridge University Press, 1991.

Wien, Thomas. "Indiens et Français, fourrures et marchandises au Canada aux XVIIe et XVIIIe siècles." In *La traite des fourrures, les Français et la découverte de l'Amérique du Nord.* Thonon-les-Bains, Haute-Savoie, France: Éditions de l'Albaron/Musée du Nouveau Monde de La Rochelle, 1992.

- "Le Pérou éphémère: termes d'échange et éclatement du commerce franco-amérindien, 1645–1670." In *Habitants et marchands, vingt ans après: Lectures de l'histoire des XVIIe et XVIIIe siècles canadiens / Habitants and Merchants, Twenty Years Later: Reading the History of Seventeenth- and Eighteenth-Century Canada,* edited by Sylvie Depatie et al. Montreal and Kingston: McGill-Queen's University Press, 1998.

Wilson, Edward F. *The Ojebway Language: a manual for missionaries and others employed among the Ojebway Indians*. Toronto: Rownsell & Hutchison, 1975 (1874).

Wogan, Peter. "Perceptions of European Literacy in Early Contact Situations." *Ethnohistory* 41, no. 3 (1994): 407–29.

Zitomersky, Joseph. *French Americans – Native Americans in Eighteenth-Century French Colonial Louisiana: The Population Geography of the Illinois Indians, 1670–1760*. Lund Studies in International History 31. Lund, Sweden: Lund University Press, 1994.

Zoltvany, Yves F. "New France and the West, 1701–1713." CHR 46 (1965): 301–22.

– "The Frontier Policy of Philippe de Rigaud de Vaudreuil, 1713–1725." CHR 48 (1967): 227–50.

– *Philippe de Rigaud de Vaudreuil: Governor of New-France, 1703–1725*. Toronto: McClelland and Stewart, 1974.

Index